Chicken Soup for the Soul.

The Dating Game

Chicken Soup for the Soul: The Dating Game
101 Stories about Looking for Love and Finding Fairytale Romance!
Jack Canfield, Mark Victor Hansen, Amy Newmark

Published by Chicken Soup for the Soul Publishing, LLC www.chickensoup.com
Copyright © 2013 by Chicken Soup for the Soul Publishing, LLC. All Rights Reserved.

The publisher gratefully acknowledges the many publishers and individuals who
granted Chicken Soup for the Soul permission to reprint the cited material.

Front cover illustration courtesy of iStockPhoto.com/chuwy (© chuwy), and
iStockPhoto.com/rangepuppies (© rangepuppies). Back cover and interior illustration
courtesy of iStockPhoto.com/lcsmith79 (© lcsmith79).

Cover and Interior Design & Layout by Brian Taylor, Pneuma Books, LLC

Distributed to the booktrade by Simon & Schuster. SAN: 200-2442

Publisher's Cataloging-in-Publication Data
(Prepared by The Donohue Group)

Chicken soup for the soul : the dating game : 101 stories about looking
  for love and finding fairytale romance! / [compiled by] Jack Canfield,
  Mark Victor Hansen, [and] Amy Newmark.

     p. : ill. ; cm.

  ISBN: 978-1-61159-929-9

  1. Dating (Social customs)--Literary collections. 2. Dating (Social customs)--
Anecdotes. 3. Courtship--Literary collections. 4. Courtship--Anecdotes. 5. Love--
Literary collections. 6. Love--Anecdotes. 7. Anecdotes. I. Canfield, Jack, 1944- II.
Hansen, Mark Victor. III. Newmark, Amy. IV. Title: Dating game : 101 stories about
looking for love and finding fairytale romance!

PN6071.D29 C45 2013
810.8/02/03543   2013937417

PRINTED IN THE UNITED STATES OF AMERICA
on acid∞free paper

22 21 20 19 18 17 16 15 14 13   01 02 03 04 05 06 07 08 09 10

Chicken Soup for the Soul

for the Soul®

The Dating Game

101 Stories about
Looking for Love and Finding
Fairytale Romance!

Jack Canfield
Mark Victor Hansen
Amy Newmark

Chicken Soup for the Soul Publishing, LLC
Cos Cob, CT

Chicken Soup

www.chickensoup.com

for the Soul

Contents

❶

~Matchmaker, Matchmaker~

❷

~Let's Forget This Ever Happened~

❸

~The Moment I Knew~

❹

~By Your Side~

❺

~Looking for Love Dot Com~

❻

~It's Not Me, It's You~

❼

~Never Too Late for Love~

❽

~Happily Ever Laughter~

❾

~Meant to Be~

❿

~Will You Marry Me?~

⑪

~Lessons in Love~

Introduction

I think every girl enjoys reading love stories from an early age, raised as we are on fairy tales and Disney movies. And I got to select and edit 101 stories about dating and love and romance for this collection! Sometimes I really love my job.

Okay, some of them were not love stories, as you'll see in the very funny chapters about bad dates, but most of these stories are about real people with real lives experiencing wonderful relationships with their spouses or boyfriends or girlfriends... after putting in the requisite time on the dating circuit.

Working on this book was a great example of what is best about Chicken Soup for the Soul—these stories are inspirational and also entertaining. Some of them will make you laugh out loud, some will give you hope if you are looking for love, some will make you nod your head in recognition if you are in a successful long-term relationship. None will make you cry. Not a single one. We are all about happiness and inspiration and entertainment in this book.

We had originally listed the subtitle for this collection as "101 Stories about Looking for Love" but after reading these stories I realized that we had a book full of modern-day fairy tales, so I changed the subtitle to "101 Stories about Looking for Love and Finding Fairytale Romance!"

I was definitely in the right mood to make this book for you. My husband and I are looking forward to two family weddings in the next twelve months—our son Mike is marrying beautiful, brilliant, and funny Emily, and our daughter Rosey is marrying Joey, who everyone falls in love with after knowing him for about ten seconds.

We had to include a chapter on marriage proposals because we lived and breathed them ourselves while we were making this book. Exactly a year ago, while all of us Chicken Soup for the Soul editors were at the wedding of our colleague Kristiana Glavin Pastir, Mike was proposing to Emily. We kept checking our cell phones that night, waiting for the news, and so nervous for Mike, who had been practicing his lines and his moves all week, even working on whipping the ring out of his pocket at the right moment.

As it turned out, Mike, who is normally a polished public speaker, totally blew it. After he ran two hours late preparing a special dinner, he finally invited Emily downstairs to a candlelit dining area, where he intended to make a speech, get down on one knee, and present the ring. Instead, Emily reported that she found him swaying back and forth at the bottom of the stairs, and then heard him mumble something like "Always... always... here," as he thrust the ring at her.

Half a year later, we lived through another nervous Saturday waiting for Rosey to call us with her own good news. We knew Joey was planning to propose on a beautiful mountain hike that day, but what we didn't know was that his plans went awry due to a late snow. When he and Rosey got to the hiking trail and saw the snow, she announced that she wasn't wearing the right kind of shoes. Now you would think that a guy who runs his own business and has traveled all over the world could adapt to this, but to a nervous man preparing to propose this was a total disaster. Luckily, when they checked into their B&B later that day, the owner serendipitously recommended that they go for a hike around a nearby lake. Joey brought the ring, but when they came to a scenic spot just right for the proposal, he blurted out loud what he meant to think to himself, and Rosey heard, "I'm *doing* this!" before he spun around and dropped to his knee.

I guess that the marriage proposal is the scariest, and luckily the final, "ask" that a man has to make — the biggest date of all. But the whole process of dating is scary, and you'll read many stories in this book about dating disasters, funny stories that are much funnier in the re-telling than they were when they happened. You'll also read about great matchmakers whose set-ups really worked, those special moments when someone realized that this was "the one," and enough "meet-cutes" to keep a Hollywood studio going for a decade of romantic comedies. I'm smiling just thinking about how much I enjoyed reading all these stories, and I'm sorry that it's over. But it's your turn now, so have fun with this collection, and keep the faith if you're single, because according to our writers that special someone may be just around the corner.

~Amy Newmark

The Dating Game

Matchmaker, Matchmaker

People are lonely because they build walls instead of bridges.

~Joseph F. Newton

Love, Off the Record

Sometimes when we're not paying attention, relationships happen.
~Lisa Kleypas, from Smooth Talking Stranger

By 1989, I had been happily divorced two years, having weathered several disastrous first dates and a few semi-relationships that failed to get off the ground. The closest I had come to a serious boyfriend was an architect who lived in New York. Since I lived in Virginia and worked in D.C. at the time, the distance between us was perfect. But this relationship also fizzled out. I was fine with that. I was happy with my work and enjoyed hanging out with friends, my family, and my cat.

So I was unprepared for an encounter with destiny when my editor-in-chief tossed a project on my desk with the command to "interview this person."

As the associate editor of an architecture magazine, I was responsible for writing features on new projects, news developments, and products. This particular design project, soon to open in Austin, Texas, was a combination piano/pool hall. Not many of those around, I hazarded to guess. Eric's Pool Hall, as it was called, was executed with whimsy and flair, and I looked forward to talking to the imaginative and witty architect responsible. I picked up the telephone.

Usually, when an editor from an architecture magazine is on the line, explaining the nature of the call, you can hear the excitement in an architect's voice when he or she is about to be published. The first words out of this guy's mouth, however, sounded like a sneer.

"What'd ya do? Pick that out of the round file?" he replied flatly.

Feeling chastened and not a little awkward and offended, I replied with as much starch in my voice as I could muster that I could tell he wasn't interested. I thanked him for his time and hung up.

As I sat there wondering what to tell my editor, the phone rang. It was Mr. Surly Guy, all apologetic and charming. He explained he had been caught short; he had tried to retrieve the project slides a year ago and been annoyed when he was told that our art department had "lost" them. As he made his apologies I couldn't help but note how warm and masculine his voice sounded over the telephone. We agreed to set up a phone interview the following day.

Typically my interviews are a mix of handwritten notes and a tape recorder used as a backup. As I had hoped, the interview was a lot of fun—more so than usual, in fact. As I replayed the tape, I was struck by the realization that we spent as much time discussing personal information as we did the article. We had actually gotten pretty flirty.

Over the next two weeks, while I worked on the piece and chose slides for the layout, I found myself excited when I had a reason to call him to confirm a fact or ask about a detail. I couldn't deny I called him more than I usually did a designer when writing up a project. Finally the article was finished. I was satisfied with it, knowing he would also be pleased with the result. A bit regretfully, I called for the last time to thank him for his time and input, and let him know when the feature would be published. I made sure to get his address to send a complimentary copy.

The following day the phone rang.

"Hey, kid. I just missed talking to you," he said.

As much as I enjoyed it too, it was obvious I couldn't have a personal conversation at work. The next thing I knew he had my home phone number, and it became a habit for him to call around ten at night. Both of us were night owls, and we'd stay on the line for an hour at a time. The nightly routine was one I looked forward to.

After four weeks, he began broaching the subject of meeting

in person. I brushed it off each time. He lived in Maryland, more than an hour away from D.C., but truthfully, I was enjoying my new telephone buddy and didn't want to jeopardize our friendship. I was afraid the bubble might burst if he was short, fat, or bald. Enjoying my flirt fantasy, I continued to put him off. After a few more weeks he finally he told me was driving down that Saturday to take me to lunch.

"I can't. I have to work," I quickly countered.

"You have to eat; I'll meet you in the lobby at noon," he said in a voice that broached no further argument.

After brief descriptions — "I'm tall and dark-haired" and "I'm tall with auburn hair" — we hung up for the night.

That Saturday, as the noon hour approached, I was nervous as I sat on a bench in the lobby. Soon a very tall, good-looking, slender man with shoulder-length wavy hair pushed through the entry doors. My heart did an actual flip-flop as these thoughts bubbled in my head: Oh no! I don't want to get married again!

Many years later, as we were having lunch with a friend, she asked us how we met. As I told her this story with my now-husband listening beside me, I laughed, since I had never told him my first reaction to our meeting.

"You don't know the whole story," he said with a chuckle.

Apparently, when we hung up after my initial interview request, he had called my boss.

"What's the matter, Don? Am I slipping? You or a senior editor have always reviewed my work before, and today I just got a call from some associate editor."

"You want to meet this girl," my editor-in-chief replied. "Don't you have a restaurant you designed up there somewhere? You should take her to lunch."

"What? I've never had to take an editor out to lunch before!" my now-husband protested.

"You aren't listening to me!" my editor replied. "You need to meet this girl."

Don Canty. My crusty old editor-in-chief. A romantic, and I

never knew it. How I wish I had learned the whole story before he died. I would have written him to thank him for steering me into a relationship with the love of my life and into a very happy marriage, now in its twenty-third year.

~Amy Gray Light

The Robes of a Prince

Love is like swallowing hot chocolate before it has cooled off.
It takes you by surprise at first, but keeps you warm for a long time.
~Author Unknown

I never expected to be single when I was sixty. I certainly never expected to be dating at my age.

I was shy, unpopular, and socially clumsy when I was a teenager. Now I've had a lifetime of experience and I'm shy, unpopular, and socially clumsy.

It is hard to meet single men at my age. Dates are few and far between, so when I do have a date I try to make it a special occasion. On my last date I dressed up, applied make-up and put on enough perfume to smell like a flower garden. My date fell asleep during dinner and snored, which wouldn't have been so bad if we hadn't been in a restaurant. I finished my dessert and woke him up. He picked his teeth with a fork and left a fifty-cent tip for the waitress. I decided to give up dating forever.

My son Shane is very devoted to me, wants me to be happy, and is terrified that if I don't get married he'll get stuck with me. Shane arranged for me to meet his neighbor George who needed help writing his memoir.

I often help people write their memoirs. I think it is important for people our age to leave behind a record of who we are and our family history. When we die, our stories will die with us and be lost forever. Sometimes writing the story of your life seems overwhelming and people need a little help getting started.

I agreed to meet George at a nearby restaurant and took along a pen and notepad to record his memories. I felt like I was doing a favor for Shane's neighbor so I wore my second best dress and didn't bother to wiggle into my incredibly uncomfortable body shaper that pushed my belly into my kidneys to make me look ten pounds thinner. I put on some make-up and applied lipstick that was guaranteed not to run into the lines around my lips.

George was short and chubby, and like most men his age he was bald, but he did have a cute little white moustache. I was two inches taller than George and he wasn't my type at all, but that didn't matter because this wasn't a real date; I was just going to help him get started writing his life story.

George was wearing the ugliest shirt I'd ever seen. It was yellow with small brown flowers on it, and to make matters worse, it buttoned on the wrong side, making it look like a woman's blouse.

Since I didn't consider this a date, it didn't matter what he was wearing, and after introducing myself, I took out my notepad and began asking him questions. Where he was born, where he went to school, whether he had brothers and sisters, what kind of jobs he'd had — I carefully wrote down every answer. In a few minutes I knew the name of his dog, the name of his third grade teacher and that his favorite dessert was chocolate cake. He'd been widowed seven years, had two grown sons and four grandchildren. His hobby was building model ships and he'd retired from the post office five years earlier.

"See how easy it is?" I asked and tore five pages out of the notebook and handed them to him. "You just need to get started and before you know it your book will be written."

"What book?" George asked.

He wasn't writing a book. My son had used that excuse to introduce us. I'd just spent fifteen minutes giving George the third degree and writing down his answers to my questions.

Now he was convinced I was crazy, but after I explained what

Shane had done we both had a good laugh. George was one of those people who laugh with their whole face; his blue eyes twinkled and the laugh lines around his eyes got deeper. Wrinkles in a person's face give them character. He had a nice laugh too, it wasn't a fake polite laugh; it was the kind of laugh that made you laugh too.

"I should explain about my shirt," George said. "My twelve-year-old granddaughter wants to be a famous fashion designer when she grows up. I bought a sewing machine for her and to thank me, she made this shirt for my date tonight. I had to wear it. I couldn't hurt her feelings. I thought about putting another shirt in my car and changing in the parking lot before I came inside but that seemed dishonest. If she asked me if I wore the shirt on my date, I wanted to say yes and that it was a fine shirt. I just couldn't lie to her."

I liked George so much at that minute I got tears in my eyes.

"Tell your granddaughter that your date liked your shirt very much and good luck with her career and that she is off to a good start," I said. "Tell her I said she could make robes for a prince."

I wanted to tell George that right now he seemed like a prince but I was afraid I'd sound stupid and it might embarrass him.

"Thank you," George said and squeezed my hand. "I knew you'd understand; your son told me you were one in a million."

I blushed. I hadn't blushed in years but I was definitely blushing. My heart was also beating faster and I hoped it was because George was holding my hand and not because I was having a heart attack.

I decided I didn't care if George was short and bald; he was a man with a good heart and integrity. He was willing to embarrass himself by wearing a hideous shirt on a first date so he wouldn't hurt his granddaughter's feelings.

"If you ask me for a second date, I promise not to interview you and ask dozens of questions." I gave him a big smile, which I hoped was flirty. I also hoped he'd think my teeth were really mine... well, they would be mine in three more payments.

"I didn't mind. I've never had a woman interested enough to

want to know my whole life story and then not just listen to me but write down what I said," he smiled back. "You're a nice lady."

And it was as complicated and as simple as that.

I met a nice man and I'm not alone anymore.

~April Knight

Good Advice

*The world is round and the place which may seem like the end
may also be the beginning.*

~Ivy Baker Priest

I found Joanne sitting on her bed. Her hair had not grown back since her last chemotherapy, and her face had become thin and gray. With a flick of her finger, she ordered me to her bedside. "Good to see you, Janice J," she said, her brown eyes fixed on me. "Thanks for coming so far to see me while I'm on my last legs." She wiggled her legs under the covers and we both laughed.

I sat with her while friends drifted in and out of the bedroom. Over the years, her friends and I had met or heard of each other, so we chatted about better times we'd shared with Joanne. Then, with a wave of her hand, Joanne ordered us all out of the room.

While she rested, her other friends and I sat with her husband, Alan, and spoke of how Joanne had lit up a room with her stunning looks, charm, and fun personality. A friend started to cry. "What will happen to Alan?" she asked. We all knew Alan was helpless around the house and uncomfortable in social situations.

Alan said, "I'll learn to manage without her. Somehow." I believed him.

The morning before my return to Oregon, Joanne called me into her room for a private conversation. "Janice J, you are looking good today."

I blushed, remembering how challenging fashion had always been for me.

"Remember all those hours we spent shopping together?" She leaned closer to me. "I want you to remember the advice I've given you and follow it."

I nodded. I'd do anything Joanne said I should.

We had met shortly after her arrival from India and explored Los Angeles together as young single women. She'd married a prominent physician while I'd just separated from a disappointing husband.

"And one more thing," Joanne said. Her dark brown eyes did not look at me with their usual boldness. "Come back here for the memorial service. To take care of Alan. He's comfortable with you."

"Of course," I said. But you'll be gone, I thought.

"Promise?" She finally looked directly at me. I noticed dark circles under her eyes.

"I promise."

On my flight back to Oregon I mentally said goodbye to Joanne. The cancer she'd lived with for a dozen years would finally take her life. She and I should have had more time together. I cried.

Alan called a few weeks later. "Joanne passed away," he said. "Peacefully."

"I'm so sorry." Images of her flashed through my head. Her beauty. Her outrageous personality. Her love for her friends.

"She wanted you to attend her memorial service," he said. "Can you be here by Saturday afternoon?"

I stammered.

"You're welcome to stay here."

"I'll be there," I said. "Thank you for the hospitality." It would be difficult to get time off. But I had to. I had promised.

Alan's brother picked me up at the busy Los Angeles airport. When we arrived at Alan's house, Lettie, Joanne's friend from North Carolina, gave me the strangest look. We'd never met, just heard about each other. Lettie had been present for Joanne's death.

Alan, his brother, Lettie, and I drove to the crematorium to pick up her ashes. Then we went to the marina to meet friends and go out in Alan's sailboat. We all had tear-stained faces and sat stiff and numb in the cockpit of the sailboat. Alan didn't put up the sail, only turned on the engine. His brother became seasick. I felt nothing.

Alan asked me to open the container with the ashes and hold it at the ready for him. I peeked inside at the white-white sand. He dumped the ashes overboard, and friends tossed roses in with the ashes. I expected Joanne to spring from the water in her full exotic beauty and tell us this had all been a bad joke, and she was back now. The ashes sunk but the roses floated for a while. Alan turned the boat around.

The next day we prepared for the memorial service. Alan and his brother wore white silk mourning clothes from India and the others wore all white. I had not known about this custom so I wore a somber navy blue. The physicians Alan worked with were there with their families. They sat on one side of the aisle and friends sat on the other. The minister and a swami from India both spoke. The swami said Joanne had been a teacher to him in her final days.

Back at Alan's house, I said to him, "If people ask, 'what can I do,' tell them to invite you over for dinner."

He nodded and took my e-mail address.

When I returned to work in Oregon, I felt different.

Alan wrote, and we became fast friends. On my visits to stay with Joanne, I hadn't spoken much to him, but as we talked online, I realized I was interested. I was also beginning to realize that Joanne had set us up!

When our e-mails got hot and sexy, Alan said we should put our friendship on hold.

The next week he wrote back and asked to visit. I took him hiking in the Columbia River Gorge.

I visited him in California, and he took me to Catalina Island on his twenty-seven-foot sailboat. We sat in the cockpit enjoying the sunny day, the calm ocean, and each other. I felt fortunate to have connected with this handsome and accomplished man. Then I went down into the cabin to fetch sunscreen.

I smelled mildew and diesel. I stared at the corrosion on the stove and grime around the edges of the carpet. I took a deep breath.

I can do this, I thought.

On our way to Catalina Island, the endless blue sky made me feel connected to the world, and the sunshine warmed my face and arms.

I watched him steer the sailboat, making small corrections to keep the sails full of wind. I sat on a hard bench and, as the waves got bigger, grasped the smooth fiberglass edges of the cockpit to stay upright. I tried not to look terrified but felt bile rise in my throat.

Alan said, "This is nothing. There've been twenty-foot seas here. This is maybe four."

"Have you been in twenty-foot seas?" I asked.

"No."

If he'd been prescient, he would have seen them in our future.

I hung on.

That night, we snuggled together in the V-shaped berth at the front of the sailboat and delighted in how free we felt and how together we were.

A few months later, I moved to California, and we were together all the time.

Thank you, Joanne.

~Janice Johnson

Grocery Store Cupid

I think the world is run by C students.
~Al McGuire

I zipped into the grocery store and grabbed a shopping cart on a quest to restock my bachelor pantry. The first person I encountered was Jess, a bagger who had recently completed my college public speaking class. He held the distinction of "Shyest Public Speaking Student Ever" in my book, barely squeaking by with a C.

"Hey, Jess. How's it going?"

"Hello, Mr. Hughes." I was surprised he even spoke.

With summer school starting in a matter of days, I needed provisions. I was twenty-six and lived alone, still waiting for "Ms. Right" but with no prospects on the horizon.

I filled my cart with all sorts of goodies and ended up in the frozen food section, where I opened the freezer door to survey the pizza choices. I felt someone behind me and turned to find Jess, standing with his open wallet in hand.

"Can I help you, Jess?"

"You're not dating anyone, are you?" He handed me the wallet, open to a picture of a beautiful lady. "I think you might like my sister Kathy."

Had I entered another dimension? My quietest student ever was now here in the frozen food section trying to fix me up with his sister. Evidently Jess had been eyeing me throughout the semester as a possible match for her.

"Uh, she looks nice." I looked around for a way of escape, but none existed.

"She works at the beauty school—you should call her there, maybe take her out sometime."

"I am between relationships now, so I might just do that." I didn't tell him I actually had been between relationships for many, many years.

I handed the wallet back, and Jess returned to his duties. I finished shopping and paid for my groceries, assuring Jess that I would call his sister. I returned to my lonely apartment and ate my usual bachelor dinner of frozen pizza, still incredulous that Jess had suddenly found his voice as a matchmaker.

I looked up the number to the beauty school. Maybe I would call, but... maybe not. As outgoing as I was around my students and my friends, I was as timid as Jess when it came to women.

A few days later summer school started, and I dedicated myself to work. Two weeks passed, and I forgot about my frozen food match.

One morning in the middle of class, someone knocked on the door. I was shocked to find that it was Jess. I stepped into the hallway and asked if anything was wrong.

"When are you going to call my sister Kathy? Here's a better picture." He handed me a 5x7 photo of the beautiful lady and a slip of paper. "Here's her phone number at work. Call her."

"Okay, I will." I handed him the picture. "I need to get back to my students."

Jess couldn't resist one more plea. "Call her."

I returned to my class, amazed once again at the audacity of this student. That evening I sat in the office with three friends, making dinner plans.

"You need a date, Carlton," one said.

I pulled the paper out of my wallet. "Well, there is this one lady."

In a whirlwind, one friend grabbed the paper, another one dialed, and the other one asked for Kathy and handed me the phone.

It all happened so fast I wasn't sure what to do, but I blurted out that I was Jess's teacher and he had told me about her and would she like to have dinner with me and some friends tonight?

And... she turned me down.

She explained she had been cleaning the school all day and looked "dirty and awful," plus she had to leave early the next morning for a conference. She apologized and encouraged me to call again sometime.

My unluckiness in love continued.

A week passed, and I was facing another dateless weekend. I pulled the paper from my wallet again. I mustered enough courage to dial the number and asked for Kathy. This time she said yes, and we met at a local restaurant the next evening. We talked and laughed as if we had known each other for years.

One date led to another and another. Three years later, Kathy became my wife.

For me, Cupid appeared in the form of a quiet young man in the frozen foods section of a grocery store, with a photo of a lovely lady. My "Shyest Public Speaking Student Ever" is now my brother-in-law. Jess never lets me forget about that C grade, even though he is responsible for one of the greatest gifts in my life.

~Carlton Hughes

My Mare
the Matchmaker

There is something about the outside of a horse
that is good for the inside of a man.
~Winston Churchill

W hat was wrong with my mare? I led my horse out of
her stall and walked her up the barn aisle to be sure
it wasn't my imagination. I wasn't imagining things;
April was obviously limping. Great! I just paid for
her new shoes a week before and here I was at a horse show with a
limping mare.

It was the summer after my high school graduation, and with
college just a couple of months away I expected this would be my
last horse show for a while. I hoped the show farrier might be able to
offer some help—and that it wouldn't cost much since I was already
a starving student.

"Hey, Don, can you take a look at my mare? She's lame," I said
to the farrier as I gently led April next to the area where he was
working.

"No problem. Which leg is she favoring?" he asked. I pointed to
the offending limb.

"Jeff," Don said. "Come pull this shoe."

Jeff was Don's apprentice. I had noticed him at several other
horse shows in the past, but never felt like approaching him. Jeff was

a good-looking guy with a muscular build, but I never got warm and fuzzy feelings from him. In fact, I got the impression he could be mean. So, even though our paths had crossed in the past, except for a quick hello, we had not officially met.

"Hi," Jeff said. I looked behind me, assuming he must be talking to someone else. No one there, so his greeting must have been for me.

"Hi," I said.

"Pretty mare," he said, pulling April's shoe off. Maybe he wasn't so mean after all.

"Thanks," I said. We continued to make small talk while he and Don took a look at April's hoof.

"Well?" I asked.

"Just a hot nail," Don said. "She'll be good to go in a few minutes." I was relieved. Jeff finished tacking her shoe back on and then handed me the lead line.

"Here you go," he said. I took the lead line from him.

"How much do I owe you?" I asked. Jeff looked over at Don.

"Don't worry about it," Don said.

"Wow! Thanks." I began walking my mare, who was no longer limping, back to her stall. The day was beginning to look up.

Then I heard Don say, in a voice loud enough for me to hear, "Hey, Jeff, isn't that the girl you think is cute?" I was pretty sure it was Don's way of trying to embarrass us both; but still, was it possible that Jeff thought I was cute? He was becoming more and more approachable!

Now that the ice was broken, Jeff found a way to strike up another conversation, and another. Talk between us was fun and easy and we both felt a connection. I realized how much I had misjudged him and now I wanted to get to know him better.

But there was a problem — I had a boyfriend. John was my high school sweetheart but after he went away to college we had gradually grown apart. I knew it was just a matter of time before we ended our relationship. And now, having met Jeff, I was certain it was over with John. Still, I knew I would have to tell Jeff before the night was over.

"Can I get your phone number?" Jeff asked as the time came for us to go our own ways.

"Sure," I said, "but..."

"Oh, man, there's a but?" He could sense he wasn't going to like what was coming.

"Well," I continued, "I sort of have a boyfriend."

"Sort of?"

"Yes, but, it's pretty much over." I said the words, but I could see by Jeff's expression that he was too honorable to ask a girl out who already had a boyfriend. And, of course, he was right. I needed to do the right thing. I did give Jeff my phone number... but he never called.

Months passed and during that time I did break it off with my boyfriend. Even if I hadn't met Jeff, I knew it was over between John and me. I assumed I had missed my chance with Jeff until my mother came home with some news.

"I ran into that horseshoer, Jeff, the one you met at the horse show in June," my mother said.

"Really?" I leaned in to hear more.

"I invited him to come over for dinner and take a look at the horses. I told him I thought you would like to see him again."

"What did he say?"

"He said, and I quote, 'I thought she had a boyfriend.'"

"And?" The suspense was killing me.

"And I told him you didn't have a boyfriend anymore. He's coming over Saturday." Ah, my mother the matchmaker... my mother, and my horse. After all, if it hadn't been for April, Jeff and I probably never would have met at all.

Jeff came to our home that Saturday and I kept him company while he made new shoes for our horses. We talked about our families, our interests, and books. I was surprised to find out that this big, hunky man actually liked to read a romance novel now and then!

He joined my family for dinner and afterwards we all watched a movie on TV. It was *Superman*, starring Christopher Reeves and I remember thinking I had my own Superman right there in my house.

But the question still remained—would Jeff actually ask me out on a date, or was I just a new horseshoeing customer?

At the end of the evening I walked Jeff to his truck. I had felt comfortable talking to him all day but now I suddenly felt awkward as we began saying our goodbyes. This guy that I once thought might be mean and unapproachable had captured my heart and I hoped that this was the beginning and not the end.

Well, it was the beginning. Jeff did ask me to go on a date, and a couple of years later he asked me to marry him. And wouldn't you know? Just when I would be able to get my horseshoeing done for free, I decided to sell my mare. Life was getting too busy to give her the attention she deserved—plus, we now had a wedding reception to pay for. It turned out that instead of getting a new horseshoeing customer, Jeff got a wife!

~Lynne Leite

The Little Matchmaker

Strangers are just friends waiting to happen.
~Rod McKuen

The other day, Mom told me that my brother might be getting a dog. I asked why, since my brother is in the middle of a divorce and lives in a rental house. A dog seemed like the last thing he needed.

"He wants to do it for the boys," Mom said. "Give them something their mom won't allow." We were both quiet for a minute, thinking about my nephews. Then Mom brightened. "Plus, with a dog he can meet women at the dog park. That's how they do it these days."

I refrained from mentioning that I had a far better idea of how dating was conducted than my mother ever did. The only person she dated was my dad—back in the early 1960s. I, on the other hand, didn't get married until I was thirty. Fourteen years later, I'd become single again. But her comment got me thinking. I had an energetic dog in need of exercise. Why wasn't I going to the dog park?

Then I remembered that I own a Husky who plays a little rough for the average non-sled-dog owner. Commenting on my dog's ability to body-slam an unsuspecting Border Collie was never going work as a pickup line.

A few days later, my daughter and I went to our favorite fish taco place for dinner. We were halfway through our meal when a cute middle-aged guy walked in. He caught my eye briefly while he waited in line at the counter, and I could tell there was a spark. Or maybe that was the jalapeno talking.

Besides, no guy was going to pick me up while I ate tacos with my autistic nine-year-old.

After Cute Guy ordered, he stood by the counter. Then he walked past our table. Katie looked up and smiled her brightest smile. "Hi," she said, loud and clear.

Cute Guy paused and turned around. "Hi," he said, coming over to our table and bending down to Katie's level. "What's your name?"

Katie was not expecting this. She started sucking deeply on her soda and smiling at Cute Guy from around her straw.

He laughed. "So that's it? You just wanted to say hi?"

Katie smirked. Cute Guy turned to me. He had gorgeous blue eyes that crinkled when he smiled. Wow. He was even better looking up close. "My daughter used to do that too. Say hi and then get shy." He glanced over at Katie. "She really is beautiful. She must get that from her mom."

My daughter is adopted, so there are many ways I could have answered that statement, but I kept it simple and said thank you. I might have blushed.

He asked again for Katie's name while she silently pulled on the straw. "Oh," he said with a laugh. "I can see you're just toying with me like all the other guys."

"Actually," I said. "I think you might be the first stranger she's ever spontaneously greeted." Cute Guy looked surprised. "She has autism," I said. "So it doesn't come naturally for her like it does for other kids."

Cute Guy didn't bat an eye at this revelation. "Wow," he said to Katie. "I'm flattered that you decided I was worthy of your very first hello. You did it like a pro."

Katie beamed at him. I could tell she was thinking, "Now THIS GUY would make an EXCELLENT daddy."

"Hey, Katie," I said. "What's your name?"

"I'm Katie," she mumbled from around the straw.

"Hi, Katie," he said. "What a beautiful name for a beautiful girl. I'm pleased to meet you."

She burbled into her soda and Cute Guy laughed. "She's a sweetheart. You've really done a great job with her."

I wanted to marry Cute Guy without even knowing his name. I glanced at his hand resting on the table. No ring.

The guy at the counter called Cute Guy's number. "Sorry," he said. "Got to go. See you later, Katie."

Katie grinned. "Hi," she said.

Cute Guy and I both laughed. He flashed his gorgeous smile, winked, and walked away. I was basking in the glow of this unexpected encounter when it dawned on me that Katie had managed to pick up a guy on my behalf.

Cute Guy grabbed his food and headed for the door, stopping briefly to wave goodbye. I caught a flash of metal from what I belatedly realized was his left hand. Was it a ring or a car key? It didn't matter. Who needs the hassle of the dog park when my daughter can reel them in with a single word?

~Cynthia J. Patton

"Hey, buddy—try a real dog next time."

Bulletin Board Matchmaker

You know when you have found your prince because you not only have a smile on your face but in your heart as well.

~Author Unknown

After I was the guest singer one Sunday morning at a small church, a nice woman there decided it was time to advertise my single status to the congregation. Unbeknownst to me, Mrs. C put my phone number up on the church bulletin board, with the words, "Call her, boys! She's available!" written boldly in large letters.

That afternoon I received two phone calls. The first one came from Dave. He asked me if I would like to go to High Park, a huge park in the city of Toronto comparable to Central Park in New York. I agreed to go out with him the following Saturday. Immediately following his call, Jim phoned. He wondered if I would like to go to a hockey game with him. I hesitated because it was on the same day as my date with Dave. Not one to give up, Jim said his event was at night and so I could still go out with him. I agreed. I now had two dates with two guys on the same day. I was excited and a bit anxious about how this would work.

The day of my dates arrived. Dave and I took the bus downtown to the park. While we strolled about, I confessed to him that I had another date that same evening. When he found out who my second date was he became agitated.

"You can't go out with him! He's my best friend."

My conscience kicked in. What was I thinking dating two guys on the same day? Worse, they were best friends!

Dave continued to press his case. "If you go out with Jim, you will ruin our friendship."

Oh, dear! What's a girl to do? I did not want to destroy a friendship, but at the same time I didn't want to hurt Jim's feelings. However, the more I thought about it, the more I realized this was an impossible situation. I had to break my date with Jim so that I didn't cause a rift in his friendship with Dave. I promised Dave I would break the date. He was visibly relieved.

When I arrived home I immediately phoned Jim to break our date for that evening. When he asked why, I told him.

"What are you talking about? He's not my best friend. I barely know him."

Confusion set in. Was Jim lying just to get me to go out with him? Or was Dave lying to me? I wavered, almost giving in, but then I remembered my promise to Dave not to go out with Jim and so I stood firm. Jim's response was touched with anger. He finished the call by saying, "You'll find out soon enough he is not the guy for you. When you're done with him, call me." The sarcasm in his voice followed by a sudden dial tone told me I would probably never hear from Jim again.

Clearly he was hurt and angry, but I felt a weight come off my shoulders. Dating two guys at once was not my thing. Since Dave and I had hit it off, I felt I should at least give our relationship a chance to see where it would go.

But Jim was right. It didn't take long for me to realize that Dave was not the guy for me. Wishing I had never turned Jim down, I wondered what to do about it. I was too embarrassed to phone him and ask him out and so I thought I would never hear from him again.

Then, after church one Sunday, he called.

"I hear you're not dating Dave anymore. Do you want to go out with me now?" he asked.

I breathed a sigh of relief. I said yes and we went to a concert together the following week. We had a wonderful time and as the weeks went by and more dates followed we grew closer. In time, I began attending Jim's church. One Sunday as I waited for Jim to bring the car around, I found myself perusing the bulletin board. To my horror I found my phone number still pinned on the board! Red with embarrassment I quickly tore it down just as Mrs. C came around the corner.

"So," she said, "you found your match did you?" She smiled knowingly and walked out the back door.

Six months later Jim and I were engaged and our matchmaker gave me my first wedding shower. Jim and I have been married now for thirty-one years and have two incredible kids. Mrs. C passed away many years ago, but I will always be thankful for the day she pinned my phone number to the church bulletin board.

~Laura J. Davis

The Set-Up

Are we not like two volumes of one book?
~Marceline Desbordes-Valmore

"Hey! I wanted to let you know Dawn's nephew, John, will be here tonight. I didn't want you to think it was a set-up or anything."

Patrice was so cute when she lied.

My close friend and co-worker Patrice knew about my former fiancé breaking off our engagement. Heartbroken, I had sworn off dating and was taking some "me" time, but she remained convinced I would find someone.

My other co-worker, Dawn, had also recently heard my woes. Unfortunately, that led her and Patrice to start scheming about my love life.

Dawn had also shared her nephew's heartbreak story with me. John dated a woman whom he did errands and cleaned for, but she didn't appreciate him. I admitted it would be nice to have someone take care of me and, if he was such a good guy, the girl was nuts to treat him so badly. Dawn often mentioned it was too bad John lived so far away in Baltimore.

He had also recently sworn off dating after breaking up with the ungrateful girl. I didn't give it a second thought when Dawn told me about it because he lived so far away.

Tonight, I only wanted to spend time with my friends, not be forced into conversation with someone I didn't know. "No, absolutely not," Patrice assured. "John's here for the weekend and they're going to bring him. There is no pressure! Come and have some drinks."

I didn't care. Even if it was a set-up, I was not dating. I was, for the first time ever, okay with the reality that I might never marry. I had my own home and my dog for company; I could come and go as I pleased and could support myself. I believed my life was pretty perfect the way it was. Besides, John lived in Baltimore. He certainly wasn't moving up to Middle-of-Nowhere, Pennsylvania.

Having convinced myself, I grabbed my coat and headed out the door.

Within minutes of my arrival, the unease returned. Patrice wouldn't look me in the eye, and she began to babble as she busied herself in the kitchen.

"You need to relax. You'll meet him, have a good time and he'll go back to his house and you'll go back to yours... If nothing sparks then you go on with life as usual," she said, barely taking in a breath.

Although she was right, her words and actions did little to relax me. My life was fine as it was, I reassured myself. I always looked forward to these nights as a way to relax and let myself just "be."

However, tonight would be different. My relaxation time was about to be invaded by a newcomer. I felt myself putting up the defense shields.

I headed outside to see what Patrice's husband was doing. Vinny was arranging chairs around their fire pit, which served as our party space. He seemed oblivious to any set-up. I helped him wipe off the cobwebs and dust off the chairs.

Dawn and her husband arrived and greeted me warmly but quickly escaped inside to Patrice. Their nephew leisurely made his way over to ask if we needed assistance. Not bad looking. Kind of geeky, but he was cute and had nice blue eyes. I tried to focus on wiping down another chair.

Vinny introduced himself, and me.

"Go get yourself a drink. Just follow your uncle," Vinny added, as he winked and motioned towards me, "and don't forget the lady." I rolled my eyes and tried to look uninterested as I continued to wipe down a chair. Vinny wasn't so oblivious after all.

A few moments later John returned with a couple of bottles.

"For the lady." He bowed slightly as he handed me my drink. What a nerd, I thought, but inwardly smiled at having some attention pointed my way. I mumbled my thanks and quickly retreated to a chair on the opposite side of the fire. I was not going to get excited about something that would not happen.

But within the next hour, I changed my mind. John and I were tossing jokes back and forth like old friends. It seemed so comfortable that I let down my defenses.

Then it happened: He made a joke in reference to a movie, and I was the only one who laughed. No one else got the joke. He looked at me and smiled.

"She got it!" He pointed to me.

My heart thawed a little. I was having a ton of fun with this guy.

This went on for a few hours. He would make a joke and I would laugh or I would start a conversation and he would continue my point of view. The weirdest thing was that John and I were already finishing each other's sentences. More than once we eyed each other after these moments as if to say, "Are you thinking what I'm thinking?"

"Get out of my brain!" he said after I had completed yet another one of his thoughts.

I'd never clicked with someone like this.

Then, suddenly, it was over.

My mood crashed as John and his aunt and uncle said goodbye and gathered their things.

He was on his way back to Baltimore.

He lived in Baltimore. That was over 180 miles away. Once again I had let myself hope for something more and now was faced with the reality of being alone. My giddiness ceased, and I sobered up to the reality of the situation. Even though he seemed the perfect match to me, we had many miles separating us.

As John turned to leave, his eyes lingered on me for a moment, but before I could think about giving him my e-mail or number, he was gone.

However, the connection was just too much to dismiss. A few days later, I obtained his e-mail address from Dawn and sent a tentative note.

"Hey," I wrote, "was it just me or were we hitting it off the other night?"

"I agree," he wrote back. "The way we connected the other night was a bit... odd. I felt like I had known you for years instead of just hours."

We began conversing every day. Before we ever had a real date, we knew almost everything about one another. One month later, when we did have our official first date, it felt like we had known each other forever. Within six months we were each considering moving to be closer to the other.

Patrice and Dawn always have claimed they didn't set us up that night, but it's really just a joke now, because three years later we were married and settled into our home in Middle-of-Nowhere, Pennsylvania.

People always say that you find your perfect love when you aren't looking. In our case, it was so true. Neither of us thought we needed love in our lives, but our friends saw the potential for happiness.

Even if it was a set-up.

~Sue Fairchild

The Dating Game

Let's Forget This Ever Happened

If you want to make God laugh, tell him about your plans.

~Woody Allen

Fateful Date

After God created the world, He made man and woman. Then, to keep the
whole thing from collapsing, He invented humor.
~Bill Kelly

t was a first date to remember, or to forget, depending on your perspective. Being shy, I did not date that often in high school and I wanted everything to be perfect to impress what was, to my teenaged eyes, the most beautiful and interesting creature in all creation.

Taking her out in my beat-up old pickup would not be so impressive, so I begged my father to allow me to use his SUV, the first new car he had ever owned. He put off his answer several days, leaving me in agony, which I almost think he enjoyed. Just as I was debating between using pneumonia or typhoid as an excuse for calling off the date, my father relented.

Friday, the day of the date, arrived and I was determined to let nothing go wrong. That evening I dressed in my newest pants and a nice, crisply ironed shirt. While paying for the gas I bought mints that advertised not just fresh breath but the freshest breath. I wanted no detail left to chance.

As I pulled up in front of her house, I double-checked everything, including how I looked in the mirror. Hair was okay, nothing hanging from my nose, but my lips looked strange, especially right at my mouth. I opened my mouth and was mortified to see that it was green! It was a dull, sickly shade of green. I stuck out my tongue and it was green, too! A detail not mentioned on the package: "freshest breath, but they make your mouth green."

I panicked and was about to drive away from her house when I saw my date come out her front door and stand on the porch. Instantly I was producing gallons of sweat. I couldn't just drive away, but I couldn't go talk to her with a green tongue and blotches of sweat staining the underarms of my once crisply ironed shirt.

She looked puzzled as I slowly got out of the car, smiling a very tight lipped smile at her, waving nonchalantly as possible as anyone can who keeps their elbows locked to their sides. I stammered a weak hello and motioned to the SUV, being careful not to raise my arms by more than an inch.

The first thirty miles of the forty-mile trip consisted of me giving short, tight-lipped answers or asking short questions, with my head turned slightly to the driver's side window, hoping she would not see my greenness. The green seemed to be fading from my lips, from what I could see in the driver's side mirror that I had repositioned. I was beginning to relax just a bit, thinking that I might just get through this. At the next gas station I would stop, pretend to get some gas, and get a drink of water to rinse what I could of the greenness from my mouth.

Eight miles from the pizza place, a deer bounded onto the road. I swerved slightly and stomped on the brakes to avoid it. Unfortunately, the swerve and braking put the car into a sideways skid across the road. When the front right wheel went off the opposite side of the road, I felt the sickening feeling of the SUV starting to tip. It was as they say it is—slow motion—car sliding, slowing tipping on its side, threatening to roll.

But it did not roll entirely. Instead, it came to rest on its right side and slid down the gravel off the opposite side of the road. Of course, my date and I fell in a heap together against the passenger side door. Had it not been for the image of my father strangling me, it might have even been a bit romantic.

We untangled and stood up, feet on the passenger door, as the SUV rested on its right side.

"You okay?" I asked.

"Yes, I think so," she said in a surprisingly unshaken voice.

"My father is going to kill me."

She did not respond, probably taking my father's side at that moment.

"Let's get out of here," I said, trying to open the door above me. Opening a door from underneath, with nothing to stand on other than one foot on a headrest and one slipping along a now vertical dashboard was not an easy task, but I did prevail after several attempts.

"Here, let me boost you up," I said.

She made her way out and crouched on the left side of the car, trying to figure out how to climb down from the side.

I was becoming increasingly upset with our predicament. As I was climbing up and out, I could see my date was confused, moving along the side of the SUV trying to figure out how to get to the ground.

In frustration, I shouted, "Just jump!"

And amazingly she did. Directly into a ditch of waist-high water. I did not expect the splash or the set of words that followed from my perfect date's lips. It was like the water had brought out the sailor in her.

At that point I made two critical mistakes. First, I burst out laughing and second I said, "Well at least I know where NOT to jump." This did not seem to impress her.

I hopped off of the back of the car and walked to the ditch just in time to take her hand, helping my companion up and out of the ditch. I must admit, she still was lovely in a wet, muddy, weeds-hanging-on-you kind of way. She was very angry though, despite my numerous apologies.

Still, I couldn't stop giggling. A bus stopped to see if they could help and found the two of us, me still trying to stifle my laughter and she trying to stifle something less kind. I am sure they thought we were both lunatics—we played and looked the part well.

I did have some good luck, though. My father did not kill me that night. In fact, he was fairly understanding. And as for my date? Fate takes unexpected turns. Eventually she became my wife.

~Daniel James

Love at First Puke

Love is a game that two can play and both win.
~Eva Gabor

"Heads, you meet me in Chicago. Tails, I come to Zion." Please-oh-please be heads, I thought. What in the world would I do in this sleepy little town to impress a guy I'd just met yesterday?

"Well, I guess I'm coming to Zion!" David announced through the phone.

"Great!" I faked enthusiasm. "See you in a couple of days."

I hung up and started wracking my brain. The coffee shop? Boring. Bowling alley? Maybe a decade ago when we were in middle school. A walk near Lake Michigan? Too romantic for a second date.

Then I remembered my dad's friend who raced sailboats on the lake. The previous summer, I'd gone along as "rail meat," moving from one side of the boat to the other to help shift the sailboat's weight as we made turns in the racecourse.

I asked Dad to get David and me an invite from his friend for that week's race. He did. He also got himself an invite, which meant my winning date idea would now include my father. Oh well. There was no time for a Plan B.

"Are you sure you don't want to take something for motion sickness?" I asked David a couple days later as we drove toward the lake. He had never been on a sailboat before, and I knew from experience that the lake could get pretty choppy.

"Nah. I'll be fine."

"You'd make quite an impression on me if you got seasick," I teased.

Ten minutes later we arrived at the harbor, leaving the muggy August heat behind. A refreshing wind whipped off Lake Michigan. Waves splashed against the sides of the docked boats and knocked them against the wooden pier.

"It's a rough one!" called Brian, the sailboat's captain. "They considered calling off the race, but we're going to give it a try."

I nudged David's arm. "Last chance for the meds..."

He shook his head. "I was born for this!" he said, and he hopped aboard a sailboat for the first time in his life.

After a few minutes of puttering through the harbor, we bobbed out onto the open lake and the boat rocked in eight directions at once. Oh! My stomach didn't like that. Good thing I took the motion sickness pills.

Crash! A wave tumbled over the side of the boat and drenched everyone on board. David laughed. "This is awesome!" he shouted over the loudly cracking sail.

David and my dad helped Brian wrestle the sails to get the boat to the starting area. The lake threw two more waves over the side and they laughed—Tom Sawyer and Huck Finn on a nautical adventure.

When all the sailboats were more or less in starting position, a bullhorn blasted through the wind, and the race was on!

"Left siiide!" shouted Brian over the snapping sail and crashing waves. We tripped and banged into each other as we scrambled to the other side of the boat, which was rocking wildly in all directions.

"Right siiide!"

Someone slipped and fell full-force into David's lap. Everyone was dripping wet and laughing. I laughed, too, and ignored the funky feeling that lingered in my stomach. I'd been on a sailboat at least a dozen times before and never had any problems.

The wind settled down a bit and things got quiet as we sailed into a straightaway.

"We're in third place!" called Brian. "Good job everyone!"

David turned around and grinned at me from the front of the boat.

Not a bad second date, I congratulated myself.

Suddenly, my stomach lurched. I grimaced and put my hands on my belly. It lurched again.

This can't be happening, I thought. I scrambled to the back of the boat and leaned over the railing. A stream of vomit disappeared into the churning wake behind the boat.

I don't remember making my way down into the hold. I don't remember where I got the plastic bag. I don't remember how much longer we were out on the lake. But I remember the number of times I puked into that bag. Thirteen.

"Down below is the worst place to be," I heard someone say from up on deck.

"She should come up here and focus on the horizon," declared someone else.

They could say whatever they wanted. There was absolutely no way I was going to stay up there and let David watch me throw up all over myself.

A pair of legs appeared on the ladder that led down into the hold. I considered hiding my barf bag but decided it would be wiser to keep it within reach.

I wrinkled my nose and winced up at David. His face was all concern and compassion. He put his hand on my leg, and romantic butterflies quivered in my already churning stomach.

"Is there anything I can do?" he asked.

"No. Thank you," I said. "You really don't need to be down here. I'm sure it reeks."

"I want to tell Brian to turn the boat around," he said.

"No way!" I replied. "We're in the middle of a race!"

Somehow, I survived the race. Somehow, there was a third date — and many more after that. And twenty-two months later, with our feet planted on the delightfully solid ground of a mountainside, David asked me to be his wife.

During the months we dated, people often asked how we met. The sailboat story usually came up. "I was so impressed with her when she said we couldn't drop out of the race," David would say, making me sound like a champion instead of a pathetic invalid. I adored him more with each telling of the story.

One day, with our wedding date approaching, David made a confession. "Remember that time I flipped a coin to see whether you'd come to Chicago or I'd go to your town?" he asked.

Of course I remembered.

"Well, I was curious to see where you were from and meet your family, but I didn't want to sound too eager."

"Yeah...?" I could see where this was going.

"So... I really did flip a coin. But it wasn't heads."

David hurried to explain that he hadn't actually lied. He had never said whether the coin landed on heads or tails; he'd just announced that he would be coming to visit me. I was mad, but only a little and only for about two seconds.

I've sometimes wondered what might've happened if that second date had been in Chicago like the coin toss said it should be. We would have had nice dinner out, perhaps. Or maybe strolled along Navy Pier and watched the choppy waves from a safe distance. But then I wouldn't have had the opportunity to impress David with my determination to finish the race, and who knows what would've happened? So it was worth suffering through the queasiness. Ten years later, we're still married, still in love—and still haven't gone sailing again.

~Karen Martin

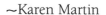

Investment Banking

Hope is the poor man's bread.

~Gary Herbert

Jennie had clear skin, ocean-blue eyes, and an acrylic nametag that read, simply, "Jennie." From where I stood in line, the bank's fluorescent lights bounced magically off her golden hair. I imagined her wearing suede boots, but of course there was no way of knowing—the counter was chest-high—and there was that bulletproof glass.

Recently freed from college, I was spending nights on a friend's cat-urine-stained futon, earning a biweekly check doing freelance jobs for Dick Clark's production company. At the time, I yearned for anything to which I could anchor my life; in my twenty-two-year-old mind, nothing was more grounding than a capital-G Girlfriend.

So when Jennie called out to me from behind that counter—to untrained ears, it simply sounded like "next"—I floated toward her and presented my check.

"Are you in the entertainment industry?" she asked, thumbing the embossed Dick Clark Productions logo. Her fingernails were fire-engine red.

"Yes."

"Do you know Dick Clark?"

"I see him from time to time," I said. True enough—I'd caught many glimpses of Dick Clark walking from his office to the limousine.

"How do you want it?"

I blinked.

"Tens and twenties okay?"

"Sure." I also would have accepted singles, pesos, euros, or pork bellies.

I wasn't holding up my end of the conversation. I was too distracted by the parallel world in my head, in which Jennie and I were window shopping for coffee tables.

And then, just like that, there were bills in my hand. The ride was over.

Jennie's big eyes met mine.

"Thanks, and come again."

Come again. That was nice.

As we parted ways, I felt her warm eyes follow me. Or maybe they'd just turned off the air conditioning.

Two weeks later, I returned to the bank with swollen confidence and ironed jeans. I brought a personal check of my own as an ice-breaker. It wasn't from Dick Clark, but it would have to do.

But this time there was no line. I could see Jennie casually playing with her hair, waiting for attention. It was all happening too soon.

I read a brochure about home equity loans. I killed some time at the ATM. Nervous, I double-pressed the zero and withdrew $200 instead of $20. I didn't even know I had $200.

There was a short line now, and I took my place. Jennie was serving a pudgy man in cargo pants. I planned my openings:

"Tens would be fine. So would your phone number..."

"How about you help me spend this..."

"I don't usually ask out complete strangers, but..."

The line moved, but Cargo Pants apparently had all the time in the world, and was still chatting up Jennie. Was he withdrawing his entire account in nickels? Making a third-world debt repayment?

Or was he focusing his squinty eyes on her and saying, "I don't usually ask out complete strangers, but..."

At this rate, my trajectory would have put me in the care of a stick-figured woman named Lupina; I had to redirect my fate.

I let a hefty woman in a polyester sweater pass ahead of me, then sized up the business suit behind me.

I looked back at the counter. Cargo Pants was gone. Instead of heading for Lupina, Polyester turned toward Jennie. I grabbed her by the shoulder.

"Mind if I go ahead? She's... she's my sister."

Though clearly confused, Polyester just nodded. I trotted toward Jennie, holding the check out like a golden ticket.

"Hi," Jennie said.

"Hi" is miles from "Hello." Everyone knows that.

"Can I cash this, Jennie?"

I swallowed hard as she took my check and punched up my account.

"Listen," I said. "I don't usually do this, but... would you be interested in the idea of maybe having dinner on me? I mean, with me. With me. But still, on me, of course. Maybe we can go to that new French place, Liaison Paris?"

Jennie scrunched her eyes at her screen.

"I'm flattered, but I don't think so."

I wasn't about to give up.

"I know we hardly know each other, but I thought we hit it off last time talking about Dick Clark and the... tens and twenties..."

"I don't mean to embarrass you, but are you sure you can afford it?"

A bead of sweat dripped down the side of my T-shirt.

"Hmm?"

"I can't cash your check. Insufficient funds to cover." She looked at her screen.

"According to this, I think you owe us money."

I felt twenty-two pairs of eyes on me. And there were only six people in the bank. Dick Clark had left the building.

"Owe you money? No, there's a mistake. A rounding error. You're in finance. You understand."

No more than two minutes later, I was outside the bank. I knew I could never return.

The next closest bank branch was miles away, but I made the trek, knowing I couldn't step into Jennie's branch for the rest of my life, or until I had facial reconstructive surgery, whichever came first.

If you've ever changed banks before, you know it's no picnic. But two things made it easier: One was direct deposit. The other was a raven-haired young woman who worked at the new accounts desk and smelled like flowers.

She gave me a free magnet. I think her name was Mia.

~Joel Schwartzberg

Disastrous First Date

Love is an act of endless forgiveness, a tender look which becomes a habit.
~Peter Ustinov

I concealed myself in the toy department aisle, pretending to straighten shelves filled with board games. It seemed ironic that a stack of *The Game of Life* hid me as I peered around an end cap. After all, I was straining to catch a glimpse of the man who made my heart flutter in a way I'd never felt before.

Russ walked into the office to speak with my department manager, and I took that opportunity to step out of the aisle and slip into the stockroom. I hated that stockroom and usually avoided it at all costs. It was dirty and dimly lit, and I was sure I had seen a mouse or two scurrying in the far corners. But... it just happened to be located next to the manager's office. I hovered in the vicinity of the office with the excuse that I was looking for a particular game to restock. I couldn't have been more transparent, but I didn't care. It was one more opportunity to "bump into" this man who had become the object of my affections.

I was seventeen, with big plans. My eighteenth birthday was a few months away, and so was high school graduation. A college acceptance sat on my desk at home. The last thing I needed at this stage of my life was a serious relationship. Too many things were changing all at once.

But my attraction to Russ was stronger than anything I'd felt for anyone else. Odd, considering we hadn't really conversed apart from a casual "Hi" or "Ray is in his office."

Russ was a friend of my boss, Ray. They had attended high school together and stayed in touch. Russ stopped by the department every few weeks, and I made sure I was working on something that just happened to be close enough to say hello.

Casual conversations developed into a first date. Well, not much of a date, really. Lunch at Burger King. The most embarrassing combination lunch and first date in the history of the civilized world.

He drove me to the restaurant in his one-year-old imported sports car. It still had that "new car" smell. I sank into the bucket seat and watched him masterfully handle the stickshift, all the while wishing the drive would last longer.

We ordered our burgers and grabbed a table by the window. I smiled and chatted with Russ, trying to get to know him better. But just a few minutes into our lunch, a quick glance out the window froze my smile even as the heat rose in my face. My boss, who had not been at work when we left, zipped into the parking lot. He pulled into a space, literally leapt from his car, then jogged into the restaurant.

What was he doing here? I prayed that he just happened to stop by for lunch, but I knew better. We watched as he approached our table. He stammered and stuttered and pretended our meeting was a coincidence. All the while I wondered what he knew about his friend that gave him enough cause for concern to follow us to lunch. Hmmm. Were my instincts wrong? Did Russ have a dark past? Was he the "love 'em and leave 'em" type? Would he have tried to take advantage of me?

Please! Could this date get any worse? Sad to say, it could... and it did.

After a few more awkward moments, my boss left. We finished our lunch, but before we departed, I needed to make another purchase. I had promised two co-workers I would bring back takeout for them. With two more lunches bagged and two large sodas anchored in a cardboard cutout on the floor between my feet, Russ helped me settle into the front seat of his car. Did I mention his car was a one-year-old imported sports car?

A five-minute drive brought us back to the store. I opened the car door, hoping the embarrassing interruption wouldn't doom this relationship before it had a chance to begin. Instead of dreaming of the future, I should have paid more attention to the present. With one clumsy move, I knocked over the two large sodas sitting at my feet. The flimsy plastic tops popped off and two thirty-two ounce sodas released their contents in a miniature imitation of Niagara Falls.

That fancy little car mat didn't stand a chance. Cola spread over the mat and seeped into the carpeting on the floorboards. It splashed onto the inside of the car door and up onto the stickshift console. A few drops even made it onto the dashboard.

Yet this still wasn't the lowest moment of the date. The worst part was my reaction. I took one look at the spilled soda and another look at Russ's horrified face, and I began to giggle. Not a quiet peep or two. No. Uncontrollable, nervous giggles bubbled out of me, louder and louder. I clapped a hand over my mouth, to no avail. His new car was ruined, our first date was a disaster, and all I could do was laugh.

I tried to apologize, but the words wouldn't come out. Not that Russ was listening to my babbling at that moment. He was too busy grabbing napkins and desperately attempting to sop up the puddle of cola that now tarnished his spotless car. I did mention it was a one-year-old imported sports car, didn't I?

In between my humiliating giggles, I tried to assist him with the cleanup, but I was already late in getting back, and my laughter wasn't helping the situation. So, at his request, I left him there in the parking lot. His car was stained, his pride injured, and my hopes for a second date were dashed to pieces.

I slunk back into the store. When my co-workers asked about their lunches, I just shook my head and told them they'd have to grab something from the store's snack bar. After clocking back in, I hurried to one of the aisles and hid, wishing the hours would fly by so I could leave before my boss could ask about our date. I didn't worry about seeing Russ—surely he would never want to talk to me again.

But I underestimated him. Fifteen minutes later, he found me in the toy aisle. With a smile that lit up my world, he reassured me the damage was minor, and that he understood my nervous giggles... and he asked if he could take me to lunch again sometime.

We married between my sophomore and junior years of college. I knew the day of our lunch that this was the man for me. Marriage requires a commitment that places each other above all other earthly relationships and attractions. That day, Russ proved I was more important than his new sports car.

And I have a puddle of soda to thank for that lesson.

~Ava Pennington

What Was I Thinking?

Success consists of going from failure to failure without loss of enthusiasm.
~Winston Churchill

Before getting married, I liked to think that I was a pretty good dater. After all, I had been doing it for years and I always figured that practise makes perfect.

I made it a habit to ask out women whenever the opportunity arose. My thinking was that if I was to get better at this, I had to keep doing it.

For the most part, this approach worked. The more I dated, the less nervous I was. I became skilled at the art of conversation and was soon an experienced dater. Or at least, so I thought.

I hoped that all of this dating experience would prepare me for the eventual day when I met the woman of my dreams. Whoever she might be, I reasoned, I would be ready. I would not be my previously nervous, tongue-tied self, but instead would sweep her off her feet with my charm and savvy conversational skills.

And so it came to pass that I met my potential Ms. Right. I was sharing a house with my sister who had a friend who had a sister named Cheryl. The friend and her sister happened to stop by one day and I was smitten.

Despite my wealth of dating experience, I was quickly reduced to a gibbering idiot. I offered them dinner and ran around like a headless chicken doing my best to prepare an edible meal. The cool, calm, suave relationship expert I thought I had become was nowhere to be found.

Somehow I managed to survive our first encounter without completely tripping over my tongue or drowning in a bath of my own nervous sweat. In fact, it looked like I might have actually salvaged victory from what initially had appeared to be overwhelming defeat when a few days later I phoned Cheryl and she agreed to go out on a date with me.

Now when someone is smitten like I was, the logical thing to do is plan a can't-miss date that will convince the object of your affection that you are the only man for her. Unfortunately, despite my lengthy dating career, I seemed to instantly forget everything I knew about burgeoning relationships and how to cultivate them.

The first part of our date wasn't bad. I took Cheryl out to dinner. I figured this would be a chance for us to get to know one another. Sadly, the only thing she got to know was that she was dining with a nervous, chattering idiot who couldn't shut up. It seemed that my extensive dating experience was of little use when I was love struck.

Still, dinner wasn't a complete disaster and I had planned a second part of our date: a movie. And not just a movie at a regular cinema, but a special showing at the arts center in our city. The movie would be shown on an extra large screen and would be backed up with a symphony-class sound system.

Now a rational man trying to impress a woman with a movie would probably choose a love story or a romantic comedy. But since infatuation had short-circuited my reasoning ability, I chose instead to take Cheryl to a special showing of the movie *Apocalypse Now*, which, I can now attest, does not appear on any woman's top ten list of first-date movies.

From the gloomy napalm-filled opening scene backed by The Doors singing "The End" to the final gruesome encounter between the two main characters, the movie is the complete antithesis of a feel-good romantic comedy. As the error of my choice became manifest, I could almost hear Cheryl mouthing the final words of Marlon Brando's character Colonel Kurtz: "The horror, the horror."

Needless to say, the date didn't end well. I still persisted and tried asking Cheryl out again a few days later but the answer was understandably an unqualified no.

Unlike *Apocalypse Now*, however, this story has a happy ending. Five years later, Cheryl and I reconnected and started going out. Apparently enough things had changed in the interim, including my choice of date movies, that I was given a second chance.

We've now been married for almost twenty years and I expect we'll be together for twenty more. So long as I don't rent a copy of *Apocalypse Now*.

~David Martin

14

Speed Dating
in the Slow Lane

Nobody grows old merely by living a number of years.
We grow old by deserting our ideals. Years may wrinkle the skin,
but to give up enthusiasm wrinkles the soul.
~Samuel Ullman

I recently relocated to a new town and was more than ready to get into the social swing of things. So it was with an enthusiastic spirit of adventure that I read of the "Valentine's Day Speed Dating Over Fifty" event at our local community center. I grinned ear to ear. I saw some serious fun in my future.

Lynda, like me, was recently divorced and, between the two of us, we'd been married over fifty-three years. We had fantastic belly laughing get-togethers and she was game for anything, so I could see a girls' night out in our future! We curled our long hair, slipped into our cutest jeans and got ready to step out. Linda had on a snappy leather jacket and a great pair of turquoise boots. I was wearing dangly earrings and a new perfume. We practically skipped arm in arm to the car.

As I pulled into the driveway of the center, I got my first nudge of worry. "The sign says SENIOR center," I remarked.

"I know," Lynda added. "I wondered about that."

Until that moment, I had pictured in my mind a sultry, dim room with long booths. Walking in the door, I was shocked by the fluorescent-lit room filled with flimsy card tables and—I am just going to say it—lots of old people. Some really old people. I am fifty-eight and certainly no youngster. Still, I was ill prepared.

Name badges affixed, we swallowed hard and looked around. We chatted with Gladys, a lovely woman with a great mane of champagne-colored hair who looked a bit like Walter Matthau. Lynda leaned in and wondered if it would be rude to simply leave but I thought it would be hard to get out without being obvious. So we kept our smiles firmly fastened to our faces and, as the saying goes, we let the gentlemen start their engines.

The rules were simple: Four minutes to speak with each person. The men moved from table to table. (That took some time. We changed it the second half because the women could get up and down easier.) There was a list of suggested questions to help break the ice: "If you could be any animal, what would you be? "Tell me some things on your bucket list." "If you could be anywhere else but here right now, where would you be?" (Okay, that last one wasn't on the list.)

My first fellow was a massage therapist. I know this because he brought his framed certificate to show me. Also, he gave me his business card right before he moved on.

The second gentleman wasn't actually supposed to be the second but he was so hard of hearing he didn't hear that he was supposed to move to his right. He just sized up the prospects after his first "date" and walked over to my table. He had taken the bus there, he shouted, and needed a ride home, but the lady at the previous table offered to give him a lift. He was looking for a roommate because he couldn't afford to buy a house and he didn't want to live with his daughter anymore.

Next came Michael, a gracious gent with a green leprechaun fedora who spoke with a marvelous British accent. He and his wife Mary had been married forty-eight years until she died a year ago. He missed her so much and his rheumy eyes filled as he spoke of her. I started to hyperventilate because I wanted to cry, too.

Jack was a "cattle rancher." "How interesting," I said. "How many cows do you run?" "Six," he replied with a straight face. Ranching was hard work, I agreed.

We took a break and it was like a sixth grade dance — the men were clumped into one corner and we women clustered together in another. Gladys' eyes were bright as she rushed up to us. She had one distinct prospect, a much younger man "with a good head on his shoulders." "What do you guys think?" she asked conspiratorially. "A lot of these guys are hard of hearing," she added, sadly shaking her head. "It's an epidemic."

Margaret, a decidedly unhappy participant, was hunkered down in a chair, arms crossed tightly over her chest looking like she'd been sent to the principal's office. "I did this three years ago and it's taken me three years to get over the trauma," she fumed. She was mad. I am glad I didn't have to spend four minutes alone at a table with her. Hell hath no fury like a woman bored.

Lynda and I compared notes. She is a social worker who counsels those recently diagnosed with cancer. "I feel like I am working tonight," she whispered. She told me about one man who lost his wife thirteen years ago and who started crying when he talked about her. Another guy liked her so much that he told her she was the most beautiful woman there and he "really liked her make-up." Oh, and by the way, one of the guys there was her second cousin. She and I were exhausted. We looked longingly at the exit, but instead plastered smiles back on our faces and found our tables.

My next adventure was Harold, a spitfire Hawaiian with a long gray ponytail. He reminded me of the turtle from *Finding Nemo*, with his surfer-dude drawl. At the beginning they'd given us a paper on which to write each person's name and then to discreetly put a check mark in the yes column if we wanted the facilitator to provide them our contact information. Harold was having a ball, not caring if a woman was fifty or eighty years old. He had checked the yes column for every single woman.

That night, I learned how difficult it is to dip your toe into the dating pool after so many years of lying safely on the beach. But I also learned that this gloriously inept group of daters and myself were all in the same boat. We wanted to make a connection. We chose not to be alone. And you know what else? We put ourselves out there. Each and every one of us got all gussied up and allowed ourselves to feel a bit silly and ill at ease, while clinging to the idea that someone special could be around the next corner.

Cupid may have his work cut out for him, but I remember that evening as a gift, and an opportunity to appreciate that we're all in this together.

~Maureen Buckley

"I don't want to stand here talking to you but I'd be happy to walk you over to another person."

15

A Toe-tal Disaster

Humor is merely tragedy standing on its head with its pants torn.
~Irvin S. Cobb

I was always a realist when it came to love. I didn't believe in destiny or the idea of soul mates. I considered it a lot of superstitious hooey. That is, until it happened to me... a date that went so horribly wrong, the only possible explanation was that our union was cursed.

When I first saw her, I was dumbstruck. She seemed to be my dream woman in every way. Everything she said and did was just so... wow. She could have worn a potato sack and it would have looked like high fashion to me. She could have read an insurance policy and I would have savored every word that poured from her sweet lips.

After ogling her with the glazed expression of a barn animal for a few weeks, I finally got up the nerve to ask her out on a date. I was ecstatic when she said yes. I walked home ten feet off the ground.

The first sign that something was amiss came when I called to confirm our date. She said she had severely stubbed her big toe and was thinking about canceling. It wasn't broken, she said, but it had swollen to twice its normal size. My heart sank, thinking she had changed her mind and made up the toe injury as an excuse. However, when I said she would be sitting most of the night — in a car, restaurant, and theater — she agreed to keep our date.

Sure enough, when I came to pick her up, she was wearing open sandals and the big toe of her right foot was heavily bandaged.

The first sign of the curse came about halfway into dinner. It was one of those restaurants with singing waiters. One broke into song so I lifted my chair to turn around, not noticing that my date had extended her leg under my chair to rest her toe. As I set down the heavy, wooden chair, one of the legs and all of my weight came down squarely on her injured big toe. She let out a yell that was louder than the singer's amplified voice. The other diners thought she was launching into a duet with him. I apologized profusely, but she was in so much pain, she couldn't respond. Eventually, she recovered and forgave me. After all, I couldn't see her unnaturally outstretched leg under my chair. But I still felt like a putz.

After dinner, we drove to the theater. At least we would be safe there, I thought. No such luck. As the theater filled up, a large woman shimmying along our aisle to her seat stepped on the same toe with her heel. My date screamed for the second time that night. This was becoming downright mysterious. I was starting to think someone had a voodoo doll of her and was repeatedly stabbing the big toe with a pin.

I didn't think her toe could swell any more than it already had. I was wrong. When the lights came up in the theater and I got a good look at it, I almost screamed, too. It looked like something out of a cartoon. I suggested taking her to the emergency room. She refused, saying she hated hospitals. However, my growing concern must have struck some chord in her heart because she asked if we could go to my place. I had mentioned that there was a swimming pool at my apartment complex, and she thought submerging her toe in the water might make it feel better. I was glad she wanted to spend more time together despite the bumpy start we were having.

It was a warm, summer night and the front yard grass was still wet from sprinklers. She took off her sandals and walked across the cool grass.

"Ahh, that feels nice," she said, finally feeling some relief from the pain. I was as relieved as she was until she kicked a sprinkler—yes, with the same big toe—and screamed in agony yet again.

"Ah, come on!" I yelled to whatever force was calling down such misery on her unfortunate toe.

I picked her up and carried her to the pool. She sat on the edge, put both feet in the cool water and said, "I don't usually drink, but I think a little alcohol might numb the pain a little."

I told her I would bring her something.

"Make it a double," she said.

We sat at the pool's edge and gradually fell into lively conversation. She even forgot about her toe. Eventually, we moved to lounge chairs. After an hour or so, I realized that I hadn't let my dog Sparky out of the apartment all evening. I excused myself and went to get him. She saw me walking him to the grass and said, "Oh, he's so cute! Bring him over here!"

Then the curse struck again. To my horror, Sparky, who had never bitten anyone before, walked directly over to her and chomped down on her bandaged toe. Maybe he smelled blood through the gauze and thought it was a sausage wrapped in butcher's paper. She let out a blood-curdling scream for the fourth time that night, the kind of scream one might hear in a 1950s B-grade horror film.

Startled by her scream, Sparky took off and I ran after him, worried he might run into the street. By the time I caught him and returned, she was livid.

"Why didn't you warn me your dog was so vicious?" she yelled.

I told her Sparky had never bitten anyone before but she did not find it comforting to know she was the first.

"Please just take me home," she said. "I've had enough toe injuries for one night."

I couldn't understand why she was insinuating that her now obvious toe curse was my fault. I mean, the chair leg, the clumsy movie patron and the sprinkler I could understand, but my little Sparky latching onto that particular toe, and with such cyborg-like commitment, was proof enough for me that she and I were in some sort of Twilight Zone episode. I half-expected Rod Serling to show up and start narrating it.

With a heavy heart, I drove her and her toe home. She stuck

her foot out of the window to elevate it. I begged her to bring it back inside to prevent some other freak accident, like a vulture swooping down on it. After everything I had witnessed that night, anything was possible.

I left several messages for her in the following weeks but she didn't return my calls. A month or so later, for a laugh, I sent her a pair of steel-toed boots to protect her cursed toe. She called to thank me and we made plans to go out again.

On our next date, she wore the boots. It was a wonderful evening, a fresh start. When I took her home, she got out of the car and slammed her thumb in the door.

~Mark Rickerby

Too Good to Be True

*A lie can travel half way around the world
while the truth is putting on its shoes.*
~Mark Twain

"C an I leave this here for a second?" A complete stranger wanted to leave his beer next to my beach towel.

My best friend and I were island hopping in Greece for the summer. We didn't know him, but I found myself saying, "Yes, you can leave it here."

"Thank you," he said, and then vanished into the Mediterranean Sea.

Later that night my friend and I were exploring the alleyways of Mykonos. I turned the corner and tripped into the mystery man. My friend Julie jumped up and said, "Hey, we know you." He asked us to join him and his friends for the evening.

We made our way down the hill only to find a table of two beautiful chiseled men sitting with a bottle of wine. They glanced up. "Ladies, welcome!"

It wasn't long before I made an instant connection with the mystery man's cute older friend. He grabbed my hand and said, "Let's get out of here." He escorted me into the closest gelato shop. It was all so romantic and dreamy. He was unlike any man I had dated before, deep and cultured, with full facial hair. He scooped the cold cream into my mouth and leaned in to kiss me. Never before had I kissed someone in such a romantic way. The gelato shop felt filled with salty air and lust.

Soon, we rejoined the group and hopped aboard a little rowboat floating out to sea. We were being carted out to what I thought would be a tropical deserted island, where we would dance in the moonlight all night. I was jolted out of my fantasy when we realized we were actually headed to a giant sailboat in the middle of the bay. This can't be real, I thought to myself. This night keeps getting better.

Could I possible take this fling and turn it into a lifetime of sailing on yachts, drinking champagne, and traveling with gorgeous men? The chiseled men pulled out chocolate-covered strawberries, and I knew they had raised the bar for my romantic future.

I was on top of the world... that is, until the morning. When I woke up, everything looked different. The hot young man seemed saggy and old. As the boat rocked up and down and I looked at him, I noticed something shiny on the windowsill. I moved over to get a closer look and realized it was a wedding ring. On Mr. Wonderful's left hand, I saw a tan line around his ring finger.

All of a sudden, my perfect night turned into a big fright. Had I actually just made out with a married man? My mind raced through the evening's events. I wanted nothing to do with Mr. Fanta-Sea.

I grabbed my dress and friend and dived into the bay, hoping to make the quick swim to shore. As I jumped overboard, my dress got caught on the boat. I heard a giant rip, and suddenly the entire dress was on the boat as my naked body smacked into the clear blue water. Just when I thought things couldn't get any worse, I looked up to see an entire tour boat of Italian men cruising to shore. They whistled and laughed hysterically.

Lesson learned: If it seems too good to be true, it probably is.

~Shannon Kaiser

A Dating Reminder

Every survival kit should include a sense of humor.
~Author Unknown

I was rather shy growing up, and my somewhat spotty dating record reflected that. But I didn't mind. I was studious, pleasant, and while I wasn't the most popular girl on campus, I certainly was never short of friends in college. Even then, though, I didn't linger much on campus after classes most days. I had a three-year-old niece with whom I spent those extra hours. Heather was so much fun! She was bold and smart and shared her days with me as soon as I walked in the door! Seeing the world through her eyes was, at the very least, entertaining—and at it's very best, educational.

As most families do when they have a toddler around the house, we had all gotten into the habit of reminding Heather of the Childhood Don'ts—reminders that are a part of every child's life: "Don't forget to brush your hair." "Don't go near the oven." "Don't touch the hot water faucet." "Don't forget to put away your toys." She was a quick study, and, like all children, she took great pride in her accomplishments. A lot of what she and I shared together in the evenings were her recollections at the end of the day of what she hadn't done as much as what she had! "I didn't touch the stove today." "I didn't forget to brush my hair this morning."

I finally accepted a date with a guy named Paul at our church. We were going out on the lake in his boat. I was a little nervous, but excited at the same time. I liked Paul and was hoping to make a good impression, even though my dating skills were definitely rusty. I had explained to Heather what a date was and that it was a big day for me. She listened to me wide-eyed and nodded solemnly, signifying she understood how important a date was.

Paul came to the house to pick me up that Saturday afternoon. I was ready, right on time, and as we walked out the front door together, Heather rushed up to me and gave me a big hug goodbye. She stood in the doorway, waving and calling out "Bye!" as Paul opened the car door for me.

What happened next was my own fault, really. I knew Heather took those reminders seriously. And honestly, she had done so well with her potty training she hardly ever had an accident. But like I said, we had all gotten in the habit of reminding her of those Childhood Don'ts. She didn't know any differently. I guess in her three-year-old mind, it was logical to remind me as I was leaving the house, just as I had reminded her many, many times. So it really shouldn't have been such a surprise, but just the same... it was.

As she stood there in the doorway, waving goodbye to me, she called out the most important dating reminder of all:

"Don't tinkle in your panties!"

~Ginny Dubose

Chicken Soup for the Soul

The Milk Dud Incident

Laughter is the shortest distance between two people.

·~Victor Borge

I yanked my shoes on and sprinted out the front door. If I didn't hurry, I'd miss the bus. At fourteen years old, when you have a date and nobody to drive you, missing the bus is a big deal.

Missing that bus was not an option. I'd been interested in the opposite sex since kindergarten, and finally, male attention had begun wandering in my lanky blond direction. I'd waited so long!

My home was an hour south of Seattle, traffic on I-5 considered. "That might buy me time if I miss the bus," I thought, since my boyfriend was driving south himself to meet me there. I raced from my neighborhood to the main road, with still enough time to feel my legs to make sure they were properly shaven, even though there was no chance anyone would be touching them. I inhaled deeply—not to relax, but to test whether I'd worked up a pungent sweat.

I arrived at the bus stop on time and I didn't stink. Oh, sweet success! Little did I know, it wasn't the bus I should have been worried about. I arrived at the movie theater before my date and before our two friends, who'd be joining us. It was overcast outside. I waited in comfort by a fountain, admiring its iridescent mosaic detailing, enjoying the breeze and occasional smattering of drizzle.

Joshua showed up in a leather jacket. You can't go wrong in one of those. His honey eyes and a laid-back style were exactly as I remembered. He and I had already bought our tickets and candy when

Cory and Hannah showed up. They were friends from church—our age—who'd been together more than a year. Joshua and I had only seen each other three times total.

We all sat down together and whispered through the previews. Josh offered me Milk Duds right before the movie began. If there's something you should know about me, it's this: I do not refuse candy. He might as well have forfeited the entire box. A few pieces rolled out of my hand as he poured. That was no trouble at all; I swiped my seat for the runaways and devoured them.

Almost two hours later, our group left the theater. We waited in the lobby for our rides.

"Uh, you should go to the bathroom," Hannah blurted out randomly.

"I don't have to go to the bathroom, but thanks," I replied.

Cory and Joshua circled behind me and laughed. "No, you should really go to the bathroom," Josh reiterated.

"I don't need..." I began, but he interrupted me, forcefully suggesting I go.

Once in the bathroom, I realized I had missed a Milk Dud. It had melted onto the seam of my pants, in the absolute worst spot imaginable. "Oh no," I chuckled, half-embarrassed, half-amused. "Have I been walking around like this?" I brushed the candy off and tied Joshua's sweater around my waist. He'd tossed it to me on my way in, and it was now obvious why. Unfortunately, from that point forward, Hannah often called me "Dudley Doo-Pants." On the bright side, Joshua asked me out again, and soon after the Milk Dud incident, became my first serious boyfriend.

~S.M. Westerlie

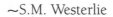

The Dating Game

The Moment I Knew

For it was not into my ear you whispered, but into my heart.
It was not my lips you kissed, but my soul.

~Judy Garland

Assigned Seats

*Once in awhile, right in the middle of an ordinary life,
love gives us a fairy tale.*
~Anonymous

I first see him in the airport in New York. He's cute. Twenty-something, dark hair, intense blue eyes. But what catches my eye is that he is carrying *Flannery O'Connor: The Complete Stories*. What kind of guy carries a book like that on a Club Med vacation? Cute Guy's book choice isn't exactly chick magnet material. But to a book nerd like me, it's catnip.

I'm vacationing with my college friend Bari. I don't see the Cute Guy again till mid-week. He's with a guy named Rich who has spent days pursuing Bari. Rich introduces the Cute Guy as his roommate. I am miffed when Cute Guy doesn't even glance at me. I shrug. His loss. But it rankles.

The last day of our trip, Bari invites me to watch Rich play in a tennis tournament. She introduces me — again — to Cute Guy, who, I know from Bari's description, has spent the last two days busily chasing Bari too. We chat between sets. We discover we both majored in English. He mentions that *Annie Hall* is his favorite movie. "Me too," I say, thinking it's too bad he likes Bari.

On the plane back to New York the next day, I pull out my copy of Henry James' *Washington Square* and start reading.

"I live near Washington Square," someone says. I look across the aisle. How did he wind up sitting next to me?

"Me too," I say. "Tenth Street and University Place."

"Ninth Street and Fifth," he says. "We're neighbors."

We talk about our jobs; when I tell him I handle publicity for authors at Simon & Schuster, he asks what's the best book I've worked on lately. I tell him it's a biography called *Max Perkins: Editor of Genius*.

"Oh, sure, he was Ernest Hemingway's editor. Scott Fitzgerald too," he says. Wow, how many guys would know that? Then he asks, "Have you read Fitzgerald's short stories?"

Excited, I nod. "'Bernice Bobs Her Hair' is my favorite."

He opens the Flannery O'Connor paperback. "If you like short stories, you have to read this one."

"You want me to read it right now?"

"It won't take long."

So I read. I feel his eyes on me. Why is he watching me read... are my lips moving? It's a test... he expects me to say something all English major-y and brilliant.

"I like the way she mixes grotesque characters with violence and colloquial humor. It's part of that Southern Gothic tradition..." Oh jeez, do I sound pretentious or what? I lean forward and hand him the book. He touches my hair gently. "You have a silver streak."

"I know, can you believe it? Going gray at twenty-five. I hate it."

"Oh no, it's very attractive." His voice is low. Intimate.

"It's my Susan Sontag impersonation."

"So now you have to tell me the worst book you've worked on," he says. I describe a novel based on a true story about a serial killer in Detroit.

"But in a weird way that has something to do with why I came on this trip," I tell him. "Even though the book was awful, I got friendly with a reporter in Detroit. I told her I was thinking of cancelling this trip because I had too much work, and she said, 'If you don't go, ten years from now you won't even remember what you were doing that week. But if you go, you'll remember exactly where you were.'"

"And now you will," he says.

"And now I will."

"I almost didn't come on this trip either," he confides. "I was all set to go camping in Newfoundland till my mother said, 'Are you nuts? Do you really want to spend your vacation in a cold damp tent in the fog?'"

"I think I like your mother," I say.

We smile. Suddenly he reaches his hand across the aisle and links fingers with me. "You are really a good person," he says, squeezing.

My heart races. I could marry a guy like this, I think wistfully. Lucky Bari.

As we're getting off the plane, Bari turns to me and says, "Do you like him?"

"I do," I admit. "But you met him first. I would never do that to you."

"It's fine!" she says cheerfully. "He's not my type."

He insists on helping me with my luggage. I see my parents chatting with a woman I don't recognize. I point. "That's my mother, but I don't know the woman she's with."

"I do," he says. "That's my mother."

"We just ran into each other," my mother explains. Our folks already knew each other? I've travelled 1,000 miles to the Bahamas to meet the boy next door?

As soon as I get back to my office I mail him a copy of the Max Perkins book. Two days later he calls; I invite him to my office. He is nonchalant as he browses my bookshelves.

"Take anything you want," I tell him.

Which he does. Because two weeks later, he asks me to marry him.

And I do.

~Liane Kupferberg Carter

More Beautiful than Tolkien

And he took her in his arms and kissed her under the sunlit sky,
and he cared not that they stood high upon the walls in the sight of many.
~J. R. R. Tolkien

My name is Elissa, and I am a rabid fangirl. And that's okay! Thanks to my fangirlish tendencies, I'm also a wife.

It started when I was eight years old. My favorite childhood memories involve my dad coming into my room every night to read to me, even long after I was able to read on my own. One night, he brought with him a well-worn paperback book with a creepy cover.

"*The Hobbit*?" I asked. "What's a hobbit?"

His answer, or rather, J. R. R. Tolkien's answer, shaped my adolescent life.

A few years later I tackled *The Lord of the Rings*, which was even better than *The Hobbit*. I read more of Tolkien's works. With my dad's guidance, I cited *Unfinished Tales* in my tenth-grade English paper on *The Hobbit*. I bemoaned the atrocities inflicted on the plot when the *The Lord of the Rings* movies came out. I spent the summer before my senior year of high school studying Quenya, the High Elven language of Middle-earth. I copied my favorite passages from the books and carried them everywhere in a notebook. With few exceptions, I hid the extent of my obsession from everyone.

This was particularly true once I arrived at college, and it often proved to be a good decision. Once, when a friend and I discussed a boy we knew, she jokingly said, "He probably doesn't want to date you because you speak Elvish!" It could have been true.

Even though I really thought her comment was funny, and even though I wasn't particularly interested in the boy in question, it wasn't exactly what I wanted to hear. It was my second year at college, and dating was a very sensitive and frustrating subject for me.

Despite my crazy obsession, I was as boy crazy as any girl. Maybe the obsession made things even worse. In his books, Tolkien told the most beautiful love stories. I wanted a love as empowering as that of Beren and Lúthien, as life changing as that of Thingol and Melian, as natural and sweet as that of Faramir and Eowyn, and as resilient as that of Aragorn and Arwen. But the whole "Love At First Sight" thing works better in Middle-earth than in real life, where you have to fall in love the hard way—that means dating. And, well, dating didn't seem to be working out for me.

Everything changed when my friend Natalie decided to invite her brother, Tom, to our weekly dinner group.

I had heard impressive rumors about Tom: he was unnaturally smart, creative, and interesting. After a few minutes of face-to-face interaction, I could see the rumors were true. Beyond that, he was cute. However, I was convinced that we had nothing in common, and that made it harder to get to know him. Our conversations were stunted and awkward. I ended up trying to ignore Tom completely, and to avoid drawing attention to myself.

We played *Speed Scrabble* after dinner. I'm not very good at *Speed Scrabble*, and whenever I'm falling behind, I tend to just lay out the coolest words I possibly can. During one round, I had several of the races of Middle-earth, and with a little effort and luck I could spell a few others. It wasn't a very practical way to play the game, but I thought it was pretty cool, and I had a sudden urge to show off my grid, but I was trying not to draw attention to myself.

But then I had another, much stronger thought: You're in a safe place, and you have nothing to lose.

So I spoke up. Of course, no one was interested.

Or so I thought. After a few uncomfortable moments of silence, Tom asked, "Who here has read *The Lord of the Rings*?"

I raised my hand. I was the only one.

"That's cool. Girls should read Tolkien."

I sat there in shock, as seconds slipped away from a moment that was definitely, definitely too good to be true.

He hadn't said, "Those movies are awesome," or even, "Girls should read *The Lord of the Rings*." He had said "Tolkien."

Tom Nysetvold was a Tolkien fan.

Shock or no shock, I wasn't letting my destiny slip through my fingers. I muttered my agreement, then mustered the courage to ask "Have you read *The Silmarillion*?" I felt obnoxious, but I had to prove that I was different from the other girls at the table. I had to show him that I was serious in my literacy without looking like, well, a rabid fangirl.

"Yep. Have you read *The Book of Lost Tales*?"

I had, though it had been long enough ago that I prayed he wouldn't quiz me on it. "Yep. Have you read *Unfinished Tales*?"

Pause. "I have not."

I prayed that he was impressed, not turned off, by the fact that I had read more Tolkien than he had.

I looked down at my tiles, carefully trying to think of a normal person response. "You should," I said quietly. "It's really good." I peeked back at him, waiting for his reaction.

He looked up from his grid, locked his amazing blue eyes on mine, and said very seriously, "We should hang out sometime."

My heart was pounding, but all I said was, "Yeah, I'd like that."

Tom just nodded. "Okay, so have you noticed parallels between the creation story in Genesis and *The Silmarillion*?"

I forgot my *Scrabble* grid completely and became engrossed in the conversation. When we were done discussing *The Silmarillion*, we worked our way through all the obligatory get-to-know-you questions. Eventually Tom had to leave, but as he did he stopped at the door. "What's your last name again?"

I told him.

He shut the door behind him, then opened it again. "And how do you spell your first name?"

"E-L-I-S-S-A."

"Got it. See you later."

One stilted Facebook conversation and one phone call later, we had arranged a date to get lunch and check out the campus dinosaur museum. The date went beautifully. Both activities gave us plenty of time to talk and get to know each other. Tom was incredibly interesting and easy to talk to, and we had much more in common than our love for Tolkien.

As the date ended, I realized I was very attracted to Tom. In every aspect, he was exactly my type. It wasn't love at first sight — it was much more practical, and that in no way diminished the magic. It was almost too good to be true, but I felt so confident that if we tried dating, wonderful things would happen.

Tom seemed to feel the same way. In the coming weeks we continued to see each other and talk whenever possible. Our relationship developed quickly. By the end of the month we were a couple, by the end of the summer we were engaged, and by the end of the year we were married. It seems like such a short time span, but Tom and I couldn't be happier, and I've learned a lot so far. Most importantly, I've learned that real love and real happy endings are more beautiful and magical than even Tolkien's stories.

~Elissa Nysetvold

In the Cards

When you love someone, all your saved-up wishes start coming out.
~Elizabeth Bowen

Outside, the card's black and white photograph showed a boy and girl holding hands and wading in the ocean. Inside, I read these words: "I waded my whole life for you."

It was perfect, exactly the card I wanted. I plucked it from the romantic section of the aisle and made my way to the checkout. To whom would I give the card? That would be a mystery for years to come.

When I was a freshman in college, I sent cards to friends and family while I was away at school. As I shopped for funny and heartwarming cards, I noticed the best ones were romantic. But I didn't have a boyfriend. So I did what any rational, prepared person does—I bought the cards anyway and placed them in a file folder labeled "cards for future reference." Then I waited for the right man to come along. I'm glad I didn't hold my breath.

Years passed, and I collected many cards. I also collected a few dates. I dated Mr. "You're the most wonderful woman I've ever met—this month," and Mr. "I'm smarter than most everyone else on the planet—including you." I'll never forget Mr. Thoughtful, the man who let doors slam in my face, or Mr. Baseball, the guy who scratched and spit like he was on a pitcher's mound instead of a date. I endured dates that smothered to the point of suffocation, and those so aloof I might as well have been alone. Occasionally, I met a genuinely nice man, but either one of us didn't want anything more than a friendship, or something about the relationship didn't feel right.

One of my girlfriends knew about the cards and my dream of being a wife and mother—before I was too old and decrepit to be a wife and mother. After each date she asked gingerly, "So... was he worthy of the cards?" To which I gave my usual response: "No. I will know I have met the right man when I can give him the cards without hesitation."

By my mid-twenties, well-meaning friends and family tried to make me feel better about my single status.

"The right one will come along when you least expect it," they all echoed.

I didn't know how to shove my feelings so far away that when my heart's desire came along, it would surprise me. I began to think that if there was one right person for each of us, my guy had already been hit by a bus or had run off with a supermodel. By the time my twenties came to a close, the dating game and I had hit an impasse. I had a file full of greetings, but in real life true love didn't seem to be in the cards.

Then I began a new career as a teacher and moved close to my school. One day I exited my second floor apartment and spied a man opening his mailbox at the bottom of the stairwell. He was tall, about my age, and had eyes the same color as mine. But it was his movie-star smile that caught my attention. We exchanged hellos. Eventually, I learned that he was my first floor neighbor, and his name was Jesse.

On another day I left my apartment and looked down while Jesse entered the stairwell and looked up. His face widened into that beautiful smile, and my heart, quite unexpectedly, skipped a beat. Apparently I had developed a crush on my new neighbor, and I didn't know what to do. Past experience reminded me that I was a flirting failure. Plus, I liked my apartment. If we dated and it was a disaster, I would have to move. I decided to wait and see if a relationship unfolded naturally.

Jesse and I got acquainted when we passed in the stairwell and parking lot. He talked about his late mother, who taught at my school and died when he was in college, and I told him about my students. I folded clothes in the laundry room while he shared stories about his niece and nephew, and he saw me in all my glory—carrying trash to the dumpster with wet hair and no make-up. We did real life versus the dating game and danced around a relationship for almost two years.

Then one muggy July evening I came home from a long day of preparing my classroom for the first day of school. Jesse sat on the front steps of our apartment building looking at the stars and moon. I was covered in dirt and paint, and he noticed that I looked tired.

"Do you need any help?" he offered.

I hesitated. It wouldn't exactly be a date, but moving our friendship beyond chatting in the stairwell and laundry room was a big step. I accepted his offer and the next night we cleaned, painted, and decorated my classroom together. I still smile at the memory of my six-foot neighbor sitting in a child-sized chair cutting out construction paper flowers.

After that Jesse and I started to date. We went for walks, shared dinners, and talked for hours. He was Mr. Romantic, holding my hand and putting his arm around me when my tears spilled down the front of his shirt during sappy movies. One evening I felt insecure about something I don't even remember now, and Jesse asked why I was worried. The best explanation I could give was, "Sometimes I need a little reassurance."

The next day the school secretary summoned me to the office. I walked down the hall expecting to retrieve a child's forgotten homework or lunch money. Instead, I pushed open the office door to find a vase of red roses. The attached card had a handwritten note from Jesse: "I thought you might like a vase full of reassurance. Love, Jesse." I was speechless. Even Hallmark couldn't have said it better. And I knew, after waiting for what seemed a lifetime, I had found Mr. Right.

He loved the cards.

~Janeen Lewis

22

Finding Florence

The most precious gift we can offer anyone is our attention.
~Thich Nhat Hanh

My children stared as the sparkling snow swirled around the red-domed roof of the miniature Basilica di Santa Maria del Fiore, possibly the most famous symbol of Florence, Italy. I shook the snow globe again, and the glittery snow fell around the replica of the historic cathedral. I wound the stem on the bottom of the globe, and Antonio Vivaldi's Baroque composition "La Primavera" played with the tinkling sound that music boxes make.

"Let me hold it, Mom! Please?" asked six-year-old Andrew.

"Me, too," said three-year-old Gracie.

I wouldn't let go. I held my treasure tightly to my heart, one of the few keepsakes I never let my children play with.

"Why is it so special?" Andrew asked.

"Your dad gave it to me for my birthday when we were dating."

Jesse and I had learned a lot about each other early in our relationship. He told me about his work and his adventurous interests like scuba diving and flying planes. He told me how much he missed his late mom. I learned that the scar on his right cheek came from a car crash when he was a child and that he didn't have a favorite color.

He learned that I had wanted to be a professional ballerina when I was five, and that when I was young, I loved the color pink so much that every year I begged for "pink" strawberry-flavored cake and icing for my birthday. He knew I wanted to write a book someday, and that I loved children.

One of the most important pieces of information he gleaned during our talks was that my favorite movie was *While You Were Sleeping*. Although it was a chick flick, he watched it with me. I had seen the charming movie years before I knew Jesse, and I related to Lucy, the main character, played by Sandra Bullock. Lucy worked as a token collector at a train station in Chicago and was lonely because she had no family. She had two desires, to meet and marry the handsome stranger, Peter, who gave her a token every day, and to visit Florence. Through a series of comical events, Lucy fell in love with Jack, Peter's brother, played by Bill Pulliam. When Jesse watched the movie with me, he didn't mind that I got a few warm tears on the front of his shirt during the most poignant part.

A couple of weeks before my birthday, Jesse said he had bought a present at the mall, and had told some acquaintances about it. One of the women in the group had given Jesse advice.

"She told me to buy you jewelry. When I told her what I bought you, she wrinkled her nose." He looked uncertain. "I hope you'll like what I got you."

"I hardly wear any jewelry," I said. "And I am sure I will love whatever you give me."

But I wondered what the present was. I rarely went to the mall, and I hadn't mentioned wanting anything from any of the stores there. What on earth had he gotten me?

The day of my birthday arrived, and I couldn't wait for the special birthday dinner Jesse had planned. When I walked into his apartment, I smelled a mixture of melted butter and sautéed onion, parsley, garlic, and chicken. That meant he had made my new favorite dish, Étouffée. This was a sacrifice because he was very health conscious and the dish has many, many buttery calories. He had covered the table with a white tablecloth, cloth napkins, and candles. We ate the delicious meal and when we finished, he served my old childhood favorite, "pink" cake.

Finally, it was time for my present. He set a package the size and shape of a shoebox on the table. I was even more perplexed. Jesse bought me shoes at the mall? Did he even know my size? I tore the paper away, and saw that the gift was from The Music Box, a store that carries specialty musical items. Still confused, I continued to unwrap. I lifted the flaps to the box and looked in at a shiny glass globe, then placed it on the table. Enchanted, I gazed at the red-roofed dome of the cathedral. I traced the carvings on the base of the snow globe with my finger—Michelangelo's statue of David, the lush Boboli Gardens, the medieval stone arch, Ponte Vecchio, and a tranquil Arno River reflecting a cerulean sky.

Florence.

I was speechless with understanding. Jesse's gift was a Florence snow globe like one that Jack had given to Lucy in *While You Were Sleeping*.

It was the most thoughtful gift anyone had ever given me. And it was more than just a snow globe; it became a symbol of another gift—Jesse's desire to understand and know me so that he could make me happy. That's what I had been yearning for all those frustrating years of dating before he came into my life. His choice had been perfect. No piece of jewelry could have replaced the gift he gave me.

Twelve years, a marriage, and two children later, I still cherish my Florence snow globe. I keep it in our curio cabinet next to the unity candle that Jesse and I lit during our wedding ceremony.

In the end of my favorite movie, Lucy found her true love, and he gave her Florence. On that special birthday years ago, the same thing happened to me.

~Janeen Lewis

23

An Unconventional Start

True love is the outward demonstration of inward conviction.
~Author Unknown

Nick and I met online. I saw his profile first, and thought he came across as a fun, genuine, and silly kind of guy. We also had a few things in common—we both worked in human resources, and the movie Nick listed as his favorite in his profile was a movie a friend of mine had worked on.

After a few days of e-mailing back and forth, Nick invited me to dinner. I thought that dinner might be a little too much too soon so I suggested we meet for a beer instead—an "interview" as I called it. I was going to be attending a networking event after work one night that week, so I recommended that we meet at a restaurant up the street from the event at 8:00 p.m.

Nick arrived shortly before 8:00 and grabbed a table. He ordered a beer and sent me a text to let me know where he was sitting. At 8:10 p.m., I was still at the networking event working on my polite exit. As I walked to my car I noticed Nick's text and responded, "Running late. I will be there in ten minutes."

Nick never received the text. As he sat there thinking he was being stood up, he decided that he would take his last few swigs of beer and leave. With only a swig left and a minute to spare, I arrived. Our "interview" wasn't necessarily eventful or amazing—we just spent an hour chatting. As Nick walked me to my car, I could tell he wasn't going to ask me out again. So I went ahead and asked him, "Are we going to hang out again soon?" He said that he would call me, and within a few days we had a real date set up—dinner at a romantic wine shop and bistro.

Our date was amazing! We had a great time sharing different items from the menu, drinking great wine, and getting to know each other. Nick must've gotten over my being late to our "interview" because I can distinctly remember noticing him scooting closer and closer to me in our booth over the course of dinner. By the end of the night, he was sitting right next to me and touching my leg with his. We had a lot of great laughs, and the list of things we had in common just kept getting longer. He drove me home and we had an amazing goodnight kiss!

One night, after about a month of dating, we had plans to hang out. He called my cell phone to figure out the details but my roommate answered. The unthinkable had happened. She told him that I was in a terrible accident and in the ER at a local hospital. I had broken three of my four wrist bones. One eye socket collapsed, my cheekbones, nose and jaw were essentially shattered, and I'd lost some teeth.

Nick asked my roommate if he could come visit me, and she told him that my ex-boyfriend received the call from the ER—and was there with me—so she didn't advise it. I didn't have my cell phone with me when I was in the accident, so the ER nurse had to find contact information for someone I knew through the white pages. Cell phone numbers don't appear in the white pages, and my ex-boyfriend was the only person I could think of who had a home phone.

Over the next seven days, Nick texted or called my roommate every single day for an update. With each conversation he asked if he could visit, and the answer was always no. After so much trauma, I wasn't prepared to see someone I'd only been dating for about a month, nor could I really even interact with visitors because of my situation. It took about four days for me to snap out of being a vegetable and become aware of what had happened to me. Nick sent me flowers every other day and continued to check on me at least twice a day.

Finally, after seven days of being in the trauma unit, plus wrist and facial reconstruction surgery, I called Nick. I told him that I was a complete mess and had no idea when I would recover. Dating me was going to be no easy task, and since we'd only known each other for five weeks, I thought it would be best if he just walked away from me. Nick disagreed. He wanted to see me and continue to date me, so I agreed to let him come.

It's hard to let someone you've known for so little time see you at the lowest point of your entire life—generally those moments are reserved for your very closest friends and family. But, he visited the next day with more flowers in hand. His co-worker tells me that he was white as a ghost the next day at work, perhaps in shock over my state.

Once I got out of the hospital, Nick kept courting me—even though I was missing teeth and the eye with the collapsed socket was completely misshapen, and my mother had to join our "dates" in the living room because I couldn't go anywhere. (She moved in with me for six weeks so she could take care of me.)

In addition to meeting my parents early on, all of this happened in early December, so Nick spent Christmas Day with my mother, my sister, one of my girlfriends, and me. I also got to know Nick's mother a bit through the frequent cards she sent me to cheer me up.

To say the least, our relationship unfolded very unconventionally. Within approximately two months of our "interview," Nick saw me in my lowest state, met my family, and spent Christmas with me. As it turns out, he was the sweetest man I could possibly have around during such a horrible time.

Exactly one year from our "interview" we moved in together, and we are now expecting our first child. There really are great guys out there—and I was lucky enough to snag one.

~Catherine Mattice

24

Not So Ill-Fated Match

Being deeply loved by someone gives you strength,
while loving someone deeply gives you courage.
~Lao Tzu

When I was eleven years old, I overheard my mother crying to her friend over the phone, "I don't think she'll ever get married and have children with such a disease!"

Those biting words would wind up haunting me for the next eight years. What my mother had been referring to was the fact that I was terribly ill with Crohn's disease, a serious inflammatory bowel disease.

Then, I met him. I was eighteen years old, and my company was hired to run a survey. When the client arrived, I was shocked. I expected a grouchy older distinguished man, and instead he was a twenty-five-year-old! My first impression—I wasn't impressed. I resented him because over the next month he drastically changed the dynamics in our once-friendly office. He was all business, with very little fun. I was counting down the days until he'd be leaving.

Then one day, completely out of the blue, the client came right out and asked me for my home phone number and asked if it would be okay for him to call me sometime. I looked at him differently for the first time. Was he really interested in me? My heart skipped a few beats.

He called me a few days later and I accepted his date and then had cold feet and nearly canceled beforehand. After all, I really didn't like this person to begin with, so why had I agreed to go out with him? And once he found out about my secret — my disease — what was the point anyway?

It was my father who told me not to break the date. "Go out with him and see what happens!"

So, with a bad attitude, I met my date at the door. As he stepped inside the foyer he handed me two long stemmed red roses. "One for you," he said. "And one for your mother," he finished as my mouth dropped open in surprise.

"You brought my mother a flower?" I asked incredulously.

He beamed this triumphant smile at me and simply said, "Yes, is she here? I'd like to meet her."

Was this guy for real?

Surprised, I explained that my mother was in bed with the flu. Nonetheless, I excused myself and ran upstairs to give the flower to my mother. Sitting straight up in bed, in between coughing, she sharply told me that under no circumstances was I to tell him I was not interested in him.

"Give it a few dates. This one sounds like a keeper!"

I rolled my eyes.

Five hours and two life stories later, it was official that we'd hit it off. Outside the office he was so different. It was the first time in my life that someone so mature and handsome had really showed serious interest in me. The next few months were a delightful whirlwind of romance. For the first time since I was eleven I began to dream of a life with an amazing person! Everything was perfect. Except my parents nagging me to tell him my deep dark Crohn's secret.

"I will," I promised. "I just haven't found the right time to bring it up."

Soon, my worst fears surfaced. He had taken me to a lovely park with a little lake that fed into a bubbling creek and set up a delicious picnic lunch for the two of us. In the background we heard children laughing, people were out with their dogs and the view from our picnic blanket was simply breathtaking. Then my stomach began to hurt, and I felt a huge Crohn's disease attack coming on out of the blue. Shocked, after a few years without issues, I ignored it, hoping that it would just go away. It didn't, and it actually only got worse. I stood up abruptly, knocking over several containers of food—surprising my date.

"What's wrong?" he asked concerned.

"I... well..." I was turning beet red. "I need a bathroom right away!" I choked out in a cross between a whisper and a yell. I was going to pass out from the intense pain, if not mortification!

What happened next was nothing shy of amazing! This man cleared the well-set picnic in record time and then drove like a maniac to find me a bathroom. Then waited in the car for me for nearly two hours as I was dreadfully sick! Then in concerned silence he drove me home. When he attempted to ask how I was, I had withdrawn into myself from embarrassment. Later he called me, and I outright lied to him.

"Oh, I'm so embarrassed. I must have the flu!" Without knowing any differently, he simply believed me.

Over the next month, as we got closer, I felt like a traitor. My parents' accusations loomed and my own sense of guilt finally pushed me into doing the right thing. I was going to tell him my secret and let him out of a relationship that had not been totally honest.

I called him one night and asked if he could pick me up, that we needed to talk. He wanted to know what we needed to talk about, and I simply replied that it was something I had to tell him in person. I was so wrapped up in my own dilemma that I couldn't see how dire this might have sounded to him.

Right on time he picked me up and we drove to a park. As he let the car idle, for a while we both just watched the children playing on the swings and the slides and in the sandbox—they bitterly reminded me of the children that I would never get to have. This was it. My one chance at happiness was being stolen away by a freak illness that I hated. However, I would do the right thing, because I loved this person enough to be completely honest with him. So, I turned toward him and began.

"I have something to tell you, and it's hard for me to say. I am telling you this because I care an awful lot for you, but you need to know the truth before our relationship goes any further. I..."

"Are you breaking up with me?"

"What?" I asked incredulously. "I, no, I mean, maybe, I don't know. Please just let me tell you something...."

"I need to know before you say anything more. I love you and I don't want to break up with you!" He was killing me! How could I say what I had to say knowing I was giving away my only chance at the life I had dreamed of?

"I love you too," I half cried. "And that's why you need to know—I have a serious chronic disease and it's been in remission but it's beginning to come out of remission and there is no cure and the only choice is for you to just move on. Find someone else—someone healthy and—"

"Do you want to break up with me?" he asked me quietly.

"Well, I... no! Of course I don't want to break up with you! But it's the best for you... you need to break up with me!" I sounded so confused and desperate. He was not making this easy. He was supposed to thank me for letting him know about my illness, drive me home and never see me again. Instead he had this amazing smile on his face and tears in his eyes.

"What?" I asked confused. "Didn't you hear me?"

"I only heard that you don't want to break up with me. I don't care what you have; we'll deal with it. I just don't want to lose you."

When I was twenty we married and eleven months later we were the proud parents of a beautiful baby girl. Over the years, two more girls followed, and today we've been married almost twenty-four years. And through it all, together, my husband and I have found the strength and courage to overcome our obstacles and embrace whatever it is life throws our way.

~Amy Schoenfeld Hunt

"Of course I want you to meet my parents.
I'd just prefer to get married FIRST."

Reprinted by permission of
Marc Tyler Nobleman ©2013

The Test

I think dogs are the most amazing creatures; they give unconditional love.
For me they are the role model for being alive.
~Gilda Radner

I'd grown disgusted with myself, and this time I was serious about not wasting any more time on a man who didn't have his head together. I'd been living with the last guy far too long, and when I got a promotion at work, I moved myself and my dog into my own place.

Then I took a good, hard look at myself. I couldn't seem to resist a man's flattery or men who were needy. Or I'd end up with men like Bobby, who would break a date at the last minute to go fishing or biking with a buddy. Or Richard, who was saving money to get tickets for us to see a concert, then blew it on a new motorcycle. Or Ronnie, who had "been hurt" and was afraid of getting hurt again (oh, please).

In the last ten years or so I'd dated commitment avoiders, men who'd tried to change me (seriously, one wanted me to dye my hair red), cheaters, or men who had the intelligence of a boiled potato. More recently one guy literally threw my dog off the couch so he could sit next to me. I never saw that guy again. You can disrespect me, but don't manhandle my dog!

So as a last resort, I turned to God. I said a prayer, something I hadn't done in quite some time. I'd attended a Baptist church as a teen and, though I'd strayed from my faith, I'd never completely lost it.

I sat on my bed and pulled the dog into my lap. "Lord," I began, "I've done a pretty good job of messing up my life. I've made bad decisions about men. I've given myself away too quickly and too easily. Now I just want to meet the right man—someone I can respect and someone I can grow old with. I've made really bad choices. I'm putting this in your hands. You choose the right man for me. In Jesus' name, amen."

In the meantime I'd been at my new job for several weeks, and had yet to meet one of my co-workers, Tom Zubel. I'd seen only an empty desk and his nameplate on the office window.

"Does this Tom Zubel really exist?" I'd asked Emma. "Or do you keep his name on the office so you can keep your job as his secretary?"

"Oh... he exists all right," said Emma, making her eyes big and looking at me over the top of her glasses. "He travels a lot."

"Why the face?" I asked. "Is he not a pleasant person?"

"Oh, he's nice enough," said Emma. "Has kind of a weird sense of humor, though."

"What nationality is the name Zubel?"

"Polish," said Emma. "And he doesn't like Polish jokes!"

"I'll remember that," I said. "I don't like to offend people. Anything else I should know about him?"

"He's a confirmed bachelor!" Emma knew that I was single.

"Ah," I said. "That's good to know. I won't waste my time trying to convert him."

One Monday morning at the office a pudgy man wearing dark rimmed glasses walked in. Emma introduced him as Mr. Zubel. He was, I guessed, a little older than me, average height, with dark hair and brown eyes. His smile seemed overly bright, like he was forcing it. In fact, he seemed a little stiff to me. He was, however, nicely dressed in a sport coat and tie.

"Hello," he said and extended his hand. "You were promoted,

eh? Congratulations!" His voice was pleasant and confident. "How do you like it here?"

He was nice enough, but my initial overall impression of Tom was "not my type."

Well, you can guess what happened. We went to dinner after work one night, just a couple of workmates taking a meal together. Yeah, right. We went out a few more times, and soon agreed to date each other exclusively.

Tom said, "I'm not like those other guys you've dated. If you catch me cheating, you can shoot me!"

I really, really liked Tom, and he did, indeed, seem like husband material. I even asked my mom's advice about him. Seriously! But I was still hesitant. Was this a man I could spend the rest my life with?

When he proposed, I said, "Can I think about it?"

"Oh... okay," said Tom. I could see he was disappointed that I hadn't answered with a quick "yes!"

"Why don't you stop over on Friday after work," I said, "and I promise I'll have an answer by then."

Tom brought take-out to my place on Friday—a bacon cheeseburger and fries for him, salad and onion rings for me. We unwrapped the food at the coffee table, then went into the kitchen for some diet pop. When we came back to the living room, Tom's hamburger wrapper was empty, and the dog sat by the coffee table, licking his chops.

Tom stared in disbelief at my dog and the empty wrapper... and I held my breath. They got along okay, but Tom wasn't used to being around pets. Then Tom burst out laughing.

That was the moment I decided Tom was Mr. Right. I said yes.

~Paulette Zubel

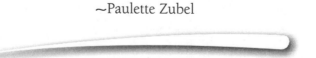

When I Realized
I Love You

When love is not madness, it is not love.
~Pedro Calderon de la Barca

The night we met you saw me first,
In the back of a car struggling out of my sweater.
I was grunting curses, not exactly ladylike,
But all you saw was a flushed face and wild hair.
You said I was an angel, but have called me trouble ever since.

Our first camping trip was a disaster.
Rain soaked air and a hole in the tent.
My stomach lurched from women's woes,
And we discovered our air mattress was a single.
Neither of us slept for two nights.

The first wedding we attended,
My hair refused to comply with the humidified heat.
And my contacts scratched my eyes red.
While we danced I tripped on your toes,
And received a blunt elbow when the bride tossed the bouquet.
I was battered and near tears by the end of the night.
You kissed me and said,
I looked like Grace Kelly.

The hotel was eco-friendly,
Lacking air conditioners, with no fan in our room.
We raided storage closets, floor by floor,
Until our bed was surrounded by gusting winds,
Yet it was the whirring of your heart I fell asleep to.

Revisiting Lake George to push our luck in the wilderness,
Dew speckled our ankles and the sun yawned for us,
Through the graying clouds,
At four in the morning on a Thursday in July.

A yen for new horizons and fresh perspectives,
Flowed in our veins and shone in our eyes.
Our supplies filled the car to bursting,
And I knew I over-packed.

The box belied the size of our tent.
A minuscule spot of blue, a mere puddle,
In verdant oceans of grass.
We romped on beaches and devoured local fares.
That night in our tent, we touched and kissed,
Our lantern casting our silhouettes of lovers into the night.

We watched fireworks over the whitewashed sand.
Each spark of light resembling stars I wanted to pluck,
And place in your hand.
A piece of the night to hold onto,
While stuck in a three-hour traffic jam,
Because I insisted we get ice cream before we left.

In the winter we stayed out late,
Throwing snowballs in the lawn,
And making forts with a spade and broom.
If we were children this would have been it,
The day to mark and compare the rest of my days.

Only when the sky began to lighten did I surrender,
Waving my snow powdered hat over my diminutive bastion.

The night we met, you called it love at first sight.
But you got my name wrong,
And I hadn't bothered to learn yours.
Love is said to be a flower in summer,
That blooms in the heart and pollinates the veins,
With happiness and perfection.

What no one ever divulges,
Is that love is found in disaster.
In the holes where rain peeks in,
And where cheeks burn with humility.
Where dancing is all missteps,
And the bouquet is never caught.
Love blooms in the winter.
Under runny noses and rosy cheeks.
Surrendering behind the battlements.

~Margaret Norway

Meeting McKenna

Love looks not with the eyes, but with the mind,
and therefore is winged Cupid painted blind.
~William Shakespeare

It was finally time for Joe to meet my daughter, McKenna. The plan was for Joe to come over to the house on a Friday after work. The two of them would get acquainted and then we would get some dinner. I had not really shared with my eight-year-old that I was dating anyone seriously. I told her Joe was a new friend that I had been spending some time with over the past couple of months.

Since my relationship with McKenna's dad had not been positive for most of her life, I think it was different for McKenna to see me so happy. We are very close because of what we have gone through together. I worried that she would not accept Joe. Boy, was I ever wrong.

During that first meeting, I tried to think of something that the two of them could do together that would be a good icebreaker. Time to get out the *Jenga* game. Joe had never played *Jenga* before and McKenna considered herself to be somewhat of an expert. It would be an especially difficult game for Joe, considering he is blind.

I watched in amazement as my young daughter explained in great detail how to play the game to a man who could not see. I witnessed a man who had never been a father react so kindly to this new addition to our relationship. They played game after game after game. At one point, Joe had McKenna put a blindfold on so that she would not have an advantage over him. I know that he was also approaching this as yet another opportunity to educate.

After at least two hours of *Jenga* playing, the tournament came to an end. Both contestants considered themselves to be winners. And they were right. Later on Joe asked me, how I did it. How did I work all day and then come home and play with her for hours? I told him that I usually did not play for hours. We generally only played for thirty to forty-five minutes.

From that first meeting on, McKenna and Joe developed a remarkable bond. He was the dad that she had been looking for and she was the family that he had always wanted. Everything seemed to click. Years later, when the three of us were at the hospital visiting a sick friend, a complete stranger said something I will never forget. She looked at Joe and McKenna and said, "There's no denying that's your baby." Was she ever right!

~Laura Dailey-Pelle

28

Silver Dime Wishes

To dare is to lose one's footing momentarily. To not dare is to lose oneself.
~Soren Kierkegaard

I never got in trouble until I started dating Justin. It was goodie-two-shoes-girl-next-door meets bad-boy-Marine-turned-preacher. There's something about a man who respects authority but doesn't fear it that gripped my timid heart and made me swoon. And you gotta love a man in uniform.

We'd been dating several months, still early enough to celebrate the monthly milestones that are long forgotten once you hit the one-year mark, when Justin surprised me with an evening to remember.

I had gotten ready in my friend's dorm room, caught off-guard by his spontaneous invitation. I twirled in the loaned dress, watching the skirt flare out, the petite flower pattern blending together the faster I spun. Five minutes before I was to meet him downstairs, I fluffed my hair, patted it down, adjusted my garments, and checked my make-up for imperfections.

Satisfied, I skipped down the stairs, blushed at Justin's look of appreciation at my appearance, and held his hand until we reached the car.

"Where are we going?" I asked. I knew my eyes were sparkling with excitement, exposing the nervous rush of adrenaline coursing through my veins.

"Can't tell ya." He smiled roguishly, and I refrained from leaning over and kissing his dimples. Wearing a dress makes me act like a lady, after all. Keeping my hands in my lap, and my lips to myself, I stared out the window and tried to imagine where we could be headed.

After about ten minutes of driving down the long stretch of highway, Justin pulled his red Jeep into the parking lot of a performing arts center. Instead of parking, he slowly guided the vehicle through the narrow stretch of asphalt leading behind the building. There weren't enough cars for us to be seeing a show, and my heart dropped to my stomach as I realized the center was closed.

We weren't supposed to be here.

Every obedient fiber in my body tensed, and I felt the tiny hairs on my arms rise as nervous tingles ran up and down my body. Justin jumped out of the car, and in three strides had my door open. The deserted parking lot warned me that we were trespassers, but one look into Justin's confident green eyes squelched my fear. Accepting his outstretched hand, he led me, half-running, across the lot to a fenced in area half-hidden from the street.

I'd been to this center before for a performance of *The Secret Garden*, but I'd never noticed the beautiful rose plot to the east of the auditorium. I felt like Mary Lennox experiencing the fruit of her labor when spring came to her tended blossoms. The buds were in full bloom, the vines growing upwards held in place by careful wire. Reds, whites, pinks, and crimson filled the small patch, and in my dress, next to the man I was growing to love, the world momentarily stilled.

Justin plucked a perfectly bloomed rose from the bush, skillfully avoiding thorns, and bowed chivalrously, presenting it to his lady. I held it gingerly in my fingertips, and unsure of what else to do, breathed in its sweetness. Taking it from me, Justin tucked it behind my ear.

"I want to show you something," he said. I looked around. Dusk was about to fall and I didn't want to get in trouble. We were still slightly visible from the road.

"Come on," he said. "Trust me."

And I did, because I do.

He led me into the wooded area along an unmarked path. The stillness in the trees added to the deliciousness of the adventure. We walked for a few minutes, chatting about nothing and everything at the same time. Then he stopped. In front of us, so perfectly like it'd been dropped there just for us, was a well.

The weathered peaked roof came to the height of Justin's shoulders. The large stones forming the round base were smooth and polished. I had to duck down to peer over the sides, but its depth couldn't be determined in the impending dusk.

Justin reached into his pocket and pulled out a small handful of change. Deliberately, he picked out two dimes and slid the rest of the coins in his pocket. Gripping one dime between his index finger and thumb, he held it up.

With a gleam in his eyes, he said, "Make a wish."

"Together," I said, taking the dime. Standing side by side, Justin counted slowly.

"One... two... three."

Closing my eyes, I held my breath, said the fastest prayer of my life, telling God that my wish was really more of a prayer. I kissed the dime and tossed it into the depths. We waited for the inevitable plop of our coins hitting the bottom, but it never came. I like to think that not hearing them land means that wishes come true. If I ever write a fairy tale, I'll stick it in there.

We lingered a while, promising to never share our secret wishes unless they came true. The growing darkness brought with it a light rain shower, shooing us out of the magical woods before we overstayed our welcome. There was enough light for us to make it back to the car, and after opening my door, Justin got in his side and started the car.

Our enchanting evening came to a jolting end when flashes of red and blue pierced through the quiet nightfall. I grabbed Justin's arm and froze. Shaking me off, he told me not to worry.

My mouth unfroze first. "Justin, Justin, Justin, Justin, Juuuustin."

The sentimental look he'd had moments earlier was replaced

with a set jaw and look of determination. The security guard, dressed in full gear—dark hat, black jacket, and a utility belt that rivaled Batman's—strode toward us. The lights continued to flash, a sign to the world that we'd broken the rules... and gotten caught.

I repeat: I never got in trouble until I started dating Justin.

The officer was at Justin's window, motioning for him to roll it down. I pulled the stolen rose from my hair and slipped the evidence of our trespassing under my seat. As the rain streamed in through Justin's window, soaking him and spraying me, I prayed for God to perform a miracle and get us out of the situation.

The rain shower became a storm. The security guard gruffly asked his questions and when the drops began beating on the plastic of his jacket, he gave us each a stern warning and glare, and trudged back to his security cart.

I don't think I stopped shaking until we were almost back to the college.

Now married with three precious sons that share Justin's dimples and mischievous eyes, we smile when we drive by the now torn down center and long-forgotten rose garden and magical well.

And as we drive, I look at Justin and let out a soft breath as I reminisce on silver dime wishes that really do come true.

~Bethany Jett

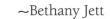

The Key
to My Heart

Love is like playing the piano. First you must learn to play by the rules,
then you must forget the rules and play from your heart.
~Author Unknown

"I f we'd met in person," he wrote, "I don't think we would have hit it off." After reading this, my father—who had signed me up for eHarmony—suggested I drop my new beau. Dad had encouraged me to try online dating after my short-lived marriage and subsequent long-term relationship ended. I was game and thought maybe online dating would give me a chance to reinvent myself. I felt my options as a thirty-something divorced mother of a special needs child were very limited.

So why not try eHarmony? It was fun each day to check my matches, from Alaska to Maine, and even to get to the point of meeting matches from Georgia or Florida in person. There was only one problem. My eight-year-old son with developmental delays always greeted my dates at the door with "BYE!" And he would push them away, literally, with both hands. Dylan is generally friendly, but he did not approve of this dating business. I had heard of single mothers who got back into the dating scene and had to work to win the children over to the new relationship, so I was prepared for this kind of reaction. But there wasn't any way to win over Dylan. "BYE" was the repeated response to any contact with my potential dates.

So I decided not to follow my dad's advice about ditching the guy who thought we wouldn't have hit it off in person. Why? He was from Alabama, had also graduated from Auburn University, and was a pastor. I felt comfortable with the similarity of our backgrounds and intrigued by the idea of being a pastor's wife. So I continued our communication via e-mails and progressed to phone calls. I have never liked talking on the phone, but with Stan conversation was easy. We would talk for at least an hour at a time. I had never even done that when I was a teenage girl. After a few months, we agreed to meet for a first date. My parents offered to watch Dylan, so that I could be the only one to meet Stan for the first time.

We enjoyed dinner and bookstore browsing. I was a former literature instructor, so he wisely chose to visit Barnes & Noble for coffee after our meal and asked for recommendations from the classics section. He even took notes. After coffee and a visit to a dueling piano bar that gave us a chance to listen to and discuss music—another strong interest of mine—we both wanted to see each other again, and soon. We agreed to meet at the tennis courts for a match the next morning, as he had to return home later in the afternoon to prepare for Sunday worship.

I was very attracted to Stan, with his dark chocolate eyes and gentle smile. Because of our many long e-mail exchanges, I felt I had known him for much longer than one evening, so I decided he should meet my Dylan sooner rather than later. I didn't want to become attached to someone who would not be able to get along with my son or who was unwilling to be a partner in addressing my son's numerous challenges.

The next morning, as I was dressing Dylan, he was very excited about meeting Mommy's new friend. When the doorbell rang, he escaped from the bathroom wearing only a diaper. My tennis date did not skip a beat—he greeted my son with a warm smile and a kind voice.

To my surprise, Dylan replied with a "HEY!" instead of a "BYE!"

Amazed, I knew this man was here to stay. Stan was the only man to have been welcomed, instead of rejected, by my sweet and sometimes challenging son. And because of that, he won my heart.

~Ginny Layton

Chapter 4

The Dating Game

By Your Side

We come to love not by finding a perfect person,
but by learning to see an imperfect person perfectly.

~Sam Keen

The Epic of Ipecac

Love is being stupid together.
~Paul Valéry

I t started out as a fine date, with the two of us spending an enjoyable afternoon together. When we arrived back at my parents' house, I offered to make dinner. Prior to proposing such an endeavor, I should have inventoried my skills — or rather, lack thereof — in the cooking department. Reflecting upon past catastrophes might have saved us some trouble.

My culinary failures were many — like the barbeque sauce incident, when my thirteen-year-old self added a whole cup rather than a quarter cup of sugar. My mom quickly discovered my sugary mistake, added more of the other ingredients to compensate, and created a lifetime supply of frozen barbeque sauce.

Because of this, I had declared a lifelong abstinence from all cooking-related activities. It seemed logical. My experiences in cookery always ended with the same outcome — disaster. So nobody wanted me at the helm of a meal anyway.

But years later, in the throws of love, my culinary revulsion fell by the wayside. Make good meals — win a man's heart. There I stood, in that mystifying place called the kitchen, preparing chicken sandwiches for my dinner date. To my surprise, the poultry cooked much quicker than anticipated. I slapped the chicken onto buns, added lettuce, mayo, and tomatoes, and voila — good to go.

But after eating a few bites, we realized the chicken tasted strange. And chewy. My boyfriend thought the meat looked raw.

"Did you cook it all the way?" he asked, eyeing the chicken suspiciously.

Of course I had. Hadn't I? The meat did look kind of shiny. I showed Mom the sandwiches. Her eyes bugged out.

"You didn't eat that, did you?" she exclaimed.

Mom's words came out part question, part disbelief, and all horror. She quickly dialed the local pharmacist, who emphasized the importance of immediately expelling all of the raw chicken to prevent contracting salmonella. He insisted on a gut-wrenching remedy—syrup of ipecac. After Mom returned with the prescribed antidote, my lucky date and I each took a dose. For those unfamiliar with the power of ipecac, internal combustion happens instantaneously. Like a match igniting gasoline, it greets the target's unfortunate abdomen without delay.

Dashing to the bathroom—our only bathroom—I encountered a closed door. I managed one frantic knock before barging in on my ten-year-old sister engrossed in reading the daily newspaper. Noticing my desperate face and hand firmly clamped over my mouth, her initial outrage swiftly dissolved into panic. My sister scrambled, flinging the newspaper and fleeing seconds before the inevitable happened. And the inevitable happened—again, and again, and again. During a brief intermission, I searched for my unfortunate dinner guest. I spotted him outside, behind a wild cherry tree encircled with purple violets, also suffering the consequences of ipecac.

Believe it or not, I actually tried my hand at cooking again. Even more surprising, my victim willingly sampled it. With watering eyes, my boyfriend graciously smiled through the first few bites of peppercorn steak—until the quarter-inch-thick peppercorn breading finally overcame his senses. After that, he kindly choked down spaghetti sauce with the consistency of mortar. I still remember the wooden spoon standing upright in the sauce.

Somewhere along the line, I started to enjoy cooking. Perhaps the challenge piqued my interest. Then miracle of miracles, my finished products improved, and eventually, people started complimenting my meals rather than feigning no appetite. But regardless of marked improvement, for a long time, whenever chicken made its triumphant appearance on the dinner table, the question always arose.

"Is it cooked all the way through?" he would ask, warily peering at the center.

His willingness to even try a bite of the bird demonstrated considerable kindness. Not to mention courage. That brave soul, who became my husband, no longer questions the safety of my chicken. But memories of that dinner date, and subsequent dinner dates when he bravely sampled my life-threatening meals, led me to a conclusion: In my experience, the way to a man's heart is not through his stomach. The way to a man's stomach is through his heart.

~Lisa Mackinder

"I think people usually have breakfast in bed on top of the covers."

Reprinted by permission of
Marc Tyler Nobleman ©2013

Mi Amor

The most precious possession that ever comes to a man in this world
is a woman's heart.
~Josiah G. Holland

"BEEP! BEEP! BEEP!" I sluggishly rolled over and hit my alarm. The time read nine a.m. It was Monday, the first day of my junior year in college. My friends and I had headed back to school a week early and celebrated the final week of summer together. Monday morning had come fast. Slowly rising, I put on a pair of gym shorts, my fraternity letters, and my backwards hat, the same thing I wore every day to class. Some people might think that I looked like an unclean, unshaven slob, but they didn't know of my recent incident. That summer, I had been the victim of a brutal assault. I suffered multiple fractures and injuries to my face and would endure a number of facial reconstructive surgeries to correct the damage. The last thing on my mind back then was school, how I looked in class, or my academics. I was just happy to be alive and in the company of my friends.

My house was a few blocks from campus, which allowed me the luxury of walking to and from class, something most students at this university did and enjoyed. I entered Baldwin Hall and ascended the stairs to the third floor for Spanish 202, my final foreign language class required to graduate. My only goal for the class was to fill the requirement. I had no idea how wrong I was.

The Spanish professor began calling out roll and the room was filled with "Aquí," and "Presente." One particular name and voice caught my attention. "Laura Miller?" I heard a faint but precious "Aquí" come from the opposite side of the room. Scanning the room I saw the most beautiful smile I had ever seen in my life. She was wearing a Truman Softball coat. I had friends on the softball team and immediately sent one of them a text message saying that there was a girl in my Spanish class who played softball and who I was going to marry. The message back jokingly said, "Yeah, right." The next few months I made small talk with Laura whenever possible, before, during, and after class.

One day I finally got the nerve to send her a message saying I needed help studying. Of course I didn't need help studying but it was my plan to spend time with her. We met in the library that night and didn't study one bit, but rather talked for hours about everything and nothing. I shared the story of my recent trauma and Laura was nothing but attentive and supportive.

As time went on, we were hanging out and going to the movies together. We developed a foundation as friends but both knew we wanted to be more. Late that November, my face started hurting pretty badly, but I just assumed I was still healing from the assault. After a week of increasing pain, I drove back to my hometown of St. Louis to get it checked out, and learned that the pain was an abscess after one of the plates they implanted into my cheek during my first facial surgery broke into tiny pieces. The surgeon scheduled surgery.

I worried that the romance I had begun to develop with Laura would be over... no one wants to have that kind of baggage so early into a relationship. To be honest, I wouldn't have faulted her for leaving. It was unclear how many more surgeries I would need and Laura had a lot to focus on with softball and school. She didn't need the added pressure of dealing with a broken boyfriend. I prepared myself for her to leave.

I returned to school a week later and to my surprise, Laura's reaction was not what I expected or feared. She did not consider walking away from the situation but rather took it head on. She was not just there for me physically, icing my face and helping me with my medications, among other things. She was also there for me emotionally, often times staying up late or pulling all-nighters, despite having early morning softball practice or a test she needed to study for, just to listen to me talk or hold me while I cried. I was on an emotional roller coaster and Laura was my saving grace.

During the multiple facial reconstructive surgeries that followed, Laura never left my side. It became clear to me that she was going to be there till the end, no matter what. I knew she was special the day I came back from my surgery and rather than running away and focusing on herself and her life, she dedicated herself to helping me through my struggles.

I am happy to say that the girl I met in Spanish class my junior year of college has been an enormous part of my life and growth as an individual. And the best part of the story? She said "yes!"

~Thomas Schonhardt

My Marathon Man

Love makes your soul crawl out from its hiding place.
~Zora Neale Hurston

I stood in a darkened Irish pub in Buenos Aires feeling infinitely out of place. As a non-drinker, non-socializer, bars didn't offer much. But a former reality star had invited me, which made me feel as though the popular girl in school knew my name.

We were both on a trip to Antarctica to run a marathon—an unusual life adventure. We would be leaving the next day for a flight to the bottom of Argentina where we would hop on a boat to travel to the South Pole. So a number of marathoners congregated that night to load up on liquid calories, which they would no doubt burn off during the race.

As I was speaking to this television starlet, in walked a tall, attractive man. He had large chest muscles and a dark blue tattoo showing underneath his tight white T-shirt. He wore a black belt with a large Harley Davidson buckle and had that dirty/styled hair that is so popular these days.

The reality star squealed, grabbed my hand and led me directly over to him. "Meet Paul," she said with an abundance of enthusiasm and pushed me directly in front of him.

I blushed and said hi while twisting my hair and avoiding eye contact. Paul stood several inches taller than I, which was saying a lot because I was six feet tall in bare feet. He had a big grin, piercing blue eyes, and when he spoke, my heart melted. He was from Sydney,

Australia and his accent made me feel a little more outgoing because I didn't want him to stop talking. So I peppered him with questions.

I learned he was a world traveler with an insatiable appetite for adventure (like me), loved Oz (me too), and lived in France (I wished I could say that). Paul asked a few questions and cocked his head to the side whenever I spoke and laughed at all the appropriate times, clearly paying attention to my words. A few times he even brushed my hair out of my face and tucked it behind my ears. His touch was electrifying.

He walked me back to my hotel room that night and, like a perfect gentleman, said goodbye at the door.

We spent the next day together, walking hand in hand along the streets of Buenos Aires, taking in a tango show, sipping hot chocolate at an open-air café and dancing together at the hotel bar while a stranger played piano.

I'd never met anyone like him: sweet with a kind smile, yet dark, brooding and mysterious all at once. I found myself attracted to him as he seemed like an everyman—articulate, self-aware, athletic and boy-next door meets the Marlboro Man.

In just twenty-four hours, I fell in love with this Australian wonder, and he felt the same, whispering those three little words in my ear.

We were forced to say goodbye before we left for Antarctica, as two small Russian boats would be traveling down the globe to the marathon and he, sadly, was not on the same ship as I. It would be three long days before I saw Paul again.

As we sailed down to the marathon site, we e-mailed each other love letters to pass the time and he wrote such caring words:

"I love your smile. I love the way you laugh. I love your enigmatic persona. I loved that you could have the courage to see possibilities, even though sometimes you expect the worst. If this isn't all just me, then for every step you take, I will take one with you. Yes we live for now in separate countries, but we have both lived abroad. There is nothing in this world that isn't possible if you have the courage and determination to pursue it."

But after a couple of days, he e-mailed a bombshell. He said he loved children; he had three—along with an ex-wife.

My eyes grew wide reading it. I asked him why, in all of our conversations, he failed to mention this colossal fact. He shot me back a three-word response: "You didn't ask."

I felt confused and wondered if this were just merely a vacation fling.

I saw Paul again at the marathon right before the race started. He stepped off his boat and speedily walked straight to me. He was freshly shaved and smelled of soap, looking like someone who put time into his appearance, not someone about to run a marathon. Just seeing him made my heart beat faster and nerves dance in my stomach, even with the information about his ready-made family.

We started the race and Paul took off running at a pace far faster than I could maintain. Obviously his muscles weren't just for show. So I figured I wouldn't see him again until the finish line.

Throughout the marathon, I climbed a glacier, fell into a mud pit, battled attacking birds and sideways rain, and carried all my own water for hours. Eventually, I slowed my pace to a painful walk, unable to run anymore. The treacherous, unstable terrain and bitterly cold conditions left my muscles aching and crying uncle. At mile twenty-three, clouds formed low over the racecourse and I let out a cry of defeat, too tired to form tears. But astonishingly, through the fog, Paul's figure materialized, carrying a jacket and smiling ear to ear.

He had finished the marathon, then turned and trudged in the opposite direction back onto the course to locate me and bring me warmth. He totaled 29.2 miles on one of the hardest marathon courses in the world, with three of those miles completely for unselfish reasons.

It was the nicest thing any man had done for me. Forget flowers and fancy jewelry—Paul hiked through freezing cold mud for me.

After I crossed the finish line, I reasoned with myself. "So he has kids? So what? You'll never meet another man like him." I literally traveled to the bottom of the world to meet the man of my dreams.

Paul and I met again back in Buenos Aires and strolled the streets holding hands. I loved the feel of his muscular arms. I loved the way he smelled of cologne mixed with leather from his Harley Davidson jacket.

After meandering aimlessly through the city, we seated ourselves at another outdoor café and I rested my head on his shoulder. Paul then began to bare his soul, telling me tales of his difficult divorce, the resiliency of his children, and how he survived brain cancer.

He was wearing dark sunglasses and I could see my stoic reflection in them, as I felt unsure of what to make of such dark life circumstances. So I just carefully lifted his sunglasses off his face, looked straight into his eyes and said, "I hope I can help you create better memories." Paul slipped his hand into mine underneath the table and whispered, "You already have."

~Jennifer Purdie

Two Metal Posts

Let us be grateful to people who make us happy, they are the charming
gardeners who make our souls blossom.
~Marcel Proust

I n my senior year of high school, I chipped one of my upper front teeth during an unfortunate wrestling incident. Not to worry. My hometown dentist placed a perfect cap upon it, and I continued to live a normal life with a healthy smile.

But years later—when the tooth next to it began to die—my dentist at the time did a super job of creating a false, four-tooth, upper bridge that perfectly matched my original teeth. Once again, I resumed a normal life with a healthy—albeit fake—smile.

In 2010, I met an outstanding woman named Kim. We established a friendship at first, and then later began dating—despite Kim living in Port Orange, Florida, and my living on Hilton Head Island, South Carolina. By Sunday, January 23, 2011, we had been conducting a long-distance relationship that consisted of meeting somewhere in between our homes once every month.

On that momentous Sunday, we met halfway in Saint Augustine, Florida, and checked into the Victorian House Bed and Breakfast Inn. From there, we walked over to Columbia, a romantic Spanish restaurant where we had eaten on a previous date.

The evening was going perfectly and we had just ordered our entrees, when the waiter delivered a basket of fresh, warm bread. We promptly dove right in.

But while I was eating a slice, my bridge suddenly came loose. Inside my mouth, I could feel it dangling atop my tongue, and I tried to remain expressionless. I excused myself from the table and luckily Kim was none the wiser. She was probably too engrossed in the bread.

Upon arriving in the men's room, imagine my dismay when my bridge fell off into the sink. I looked up into the mirror to see two metal posts jutting down from my upper gums.

I snatched the bridge from the sink, washed it off, and then wrapped it in a paper towel. Tucking it into my pants pocket, I departed the men's room.

Then I trudged back out to our table, covered my mouth with my right hand, and explained to Kim what had just happened. Have you ever tried to talk without your upper front four teeth?

Kim was fantastic! She didn't run away. Instead, she perfectly understood. She even laughed.

That night, imagine two grown adults, lying in bed, staring up at the ceiling fan... and just shaking their heads.

The next morning, we were up early—before the Victorian Inn even offered their breakfast—and went to a local dentist that Kim happened to know. He glued my bridge back in, and Kim and I returned in time to make breakfast.

The rest of our Saint Augustine date was uneventful—like nothing had even happened. We're still together, and that bridge has remained in ever since.

~John M. Scanlan

Chicken Soup for the Soul

An Unexpected Valentine's Date

*Supposing you have tried and failed again and again. You may have a fresh
start any moment you choose, for this thing we call "failure" is not
the falling down, but the staying down.*
~Mary Pickford

I f only it had been a different accident. Something more elegant, less embarrassingly clumsy. But no, I tripped over a curb and fell headfirst into a low brick wall, whacking my nose and splitting my forehead open. Fortunately, my parents lived mere blocks away. Clutching my bleeding head, I managed to pull my cell phone from my purse and dial home. My dad arrived within minutes, gave me an ice pack to press against the golf-ball-sized lump swelling on my forehead, and drove me straight to the hospital.

It was Valentine's evening but I had no plans anyway. Six months before, I had ended things with George, my long distance boyfriend of two years. He was fun and sweet, always the life of the party, but had the focus and self-discipline of a four-year-old. What I once found charming—his spontaneity, his boyishness, his tendency to make a joke out of everything—devolved into a source of stress. It became routine for him to call me at two a.m. in a panic, only half a page into an eight-page paper due the next morning, wanting my comfort. But there was nothing I could say or do to help. He needed to find motivation within himself. The next morning, he'd call and apologize and say he wanted to spend the rest of his life with me, to be partners always.

I began wondering what it would be like to have him as my partner in life. If eight-page papers were so difficult, what would a real job be like? What about mortgages and car payments and, my goodness, children? George's rosy daydreams about our future caused a tightening of panic in my chest, a need to press the escape button.

And so I did. Three weeks after my college graduation, on a sunny morning in George's childhood bedroom with the action figures on the bookshelves, I finally worked up the courage to tell him it was over. Even as the tears streaked my face and clogged my nose, I was flooded with relief.

Still, I missed him. A lot. After the break-up, all our inside jokes and shared stories, what seemed like hundreds and hundreds of them, were suddenly irrelevant. I had no one to call and say goodnight to, no one to appreciate the minutiae of my day, no one to celebrate my small successes like getting a free chai latte because it was the tenth stamp on my frequent customer card. I felt adrift in the world, a single person once again. Even though I told myself it was better to be single than to be dating the wrong person, I couldn't help but feel I'd taken a step backwards. I had once thought George was the love of my life. I had thought I was done looking.

Now it was back to square one. I moved home with my parents to save money and began working as a freelance writer. Adjusting to life after college, and single life after George, was tough. I joined a gym and began writing at coffeehouses instead of at home. I forced myself to go out some nights, even if it was just to a local open mike by myself. Slowly, I met people. Slowly, I began dating again.

Living in my parents' house gave me flashbacks to dates in high school, when boys would pick me up for school dances and I'd wait anxiously in my second floor bedroom, peeking out the window, waiting for their cars to pull up. When they did, I would hastily clomp down the stairs, yelling goodbye to my parents, running out the door. In high school my dad would always leave the porch light on, and he did the same thing now. But guys no longer walked me up the brick path through the grassy lawn to my front door; instead, they parked their cars in front of my house and said goodnight, promised to call. I would walk up the brick path alone, open the squeaky front door, and turn off the porch light. Heart heavy, feeling like an old maid, I would climb into bed and try to sleep, fighting away dreams of George. I hid my phone in the bottom of my sock drawer so I wouldn't call him.

The guys I dated sometimes called, and sometimes we went out again, but things quickly fizzled for one reason or another. Chris, a lawyer gunning for partner, told me to quit writing and get a "real" job; Kevin, a newspaper reporter, was eight years older and condescending; Ian and I had no spark.

Then I met Robert. He was a nursing student who worked weekends at the local hospital. I really liked him and we had an immediate connection, but something was holding me back. I told myself that the problem was his schedule—he was so swamped with classes and twelve-hour shifts every weekend that it was difficult for us to find time to see each other. But instead of calling him, I retreated. It was easier that way. I thought of George, and how even our best experiences were now just memories soured by heartbreak. I thought of Chris, Kevin, and Ian—I had been so excited and hopeful before my first dates with them, and it had only brought more disappointment. What was the point of putting myself out there just to get my heart broken again? I decided Robert and I simply weren't meant to be, and left it at that.

Flash forward to Valentine's Day. My dad led the way into the E.R. I shuffled slowly forward, clutching the ice pack to my forehead, blood dripping from my nose onto my white skirt and shoes. A nurse in blue scrubs rushed over to help us.

Of course.

"Hi, Robert," I said sheepishly, peering up at him from under my ice pack.

He did a double take. "Dallas?"

"She fell and hit her head against a wall," my dad explained. I cringed with embarrassment.

Robert led me to an empty bed. A doctor took my vitals and gingerly examined my head. "It doesn't appear that you fractured your skull," he said. "We'll take a CT scan to make sure. You're going to need a couple of stitches, too."

I lay back, shivering slightly. Robert brought warm blankets and spread them carefully over me. He wheeled my gurney down the hall for the CT scan. Before he left to attend to other patients, he reached down and squeezed my hand. I closed my eyes, realizing that I felt safe.

The next morning I woke up in my bed at home, bruised and sore but healing. A text message was waiting for me from Robert: "How r u feeling this morning? Wanna make sure ur ok."

I smiled and hit Reply. I didn't know what would happen—maybe things with Robert would fizzle out; maybe he would break my heart. But I wasn't doing myself any favors by holding back. I realized that as painful as my break-up with George had been, I was still grateful for the time and memories we shared together. I needed to risk heartache for the beautiful possibility of love.

I closed the text message and dialed instead. "Hi, Robert, it's Dallas. Do you want to get dinner this week?"

Sometimes you just have to let yourself fall and hope for the best.

~Dallas Woodburn

An Old Married Couple

Chains do not hold a marriage together. It is threads, hundreds of tiny threads, which sew people together through the years.
~Simone Signoret

I had met your mom about six months before I met you. She was staying in a religious retreat in Florida, where I was visiting my dad. Oh, she was lovely, so warm and fun, that I fell in love with her over the course of many shared dinners. Towards the end of my stay, she mentioned a time when her son, Ron, had come down from Harvard to visit her at this retreat. "You have a son?" I said, my heart beating a little faster. "How old is he?" I found out you were twenty-three, as was I. And, in a flash of premonition, I thought, "I'm going to marry this guy!"

I met you six months later, but I didn't know who you were. I saw you at the gift store, sporting a charming smile and golden tan in your tennis whites. Oh, how handsome you looked! You were with some people I knew, so I advanced and introduced myself. You said your name was Ron... oh, my heart skipped a beat! "Ron what?" I asked. "Ron Pollack" you answered. "Really? You're Shirley's son?" My heart was singing: "This is the boy I'm going to marry!" You later told me that as soon as I mentioned I knew your mom, you knew to be on your guard, and there was "no chance!"

Your problem was that you liked me. So, just to be safe, you told me you absolutely did not want to have a relationship with me. After that we settled into a warm and easy friendship. We found it very natural to be together; we looked for each other daily. This went on for a few weeks, and then you went back to Boston, back to Harvard.

A few months later, you visited again, and we comfortably fell back into the patterns of our friendship. You told me you had been celibate a long time, didn't want to get involved with the wrong girl. I thought that was noble, albeit somewhat unrealistic for a college boy (or grad school boy).

Again, we parted, and you flew back to school. But your problem was that you liked me. So you sent me flowers for my birthday. Then you sent me a cassette that you had recorded, a compilation of your favorite Cat Stevens songs. I held the cassette in my hands and wondered... was this the crack in the wall I had been waiting for? I thought perhaps it was. Yes, I was becoming sure of it. This was a very good sign.

We were to meet again in the summer. I was still in Florida, you were to arrive in July, I couldn't wait to see you again, my hopes rising as your return was getting closer.

A few days before you arrived, I was raped by an intruder in my home. He was wearing pantyhose stretched over his face and carrying a carpet-cutting knife, which he pushed against my throat. Miraculously, I survived. I went for help by driving myself back to the retreat, falling into the arms of a friend, shaking and shivering, my legs barely supporting me. My friend drove me to the police station, waited during my interview and medical exam, then invited me to stay in his room with double beds, so he could protect me and help me calm down. I stayed with my friend for several days, and then you arrived. My friend was leaving town, so I said, as soon as I saw you, "Ron, I need to stay in a room with you." You said, no questions asked, "Okay, you can tell me about it later."

It took me many weeks to recover from my ordeal, to be able to sleep again. The police investigation almost resulted in my rapist's capture, shots were fired but he managed to escape. So, he was still out there, knowing that I had helped the police try to catch him. I was given antibiotics for venereal diseases, and threw up my first dose. You were there the whole time, a friendly shoulder when the tears came, once even offering me the corner of the shirt you were wearing to blow my nose. We shared that room as platonic as platonic could be, and our friendship saved me.

We both decided I should get a room of my own, and I could always come back to you if the nights got too scary. So I moved out. I steeled myself, and did not go back to your room. I missed you. Your gentleness had saved me. Your comfort had restored me. I missed you, but it seemed wrong to go back to you, now that the immediate emergency had mostly passed, and my life could resume. It seemed improper to long for you.

And yet, proper or not, you as well started missing me from your room, you as well missed the intimacy of our late night talks, so you started saying foolish things, like listing the reasons why you would not start a relationship with me. Then you got even more foolish, and started listing the reasons you should not marry me. I had nothing but love in my heart for you, and every reason you listed made perfect sense to me. We spent many hours talking about it, and I saw it through your eyes; we would really not make a good couple. That was true. But then, it struck us, and we both saw it. We would make such a great "old married couple!" We had already shared separate beds, listened to each other's noises during the night, and faced adversity together. We talked at length about this great old married couple we would make, laughed at all the funny things we would say to each other if we had been married for decades, the irritating habits and usual recriminations that an old married couple like us would have, the sweetness of enduring love we would share, and the more you warmed up to the idea, the more I found your hand brushing mine, or your arm draped across my shoulders... it all seemed so natural.

I was the first one to see that this vision of being an old married couple had a chance of becoming reality. At first, an innocent participant in the game of envisioning an old age together, I was gradually returning to myself, the girl who once knew, without a doubt, without ever having met you, that I was going to marry you. "I'm going to marry this guy!" I had thought. Now it became clear to me again, and the only thing left to do, was to make you see it too. So I pushed you away, just a little bit. I told you that this talk of no marriage was getting annoying to me, and if that was a subject you wanted to discuss, we would have to start discussing it in terms of positives, not negatives. Or we could just stop discussing it. "Really?" you said. "I had no idea I was having a bad effect on you," you apologized. "Okay, we won't discuss this anymore," you promised.

The kiss happened within a day or two. It was… as I always thought it would be. I knew it must have had quite an effect on you, too, since you proposed marriage to me the very next day.

Tell me, now that we have been married for thirty years, now that we have five children and a dog, now that we say the funny things to each other that we always knew we would, don't you think we "almost" make a great old married couple?

~Mimi Pollack

36

The Muffin Man

As long as I can I will look at this world for both of us. As long as I can
I will laugh with the birds, I will sing with the flowers, I will pray to the stars,
for both of us.
~Sascha, as posted on motivateus.com

L iving in Vancouver I was accustomed to taking public transit buses to and from work and other places. Doug was a driver on the route I used most frequently, as it went past my home. Over the first couple of years I saw Doug frequently on the bus and chatted from time to time. One day, to my surprise, he asked me out for coffee. While I was not attracted to him, we went out anyway.

During our conversation I talked about how the bus service on Sundays did not start early enough to get me to work on time so I had to take a taxi. As I worked in health care, Sunday shifts were the norm. Doug offered to drive me on Sunday mornings, and while I appreciated the gesture I felt it was inappropriate and declined his kind offer. After about three weeks of paying for taxis, I happened to get on his bus for the return trip home and I—very sheepishly—asked him if his offer to drive me still stood. He said yes!

For about five months, every Sunday morning, Doug arrived to pick me up for work. Even when his schedule changed, and Sunday became his day off, he still provided me with this service. I protested that he should enjoy his day off, but faithfully he showed up. Doug would always wait at the end of my driveway and never knock on the door.

Doug began bringing me homemade raisin scones in the morning, telling me he "made a little something for your break." My co-workers noticed his efforts and encouraged me to give him a chance—even singing "Do You Know The Muffin Man?" outside of a room where I was caring for a patient. From that moment, Doug was known as "The Muffin Man."

I was not interested in a serious relationship at the time. I had been hurt too many times and had built up walls around my heart. Doug was persistent and he certainly had his work cut out for him. However, such sweetness and perseverance began to soften me and I finally gave in. We finally began dating. I found that the more Doug persevered, and the more he loved me, I began to see what a special man he was.

Two years from the day of our first date, we were married in a beautiful candle-lit ceremony in a good friend's home. It was magical. My eleven-year-old daughter was my maid of honour and Doug's two grown sons were his best men. However, every wedding has its moments. Doug was waiting for me at the bottom of the stairs, the music began, and my daughter led the way. I had cautioned her to hold on to the railing with one hand as she was descending the staircase. Then it was my turn. As I elegantly took step after step, I looked into Doug's eyes. That's when my feet came out from under me and I fell down the stairs and landed right at Doug's feet. Our guests were stunned as I got up and marched back up the stairs to try again.

Our marriage was strong despite a few struggles. We always shared laughter, and the most important thing that Doug taught and gave me: unconditional love. Even a five-month bus strike, with me being off work with an injury at the same time, couldn't shake what we had as we fought to keep our home. We were inseparable and enjoyed every minute we spent together.

Unfortunately, six years into our marriage, Doug was not feeling well. He was having trouble driving the bus and kept veering left. The afternoon of his doctor appointment, I came home from work to find my daughter fastening the buttons on Doug's cuffs. She told me he was not able to do them himself. I became very concerned when Doug couldn't remember his work phone number to call in sick.

The most life changing and difficult journey lay ahead of us. After two weeks of tests and specialist visits, we sat in the neurosurgeon's office, looked at the images of Doug's brain, and held hands as the doctor explained that Doug had a very aggressive form of brain cancer. Doug had surgery to remove the larger of two cancerous tumours, but ten days later, my daughter, Doug's sons, their wives, a close friend, and myself spent what was to be Doug's last night together. We had a glorious night all together sleeping on cots, listening to classical music by candlelight and telling stories that made us laugh and cry. I climbed into Doug's hospital bed and curled up next to my husband one last time. He tried so hard to open his eyes and look into mine.

I held Doug in my arms as he took his last breath. When I looked up at the clock, it read 12:15 p.m. That was the exact time that Doug would have finished his shift as a city bus driver.

Bus driver, "Muffin Man," persistent suitor, beloved husband, best friend... Doug was a lot of things, but to me he was—and is—everything that love should and can be. I dedicated a bench in a North Vancouver Park to Doug's honor. Sometimes I like to go there and just sit on Doug's bench. When I do, I often find myself craving a raisin scone.

~Karen Bauer

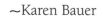

Still in Love

It's easy to understand love at first sight, but how do we explain love after two people have been looking at each other for years?

~Author Unknown

I raced through the airport bumping into passengers. "Excuse me. Pardon me. So sorry," I panted as I trotted through the crowd with a roller bag in tow. The love of my life was in a New York City hospital, and I was nearly 2,500 miles away. I reached the boarding area and saw the empty gate. A young woman stood behind the counter holding a microphone. As her lips moved I heard the announcement through the airport speakers, "Last call for flight—"

"I'm here!" I shouted. "I'm here!" I handed my crumpled boarding pass to the agent and rushed onto the plane.

I felt helpless strapped in a seat for hours while my husband Vince lay in a hospital far from home and alone. A routine business trip turned into a medical emergency when he suffered chest pains, dizziness, and shortness of breath. His condition was serious and there was talk of surgery. Vince never let me down, and now, I wasn't there for him.

I closed my eyes and tried to compose myself. A little sleep would help me adjust to the Eastern time zone, but thoughts of Vince distracted me. The news was hard to process because he was young and healthy. I thought about our love, our memories, and our future. I began to reminisce about our storybook romance.

We had met in a remote camping resort called Lo Lo Mai Springs near Sedona, Arizona. The resort, built alongside a robust creek, provided a cool reprieve from Arizona's hot desert weather. It was an oasis of beauty nestled in sycamore and cottonwood trees. The cabins, campsites, and many recreational amenities drew avid nature lovers year-round.

The owners had hired me to computerize the membership records. It was the perfect place for a Los Angeles urban girl to restart her life after ten years of disappointing singlehood. I loved the rural charm, and the scenery became more appealing when Vince joined the sales team.

He was from rural Iowa, corn-farming country, and despite our different backgrounds, we hit it off and had long conversations about our goals, interests, family, and our faith. We agreed on so many points. Vince exceeded my expectations for Mr. Right, with his gentle voice, charm, humor, and alluring blue eyes. I fell in love with him right away, and I wondered if he loved me.

After three weeks, Vince said we needed to talk. I was afraid he was going to end our relationship. "Marisa," he began, "I don't want to date you."

I stopped breathing.

"I want to marry you," he continued.

I'll never forget that surreal moment; it was the classic fairy tale.

Now it was back to reality, as I heard the aircraft's landing gear lowered. As soon as I arrived in New York, I dropped off my luggage at the hotel in Times Square and headed for the hospital to find my ailing husband.

The emergency room was bustling with weekend drama. Nurses and doctors moved swiftly, attending to patients while gurneys in the hallway were lined up with patients awaiting beds. New York cops stood guarding injured suspects. The mixed sounds of moaning patients, chatter, and the beeps and buzzes of hospital monitors added to the chaos.

I found Vince resting and waiting for more tests. Another symptomatic attack had almost put him into cardiac arrest. When I saw him, the same feelings I had years ago for a man I met in Arizona filled my heart again in the hustle of a New York City hospital.

"Hi babe," was all I could say before I started crying. "I'm so sorry I couldn't get here sooner."

"I'm okay," he said reassuringly. "They have great cardiologists here."

"I wish I could do something," I replied as I held his hand.

"You're here," he said. "That's enough."

The doctor explained the angiogram procedure, but he suspected blockage in multiple arteries and recommended immediate open-heart surgery. Just before they wheeled him away on the gurney, the nurse handed me his wedding ring. I clutched it tightly in my hand as if to protect him from harm.

After a short time, the doctor sent for me. The angiogram had him perplexed. "There's no blockage that I can see," he reported.

I couldn't believe it. The doctor explained there had been minor blockage in a small artery, but it wasn't the cause of recent episodes. Vince's doctor in California noticed the small blockage and prescribed beta-blockers as a precaution until more tests could be done. In New York, Vince started the beta-blockers and experienced an allergic reaction that mimicked heart disease. He was going to be fine.

Finally reunited, I handed Vince his wedding ring. The nightmare was over.

Skeptics may not believe two people can fall in love in a few weeks and stay in love, but I disagree. We are proof positive.

~Marisa Shadrick

The Dating Game

Looking for Love Dot Com

I've been dating since I was fifteen. I'm exhausted. Where is he?

~Kristin Davis

38

WriterChick Seeks Soul Mate

The charm of fishing is that it is the pursuit of what is elusive but attainable,
a perpetual series of occasions for hope.
~John Buchan

"How about this guy?" I asked Lucy T. Cat, who was sacked out on my desk. The computer screen showed a dating profile that wasn't half bad — okay, maybe it had more pictures of trophy fish than the fisherman, but one of the things on my wish list was "has a hobby of his own." And the other pictures got my attention, as did his math degree and writing flair.

Lucy glanced up and yawned. I wasn't sure if that meant, "He's younger than you and lives on the wrong side of the Sound," or "Pipe down, trying to sleep here."

"Yeah, you're right. It's like three hours each way." I clicked back to my inbox without sending him a message.

Dipping a toe in the dating pond after the implosion of a fifteen-year relationship, I was happy with myself but aware that, as in high school, most guys weren't looking for a nerdy tomboy. But I figured that online dating widened the pond... and, besides, I was through with trying to change myself for someone else. So I had written a quirky, geeky dating profile and become WriterChick.

There was a new message, one of those, "I think ur hot. Want

2 hook up?" e-mails that spawned more eye rolls than excitement, along with the suspicion that "hot" meant "local and female."

I shook my head. "Seriously, dude." But I shot off a quick, "I'm flattered, but no thanks. Happy hunting." Because, hey, to each his own.

They weren't all like that, of course. In a few months as WriterChick, I had e-mailed with several nice guys, and had even progressed to long phone calls with a slogan writer on the other side of the state. Things had fizzled out, though, when "Let's meet halfway for dinner" turned into "I'm beat. Why don't you pick up some take-out and come to my place?"

Um, no thanks. First date equals public place. Plus, I'm worth the drive.

After that, I'd had a brief instant message fling with an amusing fellow who claimed to be a professor at a nearby college. But he was vague on the details, I couldn't find his name on the college website, and he wanted to meet at a motel. Red flag, red flag, red flag!

I had gone on some actual dates, too, always with a friend waiting for me to check in. I went to a haunted house with a nice guy scientist and wished for sparks. I met a politician whose picture was ten years out of date, a neat fellow who was just looking for a good time, but was at least honest about it. I had planned dinner with a comedian whose e-mails made me smile, but the timing hadn't meshed yet. So far, though, none of the matches had been quite right.

"Well, that's it for today," I said, logging out. "Ready for dinner?"

It was amazing how quickly ten pounds of tabby can go from sleep mode to a striped gray blur headed for the kitchen.

The next evening, Lucy and I went through the same routine, except that this time there was a real message waiting for me, one that had me giving a little, "Oh!"

It was from the fisherman.

I hesitated before clicking. "I hope he doesn't think I was stalking him." The dating site kept a running tally of profile views, so I could see who had been checking me out... but the same was true in reverse. And, yeah, maybe I had looked at his page more than once.

"Oh, well. Only one way to find out if this is a 'hey, baby' or a 'stop staring.'"

Opening the message, I found a short introduction in perfect online dating format: he mentioned something from my profile, added a detail about himself, and invited me to write him back. Even better, he had written it like he was a crusty old sea dog, turning things playful. If he had sent me a drink, it would've been a polite white wine wearing an umbrella.

I replied in a similar tone, then focused on my other e-mails, having learned that the more pressure I put on a conversation, the more I was headed for disappointment. It was far better to take things as they came and treat life—and late-thirties dating—as a wonderfully strange adventure.

The next night, I heard back from the fisherman—a witty missive that ended with: "I'd like to get to know you better. Want to write a story together?"

Well, hello. That got my attention. It also sounded like a neat way to skip the usual twenty questions. Plonked in front of the TV with my laptop on one side of me and the cat on the other, I wondered if I should wait so it didn't look like I was haunting my inbox. Then I answered anyway, signing off with: "The story idea sounds cool. You want to start?"

His first chapter was waiting in my inbox the following morning, and I was pleased to find it a decently written setup with pirates and a lady captain. "I can totally work with this," I told Lucy, who was sitting on her window perch, watching Bird TV.

She flicked an ear back, which I interpreted as, "You've got a book due in less than a month."

I wrote the next chapter of the pirate story instead, crafting an utterly ridiculous sea battle, complete with a killer bunny and a red-skinned alien admiral who stood on the prow of his ship, shouting, "It's a trap!"

Geeky? Definitely. But I figured that if he didn't get my sense of humor, it wasn't meant to be.

His reply? "Bravo! Round of applause!"

For the next few weeks we traded e-mails, bouncing the story from sea to swamp to land and back again, complete with a hero and a romance. We didn't always get each other's inside jokes, but there was plenty of common ground. And most of all, it was fun.

Between the ferry ride and my book deadline, it was more than a month of e-mails before I headed out to meet him at the dock, driving an ugly green truck affectionately known as the Fug-150 (we had debated who drove the worst heap, which was another point in his favor). I fought a solid case of nerves, telling myself it was just another first date.

Only it wasn't.

The walk-ons were just coming off the ferry as I drove in, and I saw a guy take one look at the Fug and head in my direction. I got out of the truck, and as he drew near, I realized he was all of the six-three he had listed in his description. Bundled against the cold of December in New England and wearing a fur-lined bomber hat, he looked about eight feet tall, making me feel small and girly.

And I, a romance writer who had always thought that love at first sight only existed in books, took one look at the fisherman, this stranger I already knew so intimately, and I thought: "Mine."

~Jesse Hayworth

39

Blind Date

Put your future in good hands — your own.
~Author Unknown

Ellin bounced into Jack's Diner and headed toward my booth for our lunch date. In her high-pitched squeal, she began to speak before she sat down across from me.

"You won't believe what happened to me yesterday."

"Okay. I won't believe it. So tell me."

"I'll tell you exactly as it happened, sparing no details."

Ellin began, jumbling words in her excitement.

"You know how my daughter never lets up. At twenty-two she thinks she knows everything." Ellin mimicked her daughter's voice. "I still hear you crying yourself to sleep. It's been three years since you and Dad divorced. You've got to move on. Meet new people. Do something you've always wanted to do. Why don't you sign up on one of those dating sites?"

"You know me, Miette. That is something I swore I would never do. I'll meet people the old fashioned way — introductions. Okay, so I'm lonely sometimes, but dating websites are recipes for disaster. Last week though, as I surfed the Internet, a site captioned JDate.com caught my eye. How dangerous could it be? I took the plunge and e-mailed the first guy the site arranged for me."

I interrupted Ellin's monologue. "I'm shocked, Ellin. You're usually so inhibited!"

"You won't think that when I tell you the rest," Ellin promised.

"I got an e-mail from a guy named Jack. When he responded, he attached a photo. I hoped the grainy picture was more recent than the one I'd provided to him. He looked stern, fiftyish with silver-streaked hair, a strong chin, and straight nose. His eyes looked out over a ranch, several horses grazing in the background. He didn't look directly at the photographer, so I figured maybe he was shy."

"He sounds good," I said awaiting the next burst of words.

"He wore a faded plaid shirt and tattered jeans, a typical boomer uniform. I hoped he wasn't one of them but I decided I'd give it a try and set up a date."

"Oh, Ellin, I'm so proud of you," I volunteered.

"That's the least of how brave I was. I set up a date at The Coffee Bean and arrived early, a few minutes before four. A busy coffee shop had to be safe. If I didn't like him, I'd lose a half hour and the cost of a cappuccino. I glanced around the room for someone resembling the grainy image. Seeing no one fitting the bill, I ordered my cappuccino with skim milk. I sat in a corner hoping he'd recognize me when he arrived, even though my picture showed a somewhat thinner, more youthful woman. Everyone cheats a little, don't they?"

Without waiting for my response, Ellin went on. "I sipped my coffee as I watched the clock. Maybe he got cold feet and decided not to show up. I almost hoped so. By the end of twenty minutes, I tapped my nails against my empty cup. A man who showed up late for a date annoyed me. Who did he think he was?

"I spotted him as he entered the coffee shop a few minutes later, though he didn't look much like his snapshot. I wondered whether I should make the first move and introduce myself or wait for him to approach me. Maybe I'd just go over to him and tell him off. On second thought, I'd give him another chance. Okay, his rugged looks appealed to me."

"Ah ha," I managed to squeeze in, but Ellin didn't acknowledge my comment.

"He gave his order to the barista with barely a glance around the room. He took his grande misto over to a distant corner. What was that about? Didn't he see me?"

Ellin continued, "My picture couldn't have been so different as to make me unrecognizable. In one of the e-mails he sent, he alluded to his insecurity with women, dating back to the seventh grade when a girl teased him about his prominent ears. His confession over insecurity occurring forty years earlier, while endearing, left me with a perplexing puzzle as to my next step. He sat and began reading his Kindle.

"I took a quick look in my compact mirror and ducked behind my table as I pushed a stray lock of my freshly dyed hair behind my ear and dotted on some lipstick. Cappuccino in hand, I gathered up my courage and strode over to my blind date with all the confidence I could muster.

"I said, 'Hi. I'm Ellin and you must be Jack. What are you reading?'"

"He smiled and said, 'I'm rereading *Pride and Prejudice*. I enjoy Jane Austen, and find I can't admit it to most of my macho friends so I hide out in The Coffee Bean and read in private. I use Austen to teach tenth graders about eighteenth and nineteenth century English class distinctions. My kids lap it up.'"

"I told him it sounded like an effective teaching tool and asked him if he had seen *Miss Austen Regrets* on Masterpiece Classic last week."

"He said he missed it because he watched the Broncos game."

"I commented on Tebow's fabulous pass in overtime. Do you know what he said?" Ellin answered her own question. "He said 'I'm in love. You're a sports fan.'"

"I felt my face grow warm. He was flirting with me. Imagine."

"Why not? You're pretty enough when you stop talking for five minutes."

Ellin rushed on, ignoring me. "He asked how I saw the game if I watched Masterpiece Classic?"

"I told him I recorded it. Hadn't he heard of TIVO? I said anyone with a Kindle must be technologically savvy.

"'I'm really not too computer-literate. These gizmos throw me.

Do you use computers much at work?' Jack asked, motioning me to sit and pulling out a chair for me."

"I told him about my job as a legal secretary with the Attorney General's Office and used my job and the paralegal course I was taking at Broward Community College as an excuse for not reading much fiction.

"He asked if I was studying to be a lawyer. I told him I thought it was a bit late for that, but he said if it's what I liked, I should do it.

"We segued from our work into our love of travel. He told me he'd just returned from a South African safari. I told him it sounded exciting, though a bit adventurous for my blood. I did tell him about my trip last summer when I travelled Italy from the boot's thigh to its toe, albeit with a travel group."

Ellin went on after taking a quick breath. "We talked and talked about a million things. I can't remember everything. Only when the barista came over to our table and asked if we wanted another cup of coffee did I notice the setting sun. Two hours had gone by so fast."

"Jack said, 'I'm afraid we've worn out our welcome. How about continuing the conversation over drinks at the Sportsman's Bar next door?'

"My heart leaped into my throat. 'Why not?'

"As he scraped back his chair, he said as he stood, 'I only have a small confession to make.' An awkward moment passed. Jack looked down at his hands.

"Oh, God, I prayed. What's wrong? Don't let this cute guy tell me he's married or something. I knew the dating site promised single available contacts, but maybe he lied. Or maybe he was just being polite and didn't like me after all. I gulped, prepared to handle the bad news.

"He said, 'My name's not Jack. It's Greg.'

"I mumbled something like, 'I'm sorry, I er, thought….'

"He paused for what seemed like an eternity, but finally said, 'You seem to be under the impression I had a date to meet you here. I didn't. I always come here after my last class. When you came over, I had no idea who you were, but you were attractive and friendly and interesting, and I, um, well, figured what harm could it do?'"

Only you, Ellin. Only you.

~Miette Korda

The Reward of Taking a Risk

Prudence keeps life safe, but does not often make it happy.
~Samuel Johnson

"Clare found some guy on the Internet," Gail said, the apprehension coloring her face. Gail had been a friend of Clare's much longer than I, and it was obvious she feared for Clare's safety. She worried about her happiness, too. I didn't fret as much. Clare was responsible, wise, and independent, but since she was still single at age forty-seven she was alone. I knew Clare accepted and made friends with strangers easily, and she had a reputation for taking risks in that regard. So Gail was right to worry. But none of us, not Gail nor I nor Clare, anticipated the risk of falling in love.

"We have to trust in her ability to judge a person's character," I responded.

Gail agreed. But her concern lingered; the Internet could be a predator's stalking ground. "It's like the time she invited that couple she met online to travel all the way from Ohio to have Easter dinner with her. She's crazy."

"What happened at Easter?" I asked.

"They had a nice time. She made new friends, but she was lucky. Lunatics hunt down innocent women on those sites. As for this new guy, I think they're dating."

"Did they connect on a matchmaker site?" I asked.

"No, she was playing a game. Apparently it was in a chat room where players could communicate while logged in. He sent a private message to her—she called it a whisper—and she answered it. They've talked on the phone every day since."

A few weeks later, in typical spontaneous, friend-stunning fashion, Clare agreed to take a summer road trip with a work-related associate she barely knew. It was days after she had left her twenty-seven-year job as an emergency room nurse. An Emergency Medical Technician named John, knowing she had the time, invited her to join him on a cross-country adventure to visit his kids.

John's planned route was to take them right through Memphis, Tennessee, the exact town where Clare's online stranger lived. On a morning about one quarter of the way through the trip, Clare realized this and said, "Hey, we're gonna be in Memphis. Would it be okay to stop and meet this guy Eric face-to-face?" John agreed.

Describing the pre-meeting scene for us after returning from the trip, John said, "I was trying to steer the camper through downtown Memphis while she was trying to get ready using the tiny bathroom mirror. 'Clare, you're acting like a school girl,' I told her. The longer she worked, the more upset she got. 'You look lovely,' I assured her, 'and it's not your make-up or your wardrobe that he's going to remember after he meets you.'"

He was right. By that evening, the strangers were eating dinner together and by the next day, they were officially a long distance couple. When summer turned to fall, Eric traveled to Pennsylvania to see Clare. By the following spring, less than one year after Eric's chatroom whisper, he stuffed all his belongings into his vehicle and permanently moved north. A large group of Clare's friends were camping together that weekend, so we got to watch her as she paced the same number of miles Eric drove. When he finally showed, she spent the rest of the day smiling, making introductions, swaying in his arms to music, and talking about their future. Our worries were gone.

The two melded their adult lives together, keeping game playing at the forefront of their relationship. Whether it was a private round of *Scrabble* or a competitive match with a gathering of fellow game lovers, they challenged each other like a well-coached team.

Soon, we too were in love with Eric: his nature, his fried chicken, his southern hospitality, and his equally southern "How y'all doin'?" greeting.

For Clare's fiftieth birthday, Eric planned a surprise party. I went early to help him set up, and he seemed flustered. I thought it was anxiety from trying to fool such a clever gal. Ultimately she was shocked when she found her yard stacked with friends, but even then Eric kept sweating. Unknown to all the guests, revealed only when the cake was served, Eric had hidden a ring inside her piece. Would she be his wife?

In 2006, after many opportunities to fear for her wellbeing, Gail stood in Clare's wedding. No longer worried, she was the biggest supporter among an audience that was very much aware of the level of happiness being witnessed.

Seventeen months later, the e-mail came. "It's called multiple myeloma." Clare broke the news in writing, because it was the only endurable way. Eric fought to survive: a bone marrow transplant in 2009, heavy narcotics, weight loss, three years of doctors, and finally remission. Soon after, they celebrated their fifth wedding anniversary.

But one week later, in the middle of the night, I woke to Eric's voice calling me. It had been a dream, and I felt uneasy as I struggled to go back to sleep. You can imagine my shock when my husband called that morning to say that Eric had died.

Clare's nursing profession exposed her to the tragedy of loss on a regular basis. Her parents had died far too early in life. And, as a friend to many, she had also seen many pass. But how would she survive this? Soon, everyone was worried about Clare.

As the days passed, people began whispering, "When is she going to have the funeral?" Unwilling to contend with a bunch of dressed up, weeping people in a funeral parlor, she finally booked a fire hall to celebrate Eric's life. A box-shaped urn sat next to a looping slideshow that presented a lifetime of memories packed into less than a decade.

After lunch, Gail bravely caught the crowd's attention and got the remembrance started. She began explaining what Eric and Clare meant to her. Then, John described the road trip. We laughed at Bob's impression of Eric's accent. We cried when people couldn't speak through their tears.

Then, we all went home. Time passed. Ashes were scattered. Friends remained in place as they'd always been, but Clare was back to programming the television, washing the dishes, and watching the sunsets alone. So intense, we could almost see her pain, and there was nothing we could do to make it better.

We worry about our friends, warranted or not. We want happiness and never anguish, but the two are intertwined. In the face of such a sad ending, now when I look at Clare, I will forever see a loving Eric, too. He washed away her lonesomeness. He granted her fond memories. He proved what we knew all along: that she was Mrs. Right for someone.

After more than a year had passed, I asked Clare what I suspected others dared not: "If you knew how this was to turn out, would you do it again?" She paused for a moment. Then, with the same certainty as her response to Eric's marriage proposal, she answered, "yes."

Yes, Clare risked finding love on the Internet, and it changed her life forever.

~Ruth Heil

41

Online Discount

Mistakes are part of the dues one pays for a full life.
~Sophia Loren

I was an old hand at meeting not-quite-Prince-Charming online when I met Peter Parker (not his real name, just who he reminded me of, on my laptop screen). I decided to give him a chance. I'd been hitting the delete button on these online relationships before they'd really had a chance to start. I was going to change that.

I reminded myself to push aside my short-click attention span when Peter and I had our first date IRL (in real life). I spent a few hours with him, chatting. It was pleasant enough to lead to another date, and another. The next thing I knew, my byte-sized sample dates with Peter evolved into the whole enchilada: We became a couple.

I started to see True Frugality in action. I was all for saving a buck; I never paid full price for clothes, was a big fan of any value meal, and even downsized my online dating budget when I met Peter. After years of paying for memberships to dating sites, I had met Peter on a free site to give my pocketbook a break.

But Peter was more committed to saving a buck than I was. Most people read the weekend paper leisurely, flipping though the grocery ads in passing. Peter analyzed them as if he was discovering the true secrets of the Da Vinci Code.

"Aha! Safeway has twelve-packs of coke for $4.99 each, but over here," he said, waving the ad in the air, "it's TWO for $9.00."

"But I thought you wanted to go to Safeway to get the two bags of chips for three bucks?" I said.

"I do," he said. "I will just go to both."

To save a buck? I just kept quiet.

Now I understood how he ended up with so many groceries. He lived alone, but there was always enough food to feed a frat house. He would buy one to get one free even if he already had three at home.

He seemed to keep track of every dollar that each of us paid into this new relationship. It was irritating, but I rationalized reasons to feel good about what was behind it. I thought he wanted to make sure I understood he thought of me as an equal. He wasn't a scrub who expected me to pay for everything, and he wasn't all cave man either, not wanting me to "worry my pretty little head" about ever picking up a check.

We tried some entertainment on the cheap, like hiking. It was a beautiful day when we headed out to Peralta Canyon. We spent a couple of hours hiking into the canyon to get a glimpse of the rock formation, the Weaver's Needle. I took a picture of him with that ancient volcanic plug rising majestically in the background, and he took one of me. When some other hikers arrived, we got a shot of both of us. It was a great day.

But then, our relationship started to get as rocky as that Arizona canyon. I was starting to see that my new boyfriend was as frugal with his time and energy as he was with his money. I had a condo of my own, and really tried to do the Ms. Fix-it work, but there were times that I could've used some help. I struggled with my wrench for hours before I called Peter to help when I was fixing my toilet.

"Why don't you stay for dinner so I can say thanks?" I asked when he finally came over. It was a weekday, and we rarely spent much time together during the week, unless I went to his place. The fifteen-minute drive was an inconvenience, he'd say.

He didn't stay. And I could tell he was quite put out. So the next time I had DIY work to do in my bathroom, I did it myself. Unfortunately, I didn't have the proper ventilation in my tiny bathroom and practically solidified my lungs. Oops. I drove myself to the hospital and was admitted for five days.

Off oxygen and slowly recuperating, I called my boyfriend and asked if he would bring me some food. I don't like asking for favors, usually, but almost dying puts some things in perspective.

"You haven't gone to the store?" he asked.

"No, I still get winded crossing the living room to answer the phone."

I really tried to ignore the exasperated sigh on the other end.

"Okay, I'll be over soon."

A few hours later, he stopped by with a few DVDs from his collection and five cans of soup. I asked if he wanted to stay and watch one of the movies with me. We hadn't spent much time together lately. He visited the hospital for fifteen minutes one day (hospitals gave him the creeps) and hadn't come over much since (that long drive). He didn't stay.

When I finally felt good enough to make it to his place, we spent more time together. He cooked me a few great meals, we watched some local fireworks; it was pleasant. I was on the fence about the relationship.

I walked into his home office one afternoon in time to see him reading an e-mail with a familiar logo.

"You're still getting e-mails from Match.com, huh?" I remembered that they tried to get me to renew my membership the last time I decided to quit. It took a while for the e-mail pleas to fizzle out.

Like an employee just busted by his boss for fooling around on company time, Peter closed the window. "Oh," nervous laugh, "I tell them I'm in a relationship when they write."

"When who writes?"

"Well, you know, the women."

"Why didn't you deactivate your profile?" I knew that was possible. I had dated mid-membership before. "We've been dating for eight months!"

"But Tina," he said, in all seriousness, "I PAID for a full year."

Later, at home, I signed in to the Match site (browsing's always free) and discovered his profile. "I'm a Clyde looking for his Bonnie." Cheesy. There was nothing about him being in a relationship. But there he was, smiling away in the Arizona sun, his face a bit red, as if he'd been out all day, a big rock formation in the background....

Hey! That's the picture I took! On OUR date!

I sighed. Sometimes you get what you pay for.

~Tina Haapala

"I also just want to be friends, but with somebody else."

42

Destined to Become a California Girl

Once you make a decision, the universe conspires to make it happen.
~Ralph Waldo Emerson

I was sitting on the plane and my stomach was churning. I was traveling out to California for a job interview. I'd recently left an unhealthy relationship and was looking for a new life. I'd been applying to jobs all over the country, though I was really hoping to end up in California for multiple reasons. I had lived in Missouri most of my life, and I'd never been to California. Seeing the Pacific Ocean had always been one of my dreams. And here I was, going for my final interview with a company that seemed very interested in hiring me.

The pilot announced our descent into John Wayne Airport, telling us that it was a beautiful seventy-five degrees. As soon as they announced that we could use our cell phones, I hit the "On" button and swiftly typed out my text.

"I'm here."

My stomach was in knots, my heart was pounding, First things first—I made my way to the restroom. My phone beeped and announced that there was a new message. I was almost afraid to look, thinking he was already here....

"You're early. I'm sorry! I'm stuck in traffic. I'll be there in a few."

I put my contact lenses in, then typed out my response. "I'll meet you at baggage claim."

I made my way down to the baggage claim area, collected my bags and waited. I was in the middle of texting him again when I glanced up and saw a smiling face come toward me. His smiling face. We embraced, not sure what to say other than "Hi."

We hugged for several minutes, afraid to let go. What if it wasn't real? Or what if we had trouble talking to each other in person? We walked to his car and I strained for something to say.

"Did you know they say that there are more palm trees in South Carolina than any other state? Though I don't believe it now that I'm here...."

I rambled on and on, he didn't seem to mind. My hotel was across the street, so we went there first to drop off my stuff. I signed in as he stood a few feet away. I realized that I was letting a man I'd never met in person before accompany me to my hotel room alone. But I did know him. I felt like I knew him better than anyone else in the world. Just because we hadn't met in real life before didn't mean we didn't know each other. I trusted him.

Getting to the room, I put my stuff down on the bed and we hugged some more to avoid actual conversation. We talked and quickly discovered that we could banter back and forth just as we had done through e-mails and texts. Once we started talking, we never stopped.

We had met a year earlier via an online writing competition. The funny thing is, I assumed he was a woman. I only found out that he was a man when I accidentally called him a "she" in a comment and he sweetly told me that he was indeed a man. The rest, as they say, is history. I'd always thought he was very sweet and he soon became one of my closest friends, even as he lived thousands of miles away. Our chatting turned into text messages and those turned into phone calls that lasted until the sun came up. The first time he told me he loved me was a week before I got the call for the job interview. I told him I wanted to tell him in person, and only a few days later... I got the call that I would indeed be flying out to California. I could finally tell him how I felt, in person.

And I did. I felt just as in love in person as I did over the phone. It came naturally, even through our mutual shyness.

I'd never been to California, so he wanted to show me the sights. We visited the Huntington Beach Pier and watched the surfers, something I'd never seen back home in Missouri. Holding hands while both being very shy, we made our way down the pier and back before going out for dinner.

After dinner, we went back to my hotel for a little one-on-one fun and to indulge in one of our favorite pastimes: *Scrabble*. We played online games constantly, and to be able to play a game in real life with him was priceless.

No, seriously, we played *Scrabble* well into the night. And I kicked his butt, as always.

The next day we trekked out to the Balboa Peninsula, where we rode the Ferris wheel overlooking the water. Being kids at heart, we followed up the ride with a funnel cake and some corn dogs and we shared bits with the pigeons, laughing as they scrambled clumsily for the scraps. I put my feet in the ocean and playfully ran in the waves like the children alongside me.

He didn't mind; he thought it was cute. Or so he said.

Oh Monday, dreadful Monday... he escorted me back to the airport after my interview. We hugged some more and this time we didn't want to let go because we didn't know when or if we'd ever see each other again. I told him that I'd do everything I could to be back soon. I knew what I wanted more than anything else. I wanted to be here with him.

I got back to Missouri late Monday night and I just knew that I'd get to go back. While it excited me, it terrified me at the same time.

I turned my car on, and the radio started playing "California Girls" by Katy Perry. I laughed at the irony, but I'm not one for pop music so I changed the station.

"Hotel California." I sang along as I hit the highway and then it dawned on me... it was another California song. Laughing to myself, I jokingly wondered if it was a sign, but I brushed it off as a coincidence.

The entire week before I heard back about the job, the radio played every California song known to man. If I flipped through, I had "California Love" by Tupac, "Dani California" or "Californication" by the Red Hot Chili Peppers. On one station, they accidentally played "California Girls" twice in a row. As my nieces were in the car and liked pop music, I let it play both times.

Maybe it was just me looking for signs, but somewhere... I felt like it was telling me to go. Terrified to leave my family and everything I knew in Missouri, I needed a gentle nudge to tell me "this is the thing to do."

Then one day my phone rang. They were offering me the job in California. I was driving at the time so I told them I'd have to call them back. All the while my head was spinning and wondering if I could really do this.

"California Dreamin'" by The Mamas & The Papas started playing on the radio. The universe had given me the nudge I needed. Or rather it beat me over the head with it over and over until I knew what I needed to do. I listened.

Three years in, I still love the sand, the sun, and the surf of California. I hug the palm trees. The Hollywood sign still makes me giddy like a kid on Christmas and I can't drive down the street without thinking to myself, "I'm in California!" It still hasn't hit me that this is my home.

I'm here in California with a man I fell in love with online. We happened to be in the same writing community at the same time, we became friends and now three years later, we are still just as silly and goofy as we were back then. We've played many games of *Scrabble* and *Trivial Pursuit* in person, not just over the Internet.

I was never one to believe in fate, but this experience, this love feels like something that was meant to be. I have no doubt that the universe did everything in its power to make sure we would be together. I couldn't be happier with the way my life has turned out.

~Kristen Duvall

The Sinister Side of Online Dating

If we could sell our experiences for what they cost us, we'd all be millionaires.
~Abigail Van Buren

I took the leap of faith and decided to try online dating. It wasn't long before a handsome man sent me a letter telling me that I had a beautiful smile. I was curious, so I read his profile. It was quite intriguing and engaging. I quickly decided to respond to "smileandfun."

Before long, the mystery stranger and I were sending messages back and forth like a Wimbledon match. He said he was half-Italian and half-British. I was beginning to feel that I had met someone special as our conversations switched from the online dating site to Facebook. Soon, John and I began having extensive late evening and early morning chats on the phone.

A few weeks later, John began professing his love for me. "Promise that you'll never hurt me," he begged one night during a romantic chat.

"Don't hurt me," I stressed back.

John started addressing me by cute pet names: "babes," "sweets," and "my love." He always wanted to know how things were going in my life. My heart would pound when I got a call from him. Things were really going great for the first month. I began to trust this man so much that I opened up to him about being a breast cancer survivor with a deformity of the breast (I wanted to be honest with him). This difficult admission didn't seem to have any negative effect on our budding relationship.

John and I would fantasize about how it was going to be when we finally would meet. We'd breathlessly talk of how we were going to spend our lives together—forever. He had an antique store in Jacksonville, Florida. I quickly expressed my own personal interest in antiques.

I kept asking John, "Are you real?"

"I'm real, babes," he'd assure convincingly.

About a month into this mad, wild connection, John skillfully assessed my financial situation. "What are your monthly expenses? What are you making? Babes, you're going to be my wife. We'll be sharing everything," he guaranteed.

I was under the impression that John was financially well off, so I was embarrassed to tell him what I was making between my two part-time jobs. You'd think this would raise a giant red flag for me. But it didn't.

In early July, things really took a dark turn. One evening I received a call from John stating that he was going to a big antique sale at the end of the week in the UK. He said that he was taking $700,000 from his savings account for this trip. Eagerly, he promised to keep in touch.

John and I continued communicating on the phone and on Facebook. Then one afternoon I answered a call from him while at work. "You have to phone me right away when you get home!" He sounded distressed.

As soon as I got home I called him back, before even taking my shoes off. "I need your help!" he said, desperately. "The things I bought cost more than I had expected to pay to ship. I need you to send me $5,000!"

At first, I just thought John was kidding. "I don't have $5,000," I replied sheepishly.

For days afterwards, the pleading, the tears and the frustration hampered our conversations. "Sell some of your antiques," John said, as if I would sell family heirlooms on command. "Can't you borrow $5,000 from your friends or your grandmother?"

He became more and more desperate, until he finally said, "I don't want to die in another man's country." Speaking as though he were on his deathbed, my emotions got the best of me. I sent him some money so that he could eat. Whether this was what the money was used for, only John and God know.

When John initially went overseas, he gave me a number to call to reach him. He said if I dialed the number he gave me, it would cost less than direct dial. Of course, to add to my financial agony, when I opened my phone bill the following month it was almost $1,000! Thankfully, the phone company had seen that I was being scammed—well before I had—and had blocked the number after a certain time.

The emotional stress from this man was beginning to take a physical and financial toll on me. I was having more difficulty than usual sleeping at night and my blood pressure was out of control. Not to mention I was having issues concentrating on my job. When I expressed these issues to John, he said, "Just hang in there a little longer, babes. Don't you love me and want me home? Tell me you love me."

The last straw came in one of our final messages on Facebook. I was ranting about how I didn't believe him, when he arrogantly said, "Just send me the money!"

I was sick to my stomach. I just couldn't believe that I had exposed my soul to a man that I thought I could trust. John turned out to be a crook. I went through all the stages of grief. Finally, I came to terms with what had happened and began to deal with it.

I'm not afraid to admit that I was naïve. Just recently, I was on the Katie Couric show talking about my experience with online dating. I wanted to get my story out there so that other women who come across a man like this would think twice and ask questions before becoming emotionally involved.

I took this horrible experience and turned it into a positive learning experience. Here are a few tips: Beware of the person telling you they lost family members tragically. Beware of the person who wants your address right off the bat. Scammers will check to see if you are who you say you are, which is pretty hypocritical considering they're the ones who are lying! Beware of the person who professes his or her love within a short period of time. Beware of the person who says there is an emergency and he or she needs some money right away. Lastly, if any mention of Nigeria is brought into the conversation, beware!

~Debbie Best

Editor's note: You can watch Debbie Best's interview on *Katie*: http://katiecouric.com/2013/01/28/online-love-traps-the-victims-and-masterminds-speak-out

"He asked to see my portfolio on the first date. What kind of woman does he think I am?"

Dating 101

When you have to make a choice and don't make it, that is in itself a choice.
~William James

I flunked Dating 101 a long time ago. Yet there I was, age sixty-seven, considering entering the online dating field.

By happenstance, the day I decided to look at the online dating sites was the very day there was a free weekend on one of the more popular sites. That meant I could go online to look, to see if there were indeed men living in my area in the age bracket I thought was reasonable. I found a plethora of men looking for love. Excited, I began to fill in the questionnaires on two different sites. I wasn't sure I wanted to go live at the moment but at least I could consider their questions, form my answers and then when I was really ready, it would be easy to proceed.

As I filled in the questionnaire on one site I came to a series of questions about my ideal partner that also had a box to check off marked "deal breakers." I considered my options and decided that a deal breaker for me would be any man who was shorter than I was. I checked off that box. The question about weight was a bit of a puzzle but finally I decided that their definition of "heavyset" probably meant very overweight and I knew that was not something I was attracted to, so I checked off that box too. The deal breaker box concerning smoking was a no brainer—I had no desire to be with anyone who smoked—so I checked that box. The deal breaker box concerning drinking was also checked as I did not imbibe alcohol and had no desire to be with someone who drank regularly. A few more selections and I was done with that part of the questionnaire. I decided to stop at that point and logged off. I had not completed the questionnaire but thought I would do so another day.

The following morning, when I logged on to the site there was a message telling me that my profile had been accepted and was now online and live. Heart palpitations would not be an exaggeration as I raced to the site to look—and yes, there I was. No pictures, an uncompleted profile and worst of all, all the deal breaker boxes that I had so carefully checked off were there—as what I required. Yes! I wanted to meet men who were very heavy, shorter than me, who drank regularly, and smoked! Yikes. I couldn't figure out how it was that I was now online when I had not approved that. For a few minutes I couldn't figure out how to get my profile down, but I finally found a section of the site that allowed me to hide my profile. Whew!

I then turned my attention to the other e-mails I had received only to discover I had received about thirty hits from interested men who sent me their detailed information about their heights, smoking, drinking lives, as well as pictures showing a variety of midsection girths. The humour of it all hit and I started to laugh, and laugh, and laugh. Was this a sign? Was I meant to explore online dating? Should I just give up and remain single? Was a lasting love beyond my ability in this lifetime? What did it all mean? These questions and more flitted through my mind even while I was laughing at myself.

A day or two later I went back in to edit my profile. This time I deleted the deal breaker boxes and simply put down that I was looking for a man to be my companion, my love, and the most necessary ingredients were being spiritual and having an open heart. I think my online dating mishap was a lesson that I needed to stop focusing on the deal breakers and, instead, focus on the positives.

~Camille Hill

Worth the Risk

*To decide is to walk facing forward with nary a crick in your neck
from looking back at the crossroads.*
~Betsy Cañas Garmon

"Do you think you'll ever get married again?" a friend asked me.

I wrinkled my nose and shook my head. "I doubt it. It's hard for me to trust people, especially men." I shrugged. "I was crushed when my first marriage ended and I don't want to get hurt again."

She nodded. "I can understand that, but you don't want to create a wall around yourself. There are some really great guys out there, and you should give someone a chance."

I shrugged a second time. "If God wants me to get married again, He'll bring the right person into my life."

"Yeah, but if He does, will you even give the poor guy a chance?"

My friend's words ran through my head for weeks afterward. Her final statement held more truth than I'd wanted to admit. The truth was that I'd already made up my mind to remain single. My plan was to raise my children, enjoy my job teaching kindergarten, and protect my heart from any future pain.

That was my plan. It was safe... and lonely.

Eventually my longing for companionship won out over my desire to avoid heartbreak. I signed up for eHarmony, a website to meet other singles.

I went on a few dates and the guys were nice enough, but I couldn't see myself marrying any of them. Friends told me I was being too picky and reminded me that no one is perfect.

Of course, they were right. But I wasn't about to settle. I wasn't going to put my heart on the line for just anybody. He was going to have to be worth the risk.

I wish I could tell you that I knew it was him the moment I saw his picture, but the truth is, I didn't. I received an e-mail from eHarmony, telling me that I had a new match. I opened it and saw a photo of a nice-looking man leaning against his kitchen counter.

And there were piles and piles of dirty dishes on the counter behind him.

My first thought was that this man needed a maid, not a wife. But something inside me wanted to give this one a chance.

The man's name was Eric and he lived in a small town about 200 miles away. He was an engineer and a single father of two. Most importantly, he shared my faith, a key component that was lacking in my first marriage.

After exchanging e-mails for a week, the dirty dishes were already forgotten. Eric's good qualities more than made up for his messy kitchen. And he seemed equally impressed with me.

We decided to meet in person. We agreed upon a restaurant halfway between our homes. But that morning, there was a snowstorm, and Eric called me to insist that he make the entire drive. "I don't want you to have to drive in the snow," he said. "My truck is four-wheel drive and it will be safer this way."

I was touched by his concern for my safety. And when he knocked on my door that evening, I was shocked to realize how strong my feelings already were.

By the end of the evening, I was sure Eric was the one God had chosen for me. But a part of me was still scared of being hurt.

We introduced our children into the relationship and it only made things better. The kids clicked right away and I could already see a family forming. Everything felt right.

We took turns making the 200-mile trip and saw one another

nearly every weekend. We talked about everything, from our faith to our childhoods to what we wanted in a spouse. I felt like I'd known Eric for years, rather than months.

Four months into our relationship, Eric proposed to me. Without even thinking, I threw myself into his arms and said yes. But days later, in the privacy of my own home, I had some doubts.

"What if I get hurt again?" I feared. "I can't put my children through a second divorce."

I talked to Eric about my feelings and was surprised to find that he shared my concern. He always seemed so sure about everything.

"We've both been hurt before," he said, "and we know how awful divorce can be. Neither of us wants to go through that again." He shrugged. "So we won't."

"But how do you know?" I said with tears in my eyes.

Eric grabbed my hands. "Because I promise to love you every day of my life. I promise to love your kids as though they were mine by blood. I won't hurt you. I'm worth the risk, I promise."

I looked into Eric's eyes and I knew it was true. Loving him was a gift, and I'd be crazy to pass it up because of fear.

Eric and I married six and a half years ago. It was a small ceremony, with our children as our only attendants. Eric's best friend was the pastor who performed the ceremony. There was no fancy meal served afterward, but none of that mattered. Eric and I had joined our lives, our families, and our hearts.

These days, I no longer worry about enduring a second broken heart. Eric has kept the promises he made, and I love him more every day. I was given a second chance, and I'm so glad I didn't let my fear stop me from taking it. I'm happier than I've ever been, and I can't imagine my life without Eric.

I've learned that true love is always worth the risk.

~Diane Stark

The Dating Game

It's Not Me, It's You

The trouble with using experience as a guide is that the final exam often comes first and then the lesson.

~Author Unknown

46

Keeping an Eye Out for Love

There are much easier things in life than finding a good man.
Nailing Jell-O to a tree, for instance.
~Author Unknown

I was in my fifties when I finally decided to see if there was someone for me in the world. I had never been married, and people always told me, "He must be at the bus station when you're at the airport."

Friends told me that online dating was the best way to meet someone, and after much thought and prayer, I decided to meet only four people—and if one was right for me, I would know.

I carefully put up my profile and talked with many men online. I was very specific about what I was looking for, just basic things like common sense, understanding, and humor. Plus, I had always quietly hoped for someone handsome.

The first date was in a restaurant for after-work coffee. He told me he was a plumber at a local university and seemed like a nice person. When I met him, I soon found he was a little hard of hearing and we had to converse rather loudly. It seemed to go well until he sneezed. It was then that I saw something fly from his head and splash into his coffee cup. I was dumbfounded. It was his eyeball! He quickly stated that he had a glass eye and when he sneezed, it sometimes flew out. Of course, the whole restaurant was intrigued since he had loudly announced that his eye was in his coffee.

As I wondered what to do, and people in the restaurant were ordering more coffee and dessert to see what happened, he took his fingers and got the eye from the coffee cup, promptly popped it in his mouth and pushed it back into his head. As he moved the eye with his finger, it made little squeaking noises, and he soon asked me if it was in straight. I said it was all white. "What?" he asked loudly. And I again said, a little louder, that it was all white. He then squeaked it a little more, and asked again how it looked. The eye was "looking" at his nose, but I said it looked great, excused myself, and promptly left the restaurant. I did not go to that restaurant again for a year.

Having promised myself to meet four men, I tried number two. We met at a pizza place for coffee. He was very nice and we talked until the place closed. As he walked me to his car, he became an octopus, putting his unwanted arms around me. I told him stop meant stop, and kicked him in the knee. As he hopped around holding his knee, I left him hopping and drove off. All the while I was thinking, "God, there must be a better way."

Being stubborn, I met number three in a café and he apologized that he had posted his grandson's picture online as himself. This meeting was null and void.

Resolved and determined, I tried number four. I had a heavy heart as I looked for the "right one" to come through the door of the café. We had chatted online and he was a retired gentleman who sounded very nice. I finally saw a man at the door with distinguished white hair, and a brilliant smile. He was looking right at me. I really hoped this would work out, since this was my last chance. I really did not want to be alone in my life any longer.

As I waited for Michael, I pondered what he would be like. I said a little prayer, "God, let this one be the one meant for me." Then, as I looked up I watched Michael as he walked across the room. He was wonderful. We talked, laughed, and chatted for many hours. I briefly told him about the three men before him, and said I had one important question to ask him: "Do you have anything that flies off your body when you sneeze?" He laughed and said he was all original parts.

After six months of dating, I had found the man for me.

~Pamela Tambornino

"A woman by the name of Daniela called to let you know she couldn't make it. She also asked me to wait an hour before telling you."

47

Turkey
on the Mountain

Humor is emotional chaos remembered in tranquility.
~James Thurber

W
e met in November, and after only one date, I invited
Eric to spend Thanksgiving with my family and me.
But he surprised me by countering my invitation
with one of his own.

"How'd you like to spend the long weekend camping out with
some friends of mine?"

"Camping?" I gulped. "With your friends?"

He chuckled. "Their wives and girlfriends will be there, too. It's
a tradition that dates back a couple of decades at least."

Well, in that case, I jumped at the chance to see him interact
with his long-time buddies, and packed a small duffle bag and my
sleeping bag. He'd already explained that it was far too cold to tent-
camp so late in the fall, so we'd be sharing a trailer with several other
people.

In hindsight, I should have asked a few more questions.

It turned out that the entire expedition centered on hunting elk.
And Eric went out there with his buddies, all right, but also with half
a dozen of his former in-laws.

No problem, I thought. I can show him I'm as good a sport as any gal being thoroughly scrutinized by members of his previous wife's family.

Since none of the campers or trailers had an oven large enough to roast a whole turkey, the plan called for us to bring it to camp on Thursday morning—fully cooked—right out of the oven. The other provisions of our feast would be "potluck" from the assemblage of hunters.

At the appointed hour, I pulled the turkey from the oven, wrapped it tightly in foil, and we transported it up the snow-packed twists and turns of the hilly coast range to the makeshift hunting lodge. So far, so good.

The trailers and campers were backed into a rough circle. Tarps were strung from one vehicle top to another, forming a pseudo-canopy. All the doors opened toward the center. A burning barrel kept the common area toasty warm. Rounds of tree trunks served as both tables and chairs and were split into firewood as needed.

Midday we spread our banquet among the fir boughs. And what a banquet! Most memorable of the eclectic taste offerings was a roaster pan brimming with hamburger gravy. "It's the only kind of gravy I know how to make," said the cook with a shrug.

After our feast, we headed out for the late afternoon hunt. Two hours of bouncing and bumping over rutted goat trails passing themselves off as roads took its toll on my bladder. "I've got to go," I whispered to Eric.

He gave me one of those looks—the kind that makes you want to apologize even if you know you haven't done a darn thing wrong. A steep snow bank hugged my side of the truck, a deep gulch graced his side. He stopped the pickup right where it was. "There's tissue in the glove compartment."

I edged my way around the vehicle. Finding no shrub to protect my modesty, I squatted down behind the truck. Meanwhile, Eric checked in with the other hunters via the walkie-talkie.

"Hurry up," he hollered out the driver's window at me. "One of the guys is about a quarter mile back around the bend and heading this way."

Now, I don't know for sure if guys can do this, but somehow I managed to stop what I was doing mid-stream. Frantically, I tried to hoist my undies, pantyhose, long johns and jeans back to their proper place. "Tell him to wait a minute!" I shrieked.

At that precise moment, Eric slid the pickup into gear and took his foot off the brake, slowly rolling on down the road, away from his would-be girlfriend whose language now indicated a total lack of good sportsmanship.

A portion of my clothing still around my knees, I began to run after him like a duck to a corn feed. Above Eric's maniacal laughter I could hear the engine of the approaching vehicle. I looked back over my shoulder only to discover that forty or fifty feet of baby blue toilet paper trailed behind me.

By the time Christmas rolled around, I was happily dating some one new.

~Jan Bono

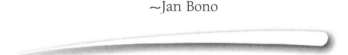

Worst First Date Ever

Nothing spoils romance so much as a sense of humor in the woman.
~Oscar Wilde

On February twelfth, Jake was getting ready to go on a weeklong trip to visit his old fraternity in upstate New York. When he said goodbye to me, he put his hands in his pockets, looking bashful.

"I probably shouldn't give you this," he said, "but you've been really sweet to me these past few days, so I wanted to say thank you." He pulled out a box of chocolates and handed them to me.

"Thanks, Jake." I was totally taken aback by the gesture, the romantic thoughtlessness of it. It was sweet. I was vegan, which he well knew, and I wasn't going to eat the milk chocolates, but it was kind. And it wasn't like Jake to be gratuitously kind.

"Well, Gary's been pressuring me to give these to random girls, so I figured I'd give one to you." He paused for a moment. "Please don't tell Gary. Actually, don't tell anyone." Another pause, then, "It cost a dollar."

Then he kissed me goodbye and rode off in his car, a 1990s pickup truck he used to cart his band's instruments.

The words echoed after he left: "Random girls." "This cost a dollar." "Please don't tell anyone."

I hadn't been expecting a Valentine's present, hadn't wanted one, but this seemed worse than nothing at all. Did he expect me to bowl over in gratitude? "Thank you Jake, thank you! This dollar candy has made my dreams come true. When can we plan the wedding?"

Yeah, it was time to find somebody new.

• • •

Valentine's Day found me alone and drinking in the campus Starbucks, drowning my loneliness in a mocha with a double shot of espresso. If you can't get happy, get caffeinated.

Gary, Jake's friend, spotted me in line, and walked over. "How are things going with you and Jake?"

"Meh." I sipped the mocha and avoided eye contact.

He nodded. "You need to find someone better. Jake doesn't care about you." Then, a smile lit across his face as he recognized someone he knew sitting at a table. "My friend Paul is over there. The comedy guy I was telling you about. You guys have to meet."

"I dunno," I said. "Isn't it a little weirdly pressured to meet someone on Valentine's Day?"

"No! It's totally adorable, man. If you guys get married, how cute would that be? You could say that you met on Valentine's."

Gary had been talking Paul up for weeks. Paul was so funny, and Jewish, and perfect for me. So Gary said. I think he was trying to wean me off of Jake, but Paul still sounded tempting.

Whatever doubts lingered faded as Gary guided me to Paul's table. He was a small guy, sitting alone at a table with his laptop. He looked like a miniature Woody Allen, complete with horn-rimmed glasses and a black gothic coat that was two sizes too big.

"This is Rebecca," Gary said. "She's interested in doing stand up comedy too."

"Oh yeah?" Paul said.

"How's everything going?" Gary asked.

Paul shrugged. "Not great. I can't decide whether to ask this girl I like out for coffee or not."

"If you like someone, I say you should go for it," I said.

"Maybe." Paul picked at the half-eaten muffin on his table.

"The baked goods here suck," I said.

"Tell me about it. But there's nowhere to get a good muffin at school."

Then I said, "I can whip together a batch of pumpkin muffins in about twenty minutes. Do you guys want to come back to my apartment?"

Paul looked at his computer. He was watching YouTube videos. Gary nudged him. "She's a good cook."

"Okay," Paul said. I grinned.

Like I always say, the way to a man's stomach is through food. Or something like that.

Back in my apartment, an hour later, Paul was scarfing down muffins with a healthy appetite. He looked at a *Sandman* poster I had up in the living room. "Do you like Neil Gaiman?" he asked.

"He's my favorite author," I said.

"Me too." Paul polished off the muffin in his hand and tossed the wrapper into the trash. My heartbeat quickened. I updated my mental checklist: Jewish. Into books. Funny. Likes my muffins.

"What are you doing Friday night?" I asked.

He shrugged. "Not much."

"Do you want to get dinner?"

"Sure. Are crepes okay?"

Gary grinned, as if to say, "I told you so."

It's hard to pinpoint the exact moment that everything went completely and utterly downhill. It started when he picked me up. Or rather, when his mom did.

I was mortified when a blue Chevy rolled up outside to find Paul in the back seat. I got in the back with him.

"Hi Rebecca," the woman driving said. "I'm Paul's mom. It's nice to meet you."

"Oh," I said. "Nice to meet you."

"Paul doesn't have his license yet," his mom explained.

I stared out the window. Paul was twenty-three, I was twenty-one, and we were being driven to a date by someone's parent. I hadn't expected that to happen ever again once I left high school.

Later, when we got to the creperie, the very first thing that Paul said after we sat down was, "So, I took your advice and asked out that girl."

I was speechless.

"She hasn't responded yet," he said. "I sent her a Facebook message."

"I'm sure she'll say yes," I mustered.

"Hopefully," Paul said. He perused the menu, totally oblivious. "The Western crepes here are my favorite."

After I got over the initial mortification, we bantered a little. He asked me if I liked my apartment.

"It would be nice if the walls weren't all white," I said. "The place is so bare, it feels a little prison-y."

Paul got quiet. "I've been in a mental hospital. That is a prison. There were bars on the window and I couldn't leave."

"Oh my God," I said. There weren't many things left to say after that. "Why were you institutionalized?"

"I have schizophrenia," he said. "I heard voices."

"Oh." I picked at my crepe.

"Are you done?" he asked. I nodded vigorously. Yeah, I was done here. With the crepe, too.

"My mom gave me money to pay for you."

I blushed. "No, that's okay. We can split it."

After that, we had to get back into the car with his mom for the long, silent drive back to college.

Back in my apartment, I called Gary.

"Why didn't you tell me he had schizophrenia?" I yelled into the phone.

"Hmm? Is that a problem for you?"

"No. But he told me in the worst way possible. Also, it was definitely not a date." I quickly summarized our evening. Gary chuckled on the other end.

"Oh, Paul," was all he said.

It's been a while, and I can laugh about it now, but that was the first worst date that I've ever had. If it counts as a date at all.

I guess it goes to show: when you date a funny guy, they always get the last laugh.

~Rebecca Kaplan

MTN

"How would you feel about going back to an
exclusively online relationship?"

Male Order

Patience is the ability to count down before you blast off.
~Author Unknown

I remember the first time I thought about ordering a man. Until recently, I had thought there must be something seriously wrong with someone who would resort to the Internet to locate love. But things had changed. I had been single for two years and as far as I could tell, the supply of men was non-existent. It was time to take more extreme measures.

Outside of work, my daily haunts included La Petite Academy and Walmart. Even though the selection of bachelors at La Petite was enormous, most of the boys were still being bottle-fed. So Walmart would have to do. I hung out in the produce section for a while, but there were no men on display there so I wandered over to the automotive department. Who could resist a clueless female needing advice on which oil grade to select? The first guy I approached had fantastic hair, fabulous shoes and most importantly—no ring. How was I supposed to know he was married and his wife was looking at light bulbs in the next row? Her cart came squealing around the corner so fast she nearly knocked over the end cap display of wood-grained toilet seats. There had to be an easier way to meet men.

It was about this time that I noticed Julie at work. This perky little thing had a lunch date nearly every day. Of course it probably had a lot to do with the fact that she was young, blond, and perfect.

"Julie, where are you meeting all these guys?"

"I joined a Christian dating service," she gushed. "You should try it. It's very affordable and they even have men your age, too."

How thoughtful.

Turned out, Julie's definition of affordable amounted to $159 for a monthly membership fee.

"Try *The Gazette*," whispered my eavesdropping co-worker. "You can place an ad for only $29.95."

"What have I got to lose?" I thought as I dialed the number.

"I'm sure you will be very happy with the results," the rep assured me. "Most professionals today are too busy to meet other singles."

It was probably just a canned speech designed to help me justify my departure from normal dating venues, but she did have a point.

I couldn't wait until *The Gazette* came out.

I didn't get one call. Meanwhile, the men waiting in line for Julie had to take a number. That's when I heard a radio commercial advertising the Twister Love Line. They say it's darkest before the dawn.

By selecting one, two, or three on my telephone keypad, I could indicate my preference for a variety of features. This was a regular Build-a-Date workshop. I ordered a Christian low-fat combo and super-sized the bank account.

I couldn't get home fast enough the next day. I dialed the Twister Love Line and entered my pin number. The cheery voice announced that I had "two new dates."

Halleluiah, it was raining men!

After I listened to each potential date give his personal sales pitch in a prerecorded voice introduction, I was advised that if I was interested, I could leave a call- back number. Unfortunately, the bios sounded more enticing than the intros. A month went by and still no catch of the day. I was growing weary and was just about to delete the entire campaign when finally I got a bite. He was 6'2" with blond hair and blue eyes. My only reservation was that his favorite hobby was ice-skating.

Was I expected to participate? Sure, waltzing on the ice sounded romantic, but for someone with about as much grace as a hippo on a high wire, anything involving balance on a razor thin blade could be nothing short of humiliating. At this point, however, all remaining logic had evaporated and I left a message. "John" called a few days later. Naturally, he insisted that we meet at Iceland for an afternoon skating session.

As I entered the rink on Saturday, I thought I must have completely lost it. The place was packed with teens and loud music played over the speakers.

What had I gotten myself into? It seemed so high school. Was I really meeting a guy at the rink? Was this the only place I can find a date?

I felt more awkward than a cat in a swimming pool, but I scanned the crowd trying to appear like I belonged.

Hmm, was that him over there?

I gave a slight smile and nod in case it was John.

"And now it's time for couple's skate," blasted the voice over the intercom.

The mystery man started his approach. As he drew closer, I froze. Oh my gosh. Please, no!

His exuberant smile flashed a missing front tooth and his unbuttoned coat revealed a never-ending sea of denim. The loose fitting jeans were actually paint-splattered overalls.

John had described himself as being "semi-fashion conscious" and he certainly didn't say anything about being dentally challenged. By now I was scolding myself. You knew better than to trust a guy's description of himself. They always exaggerate! What were you thinking? How did he get matched with me?

All of a sudden, I felt a tap on my shoulder.

Relieved at the opportunity to avoid the dapper denim dude, I whirled around.

Towering before me was a chisel-cheeked, blue-eyed wonder.

"Is your name Christy?" he asked.

"Yes..." I stammered, trying to conceal my delight. "Are you John?"

His eyes twinkled as he nodded and extended his hand to shake mine.

Bingo. My male order delivery had finally arrived. Maybe there is a FedEx in heaven after all. And hopefully they packed the bubble wrap. I was going to need some padding for my behind if my new hobby was ice-skating.

~Christy Johnson

50

Clueless

Before we work on artificial intelligence why don't we do something about natural stupidity?
~Steve Polyak

The doorbell rang. My blind date, Mr. X, had arrived. I stood up, smoothed my shirt and headed to the door. We planned to grab dinner but it was early so I invited him in and offered him a beer. We talked for a bit, finished our beers, and decided to leave for the restaurant. Mr. X excused himself and headed to the bathroom.

As I watched him walk toward the bathroom I thought, "Huh. Great smile, polite, very personable... this guy has real potential. I'm so glad my friend set us up!"

When my dream date reached the bathroom he turned around, walked to my bookshelf and in one fell swoop took a huge 500-page book off the shelf and proceeded back into the bathroom.

Oh. No. He. Didn't!

Oh my god. I couldn't believe it. Did he just bring a book into the bathroom on our first date? Ugh.

Maybe I was being too harsh. Maybe it wasn't too weird. Just a smidge weird. And a smidge weird is okay. Heck knows, I did weird things sometimes too.

I subsequently perched myself on the edge of the couch and tried to appear busy. I looked at the quilt on the back of the couch, ran my fingers over the fabric and acted oddly interested in the design and pattern of my own quilt while I waited... and waited.

Next thing I knew, Mr. X had been in the bathroom for fifteen minutes. That may not seem like a long amount of time, but keep in mind that he was a visitor on his first date and he knew I was waiting for him. Fifteen minutes is longer than it takes to get your oil changed at Jiffy Lube.

It occurred to me that maybe he was sick. Poor thing! Or maybe he was embarrassed because the apartment was so small he was worried I would hear him. For that, I had a plan. I stood up and yelled in the general direction of the bathroom, "I forgot to get the mail this morning! I'm just going to run out to the mailbox and see if it arrived!"

I walked outside, purposely shutting the screen door loudly to inform him that I had in fact left the building. I walked over to the mailbox, opened it, and checked for mail. Empty. Obviously, because I had gotten the mail six hours before. I took my time heading back to the apartment so that he would have time to do his thing.

When I walked back inside I expected to see Mr. X sitting on my couch, but he was nowhere in sight. I glanced at the clock: 5:08 p.m. Man, was he really still in there?

The possibility crossed my mind that something was seriously wrong with him, but seconds later I heard his feet shuffling in the bathroom. And—I kid you not—I also heard pages turning. Boyfriend was just fine. And he was apparently enjoying his novel while I sat there for over half an hour waiting for him.

I walked over to the mirror to check my hair and make-up. I fluffed my hair and played with my shirt. I was torn between trying to look sweet or sexy. He did a ton of charity work, so I figured he'd probably be into sweet. I pulled my neckline up a little. But charity work or no charity work, he was a man. I yanked my neckline down a little. Up, down, up down, sweet, sexy, sweet, sexy... Argh! Whatever! None of this was going to matter if he never came out of that bathroom!

It was 5:34 p.m. (exactly fifty-four minutes) when I heard the bathroom door open and Mr. X emerged from the bathroom. I politely, but eagerly, awaited his explanation for his hour-long rendezvous in my bathroom…. "I have a digestive disease," maybe, or "I ate something bad on the car ride here." Anything.

But he didn't say anything. I was greeted by an upbeat Mr. X who placed the book back on the shelf, clapped his hands together and said, "All right! Ready to grab a bite to eat?"

Feeling shell-shocked after his spending an hour in my bathroom, I continued to wait for the explanation. But the reality hit me that it was his business and there was no reason for me to know anything more than that. Forgive, forget, move on.

"Yep! I'm ready for dinner, let's go!" I replied.

Then, Mr. X grabbed his jacket, turned to me and said, "That was a great dump!"

Screech! Stop the music! Did he just say the word "dump?"

I stopped myself from bringing it to his attention that I was not his brother, his friend, nor his doctor. I was his date. His disgusted date.

We still went to dinner because I didn't feel as though I had a choice, I felt backed into a corner. In that moment, I knew there was no chance of a second date, so I decided to get this one over with. Mr. X-Lax was welcome to continue his Book Tour elsewhere.

~Gretchen Schiller

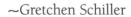

The List

Map out your future, but do it in pencil.

~Jon Bon Jovi

The sun glinted off my friend's new diamond ring as we nibbled spinach salads. I felt a bit jealous. I wanted to meet my perfect match, too.

"It's all in the list." Sue pulled a small spiral notebook and pen from her bag. "You write down the qualities you want in a guy and look for someone who has them. I met Ken two weeks after I made mine. You dictate, I'll write."

I arched an eyebrow, then shrugged. Couldn't hurt. "Single, attractive, witty, well-educated, well-employed, health conscious, family oriented. Too much?"

"Not enough."

"Loves animals, shares my political convictions, enjoys out-of-doors and road biking."

"And?"

"Seriously? Interested in cultural events, enjoys international travel." I grimaced. If men made such lists, I'd never match one.

"You're sure that's all you want in a man?" Sue asked.

I nodded firmly.

Next Sue helped me write a profile for an online dating site.

David contacted me right away. A dentist with a Golden Retriever, season tickets to Portland Center Stage, a large quantity of free air miles, a road bike and a mountain bike, he seemed to have everything on my list. My heart fluttered with hope when I looked at the profile picture of his sky-blue eyes and boyish grin. We agreed to meet the next Sunday afternoon for coffee.

When I arrived at the appointed Starbucks, a tall, well-built man in jeans and a cream-colored silk shirt got up from a table. I recognized the eyes and smile.

"Samantha?" he asked, extending his hand.

As we sipped our drinks, David showed me photos on his phone of his dog and of his recent trip to Croatia. We compared notes on bicycle rides we'd both done, and local bands we both liked. "Want to do a bike ride next Saturday?" he asked. "There's a nice ride across the Glenn Jackson Bridge. When we get to Vancouver I'll buy you dinner at my favorite restaurant."

I agreed instantly. I hadn't pedaled across the Glenn Jackson Bridge from Portland to Washington State, plus I was always up for a new restaurant. We decided on a meeting place and he gave me a nice goodbye hug.

I counted the days, met David at the appointed spot, and pedaled onto the bridge close behind him. I'd folded a little black dress and sandals into my bike pack for a quick change at the restaurant, and assumed David wouldn't be wearing spandex to dinner, either. My spirits soared as high as Mount Hood, visible off to our right.

Minutes into the ride they dropped into my biking shoes. Nine feet wide, the bike lane ran smack down the center of the freeway, with three lanes of noisy traffic on each side spewing fumes in our faces. The manhole covers spaced evenly along the path added a jolting variety to the steady uphill climb. I strained to keep up with David as we sped across the bridge. At least there would be an elegant dinner on the other side.

I followed David off the bridge, along a highway, and into a restaurant parking lot. I barely suppressed a gasp of surprise. Could this well-heeled dentist be taking me to a buffet? True, I hadn't written "Big Spender" on my list. Or "Foodie." Still. Putting on my best smile, I locked my bike to a post as he locked his.

"Wasn't that great?" he asked.

"Kind of noisy and fumy, though," I replied.

He shrugged. "When you ride faster that stuff won't bother you as much."

My chest tightened. "Rude" hadn't been on my list either.

But seated in a booth, I found myself relaxing in David's company despite our biking attire and the standard salad bar fare, overcooked vegetables, and some kind of tasteless white fish. We found that we both liked bluegrass and jazz, streams running beside mountain roads, and workdays that included quirky events. Biking speed and the cafeteria faded in importance as we made a second date to meet at the parking lot just off the bridge at Sauvie Island, and bike out Reeder Road to the strip of three river beaches.

I'd ridden several times on the island's flat roads east of the wild-life refuge, past grazing horses and cows and tidy farmhouses, then on out to the beaches. The ride would be a perfect summer evening date. When David kissed me goodnight, hips touching, lips lingering, I wished our ride were the next day.

He looked good when we met at Sauvie Island, his biking jersey matching his blue eyes. We chatted about the pleasant weather as we lifted our bikes from their racks, changed into biking shoes, and fastened helmets. "Feel free to ride ahead if I'm too slow," I said, as cyclists often do.

"We'll see how it goes."

Disappointment thunked in my stomach. This was our second date. I'd hoped for "Hey, spending time together is the point."

I chased after him for at most five minutes when he turned his head and called over his shoulder, "I'll meet you at the beach." And off he sped.

I watched the rear tire of his bike disappear around a curve in the road. "Fastest bike alive" had not been on my list.

I next saw David when I arrived breathless at Walton Beach, about eight miles out. "Hi," I called out as I carried my bike across a ridge covered with a thick stand of cottonwoods, willow brush and red-twig dogwoods.

His eyes were alight with enthusiasm. "Isn't it a wonderful

evening? I've been walking around for a while. Great weather. Great company."

I looked around the empty beach. Did he mean me?

"So hey. My brother and his girlfriend are headed up to bike Orcas Island in a couple of weeks. Want to join them?"

My first thought was, "How fast do I have to ride?" My second thought was, "Biking in the San Juans with a handsome guy could be really fun."

Before I could answer, David grinned at me, spun his bike on its rear wheel, and asked, "Ready?"

Ready for the return ride? I'd just gotten to the beach. But never mind. Maybe this time we would chat about Orcas Island as we rode.

But the minute we reached the road he got on his bike and barely got out the words "see you at the parking lot" as he rode away.

I watched him disappear, Orcas Island losing all its appeal. He had already loaded his bike and was doing some quad stretches when I panted into the parking lot.

"Want to get something to eat?" he invited as he leaned into a hamstring stretch. "Plan the trip?"

I declined as politely as I could, turning my cheek when he leaned in to kiss me.

As soon as he drove away I called Sue and exploded.

"Did you have 'courteous' on your list?" she asked quietly. "What do you want in a man? Is it on your list?"

I gulped. I got it. My list, not to mention my thinking in general, hadn't included the qualities that mattered most like "thoughtful," and "listens well." When I got home I made my old list into a paper airplane and looped it into the wastebasket, then, smiling, sharpened my pencil for something brand new.

~Samantha Ducloux Waltz

"Did I interrupt again? Sorry, I don't usually do that when I'm talking about myself."

Fairytale Romance

Make the most of yourself, for that is all there is of you.
~Ralph Waldo Emerson

There was a time when I thought fairytale romances could only exist in books, that the idea of being someone's knight in shining armor was a fantasy that could never happen. Then I met someone who helped me see that such romances did exist, and they didn't always end happily ever after.

There was this girl I had known for about a semester at college. She was cute, with a laugh that lit up the whole room when I heard it. She came into the library where I worked on campus and spent a lot of time asking me questions about books she never really got around to checking out. I got the idea she was checking me out, and one day I asked her out on a date.

"Can I take you to dinner?" I said. "I know a couple of places that are kind of romantic."

Her smile got larger and she leaned over the desk to whisper to me. "Funny you should mention romantic, because that's exactly what I'm looking for in a guy."

I felt my heart begin to beat faster. "I could be that guy," I said, almost knocking over a stack of books. "I'm the romantic type."

"That's good," she told me, "because everyone I've dated doesn't get what I'm looking for." She slid a book over to me, one she'd found on the library shelves. "What I'm looking for is someone who wants to be my Prince Charming." She squeezed my hand and suddenly turned to leave. "See you Saturday at eight!"

I looked down at the book she'd given me. The title read, *Fairy Tales*. I saw she'd marked several stories. The first was about a prince who rode up on a white horse to a tower where a princess was trapped, climbed up the tower, and carried her off into the sunset.

I closed the book. This girl really did want to have a fairytale romance for a date, and if I had any chance of impressing her I was going to have to live up to what the prince in the book had accomplished. But I wasn't a prince, and the girl in question lived on the second floor of the college dorm, not a tower, and I didn't think there was a horse within fifty miles of the place. What was I going to do?

Well, any good prince worth his crown wouldn't take such a challenge lightly. At eight o'clock Saturday night I rode up to the side of the dorm where her window faced out and climbed out of the car I'd borrowed from a friend. I picked up a pebble and threw it at the window of her room. She appeared in a moment, looking like a princess in the gown she wore.

"Good evening, princess," I said, bowing. "Come, your chariot awaits."

"Where's your mighty steed?" she called down to me.

"The car's a Mustang I borrowed from a friend," I answered. "That's as close as I could come to the real thing!"

She laughed and came down to meet me. Slipping into the seat beside me, she said, "This will do for now, but next date I want the whole package: prince outfit, mighty horse, maybe even a magic crown."

I laughed, thinking it was a joke. We had a wonderful night, but I could see a shadow fall over those pretty green eyes. Next date I'd really have to make her fairytale fantasies come true.

So I looked over the pictures in the book. I talked to a friend of mine who was majoring in fashion design and asked her to make me a real prince outfit, and a princess gown. I rented a horse from a local farmer and learned how to ride it without falling off all the time. I even found a crown in a novelty shop that I could place on my girlfriend's head at the end of our date.

She was swept off her feet by all the effort I'd made. She twirled in her gown on the hill where we'd spread a picnic lunch, and cried when I put the little plastic crown on her head. She hugged me, and the smile she showed me was a magical one.

"I can't believe you did all this," she said, hugging me again. "Now I know I've found someone who will always make my dates the fairy tales I've dreamed about."

Suddenly something caught in my chest. I stood there looking at her, joyous in the fantasy I'd helped create, and realized it wasn't me she was head over heels for; it was the fairytale prince I was playing. I took off the cape I was wearing, that had itched me all day long.

"Look," I said as gently as I could. "I can't possibly keep this up on every date we have. Sooner or later you're going to have to have just a date with me."

The light in her eyes faded. "Not with my prince?" she asked.

"Maybe someday," I said, "but it can't be me. I'm just a guy, some-one who needs someone else to like me, not an imaginary prince."

So I rode her home to her dorm, and like a prince said my good-byes with as much gentleness as I could. Perhaps, I thought, as I bounced away on my rented horse, she was imagining I was off on some kind of magical quest.

In a way, I was. My quest was to find someone who would like being on a date with plain old me. That happened, eventually, but I'll never forget the time I tried my best to be a Prince Charming for the girl of my dreams. The girl of my reality I dated later was much more fun.

~John P. Buentello

53

Chicken Soup
for the Soul.

A Heartfelt Verse
for Modern Times

Shoot for the moon. Even if you miss, you'll land among the stars.
~Les Brown

I stood in the card shop,
My heart at my feet,
While staring at greetings
All mushy and sweet.

February fourteen
Came early this year,
I don't have a "Honey,"
Or a guy to call "Dear."

I was gathering missives
For family and friends,
But I read every message
To see how it ends.

The cards were all leering
In red, pink and white,
And I couldn't find greetings
I thought were "just right."

I got quite depressed
As I stood there that day,
So I shrugged, and I sighed,
And walked sadly away.

"If you weren't quite so picky,"
Said Anna Marie,
"I'm sure that you'd find
A suitable 'He.'

"To what kind of man
Would you mail out a card?
If you narrow it down,
It shouldn't be hard."

"I'm NOT picky!" I screamed
At the top of my voice,
"I'm single, not desperate,
It's just there's no choice!

"All the good ones are married
Or live far away,
And I'm feeling quite lonely
This Valentine's Day."

"Then tell me," she challenged,
"Describe Mr. Right.
Then I'll know when I see him
Some Saturday night."

"Okay," I relented,
"Proceed if you must,
But I think your idea
Will be a big bust."

She gave me "that look,"
Stared me straight in the eye,
So I tried to imagine
The most perfect guy.

"...His hair might be blond,
Or perhaps it's quite dark,
He's tall or he's short,
But he sings like a lark."

"Go on," she implored me.
"What else is he like?
Are his eyes blue or brown?
Does he fish, does he hike?"

"I'm thinking," I told her,
"Of what's bottom line.
Getting down to the essence
Takes a great deal of time...

"...He doesn't do drugs
Or smoke cigarettes,
He likes to play *Scrabble*,
And lets me win bets.

"He might wear glasses,
Or a ring in his ear,
He speaks his own mind,
His opinions are clear.

"He'll do small repairs
And change the car oil,
His cooking exceeds
Bringing water to boil...

"Yes, he'll often cook dinner,
When home from his job,
And he'll pick up his socks,
'Cause this guy's not a slob.

"His jokes make me laugh,
I know he's quite smart,
He's romantic, sincere,
And he calls me 'Sweetheart.'

"He's kind and he's gentle,
He'd not hurt a fly,
He votes Democratic,
That's my kind of guy!"

"A Greek God!" said my friend,
Dear Anna Marie,
"When you find him, please ask
If there's a brother for me!

"Your list sounds a lot
Like a card that I'd buy
One for women still looking
For their special guy..."

"You're brilliant!" I told her,
"I could make quite a lot!
I've spent a small fortune
On cards that I'VE bought!"

So I got out some paper,
And fired up my pen,
And where my verse started,
This column will end:

"Roses are red,
Violets are blue,
Is there any such person
As Mr. Will Do?"

~Jan Bono

The Dating Game

Never Too Late for Love

You are as young as your faith, as old as your doubt;
as young as your self-confidence, as old as your fear;
as young as your hope, as old as your despair.

~Douglas MacArthur

54

An Unlikely Pair

What I need to live has been given to me by the earth.
Why I need to live has been given to me by you.
~Author Unknown

Jack is clever. And creative. And that's how we came to have dinner together three years ago. For months, we'd been Facebooking back and forth—just as friends—so naturally, when he contacted me about joining everyone for a happy hour, I accepted. It seemed perfectly legit because by "everyone," he meant many of our hometown classmates.

You see, Jack and I grew up together in a small Texas town, albeit from different sides of the track. He was a wild and reckless boy, and well, I was the proverbial good girl. I was responsible, walked the straight and narrow, and did things by the book. Jack, on the other hand, got himself into lots of trouble and as often as possible. It wasn't unusual to hear that he'd been in a car accident, a four-wheeling collision, a bloody brawl, or suspended from school. Quite frankly, he intimidated me, and I avoided him at all costs. Likewise, he didn't think he had much in common with me either, so for the duration of middle and high school, we frequented the same places and passed each other in the hallway, but I never looked his way. And we certainly never uttered a single word to one another.

That night, at a local Mexican restaurant, I wasn't sure what to make of my meeting with little Jacky Bryant who was all grown up now and sitting before me. So far, it was just the two of us, and I was secretly hoping someone else would show up soon because, well, I felt a little awkward. Sure, we knew each other from childhood, but that was over twenty years ago, and like I said, we weren't really catching up as much as we were forging a new friendship. Before our meal arrived, I hurried to the restroom to text my best friend, another classmate of ours. "Please come to happy hour, Tonia. It's just me and Jacky!"

My phone buzzed. "What happy hour?" she replied. And at that moment, I realized there never really was one. That sneak! I wrestled with my emotions. On the one hand I was sort of freaked out by his ingenious plan to hang out with me, and on the other, I was intensely flattered. Like I said, Jack is clever. And creative.

"What the heck," I thought as I returned to our table. "I am kinda hungry." I sat down with Jack and we both plowed through our fried avocados, rice and beans. Although you wouldn't know it from my size, I'm actually known for my freakish ability to suck food down like an NFL linebacker—along with any of my companion's leftovers if they'll let me. With a raised eyebrow, Jack leaned in and pointed to my empty plate. "How do you eat like that and stay looking like that?"

"Oh, I don't always eat like this," I replied, embarrassed, "and I work out at the gym with a trainer."

Jack, who'd been struggling with his weight, alcohol, and an addiction to cigarettes, looked me in the eyes and said, "I'm going to do that."

"Sure you are," I thought.

We went on to talk about the last twenty years, marriages, divorces, relationships, fitness, and pet peeves that night. Tonia never rescued me, by the way, but by the next time I glanced at my phone, much to my surprise, four hours had passed. And even though our lifestyles were still very different, I found myself sort of liking little Jacky Bryant. To be quite honest, though, I didn't really put much stock in his fitness announcement that night. Judging from his Facebook page, I knew he still partied a lot, and much like I felt in our youth, I just didn't think I could keep up, nor did I want to.

I dismissed our dinner as friendly, and I didn't give him a romantic second thought.

A couple of days later, he posted on Facebook that he'd prepared his last unhealthy meal because he'd joined a gym. "Hmmm," I thought, but fitness resolutions can be a dime a dozen, and again, I really doubted he could change the routine he'd had for the last twenty years overnight. Boy, was I wrong!

I saw Jack a few weeks later, but by this time, he'd sweated his way to a twelve-pound weight loss. At over 250 pounds, and no taller than me, it was just a small dent in the work he'd planned to do, but for the first time, I caught a glimpse of his determination. This man was serious.

Jack quit smoking and drinking, and he followed a food plan. He went to the gym religiously, and then he made an appointment with Todd, my trainer. Jack likes to joke about the first time we worked out together because when Todd put us through the exercise mill, he almost puked while I was still going strong. Jack, who lived about two hours from me, returned home and continued with Todd's workouts. One day, months later, and after we'd been dating for a while, he shared his motivation for change.

"I wanted to get healthy for a long time," he confided, "but it's hard when you're stuck in that cycle day in and day out. I didn't know anyone who worked out, didn't hang out at a bar, and didn't smoke cigarettes. When we met that night for dinner, I went home and poured all the beer out of my cooler. I printed out a picture of you from Facebook, put it in a frame by my bed, and every morning when I woke up, I looked at you and thought, 'To get a quality girl, I have to be a quality guy.' You're the kind of person I've wanted to be with my whole life. That's what motivated me to get my life straight. You didn't know it at the time, but when I met you for dinner, I was still hungover from the night before. You were my inspiration, and you saved me."

My mouth fell open. That is probably the most special compliment any man has ever paid me. Over the next year, Jack lost seventy-five pounds, gained some serious muscle mass, sobered up, and kicked nicotine. He says that I inspired him, but truly, I find him to be inspirational.

They say opposites attract, but those two teenagers from opposite sides of the tracks had a lot more in common than either of them thought. What I didn't know back then is that wild and reckless troublemaker Jacky Bryant was really just a big teddy bear underneath his rough exterior. What he didn't know is that goody-goody Vallory Jones was outgoing and adventurous underneath all that studying and good behavior. Today, almost three years after that make-believe happy hour, once an unlikely pair, we are now soul mates. Jack and I lift weights together, mountain bike, camp, cook, and a whole host of other things. We like the same music, the same foods, and we share the same thirst for life. We've faced my cancer diagnosis, his career change, and lots of other ups and downs, but his unwavering support and adoration have gotten me through the toughest of times.

Some say people can't change, but Jack has proven that people do. He insists that I came along at just the right time—a time when he'd been praying for his own transformation. We often laugh that it took us almost forty years to find each other when we ran in the same social circles for most of our lives. Sometimes I wish we could have known each other better when we were kids, but I realize now that reckless Jacky and goody-goody Vallory weren't ready to combine forces until they'd gone through twenty years of preparation for one another.

~Vallory Jones

55

Getting Married... at My Age?

Age is a question of mind over matter. If you don't mind, it doesn't matter.
~Leroy "Satchel" Paige

J ack and I met at the condo pool in 2003 while I was vacationing in a condo I co-owned with my brother and sister. I lived in Milwaukee, Wisconsin and visited the land of sun, sand, sea, surf and glorious sunsets in Florida three or four times a year.

At the pool, Jack, age sixty-six and I, fifty-seven, treaded water in the deep end while we talked about our children—my four, his six—about our grandchildren, and about the church we both attended just a few blocks away.

Not long after we met, Jack's wife Jane was diagnosed with liver disease and a year later, the following April, died peacefully in the hospital. I sent Jack a sympathy card with just a few paltry words scrawled at the bottom. How could I, who had been married, divorced, and annulled twice, and had never lived with either husband longer than seven years, even begin to understand the pain of losing a spouse you loved with all your heart for forty-three years? I couldn't come close to comprehending what must have been unbearable sadness.

The next time I visited Florida, a month after Jane's death, I saw Jack sitting alone at the pool in a lounge chair. I walked over to offer my condolences. He hugged me and said, "Thank you so much for your kind words on the card."

I wanted to know more about Jane: her life, her illness, her death. How were their children coping? What about their youngest daughter, pregnant with her second child? How was she doing?

I kept asking questions. Jack kept talking. Before long I understood that he probably needed someone outside the family to talk to and so, with the help of my many questions, Jack talked to me that day at the pool for five straight hours. We did the same for the next three days. He talked. I listened. He cried. I shared my life and background. We had things in common, Jack and I.

On the fourth day, Jack and I were in the deep end of the pool, hanging on to the ledge with our elbows, talking more about the fragility of life and the importance of going on.

Suddenly this man who had opened so much of his heart and soul to me over the past four days asked me if he could ask me a question.

"Of course," I said, curious as to why he needed permission to ask me a question.

"Would you ever be interested in pursuing a relationship with me?"

I couldn't speak. I'd been mostly single for almost two decades, since the day when my second husband Harold moved out. He had married his girlfriend the day of our divorce, then died two years later. I'd raised four children as a single parent. In nineteen years I'd dated two men, one for eight months, one for two-and-a-half years. After that I hadn't had more than one date with any man for the past twelve years. A relationship was the furthest thing from my mind.

The only thing I could think to do at the moment was raise my arms up over my head, inhale as much air as I could into my lungs, and sink slowly to the bottom of the pool. I needed time to think before I could answer that question.

At the bottom of the pool I thought, "Oh my gosh, oh my gosh, this poor man. What am I going to say? What does he mean? Why is he asking this? He loved his wife so much and she just died five weeks ago. How could he ask me such a thing? How? Why?" I asked myself over and over.

I surfaced and gasped for breath. I looked at Jack and asked, "What exactly do you have in mind?"

"I have no idea. I just know that I like talking to you. I also know three things. One, I loved my wife very much. Two, she's gone and she's never going to come back to me. And three, Jane would not want me to sit around feeling sorry for myself. She would want me to be happy. I'm a realist, that's all."

"But it's only been five weeks since she died. You can't possibly mean that you want to start dating this soon."

"No, I guess not. Besides, even if we did go out we would have to be very discreet. My children are hurting and they need more time to grieve. I did most of my grieving this past year before Jane died. Months and months when we both knew it didn't look good. She knew how much I loved her and cared for her, but she was also the type to say, 'Get on with your life, Jack.'"

He continued slowly. "I'd just like to see you, that's all."

"Well then why don't we go for a bike ride?" I suggested, thinking that seemed like a safe alternative to dating. "We have four bikes in our condo shed. I'm sure we could find one that would work for you. Let's bike over to the Gulf and go for a swim."

"I haven't been on a bike in years, but it sounds like fun. How about if I make a couple of bologna sandwiches? I have some really good German bologna and rye bread."

"That's fine, I'll make the drinks. I'd like mustard on both slices of bread. No mayonnaise," I prattled.

An hour later Jack and I met again, gathered the bikes, placed our picnic in the bike basket and took off on the two-mile jaunt to the Gulf. When we sat down on the sand on our beach towels, I opened the sandwich. Mustard on both slices. No mayonnaise. I looked at Jack and smiled. Here's a man who actually hears what I say and remembers it, I thought to myself. If you want to know the truth, I started falling in love with him at that very moment.

We were together every day for the rest of my three-week visit to

Florida. No two people have talked more than we did during those days. A month later I returned to my favorite place on earth for another three weeks. Knowing that I'd been dreaming of living in Florida fulltime for years, Jack told me about a condo for sale in his building, one that was just fifty-seven steps from his. I looked at it twice. My belief that one should follow your dreams while you're still awake and my disdain for those long, six-month winters in Wisconsin were the catalysts for my making an offer on the condo. My six-bedroom empty-nest house in Wisconsin sold in two weeks.

The next month, Jack came to Wisconsin to help me get rid of most of my furnishings at my second huge rummage sale.

We had our ups and downs over the next few years like all couples do. I even made a long list of reasons why I never wanted to marry again. But partly because we lived fifty-seven steps from each other's condos and walked in and out without knocking as if each of our condos was an extension of one big home, it was hard to be upset for very long.

However, after one misunderstanding while we were on a cruise with various members of his family, Jack decided to end our relationship. I was devastated, but we both began dating other people—he more seriously than I. He brought one woman home to his condo for eight straight months. Each time I saw her it was like a knife in my heart. I was so hurt and angry I wouldn't even speak to Jack even if he and I were the only ones in our daily water aerobics class.

But finally, in June 2011 he came to his senses. In the pool that morning he asked if we could talk. I said he could have fifteen minutes at my condo but he had to leave right after that because my cleaning lady was coming.

He came, we talked, the cleaning lady came and we finished talking at his condo for three more hours. That night he ended his relationship with the other woman. Two weeks later I went to Alaska for a month and we talked or e-mailed nearly every day. Four months after my return Jack got down on one knee and proposed at a restaurant right on the Gulf, one of our favorite places.

We were married in June 2012 in what we lovingly referred to as our "geezer wedding." I was sixty-six years old and Jack was seventy-five. We had no attendants, no ushers, no rehearsal, no rehearsal dinner. Just Jack and me walking down the aisle of our church hand in hand, married by my cousin Jerry, a monsignor in the Catholic Church.

Over 100 of our relatives and friends joined us at the church and then at our condo clubhouse for the most fun wedding reception I've ever attended in my life. We had live music, an open bar and a spread of mid-afternoon finger food enough to feed an army. My kids surprised us with an elaborate flash mob dance they'd worked on the week before to the song "Get Down Tonight." It's even on YouTube!

All in all, our geezer wedding was perfect. And Jack and I know one thing for sure. Age is a matter of mind. If you don't mind, it doesn't matter. And that is how we know for sure that you're never too old for lifelong love.

~Patricia Lorenz

Editor's note: You can see Patricia and Jack's wedding dance flash mob, called "GP & PJ wedding dance" at
http://www.youtube.com/watch?v=rEbqSntSyCo

All Over Again

For 'mid old friends, tried and true,
Once more we our youth renew.
~Joseph Parry

I was the proverbial soccer mom, and all of my friends were married. At the time of the divorce, I hadn't dated anyone but my ex-husband in over twenty-five years.

I joined singles groups but still felt too raw to go on an actual date. Staying in a large group became one more way to hide out. The invitations came in, but every time, I said the same thing: "I'm sorry, but I'm just not ready to date."

A couple of years rolled by this way. Then one day, a name appeared in my Facebook inbox that was so familiar, it didn't seem out of place at all even though I hadn't seen that name in close to thirty years.

He'd lived on the other side of my neighborhood, so we were practically children together. What was I—fifteen, sixteen when we'd first met? My sister and her boyfriend had given him a ride somewhere and we briefly shared a back seat. I thought he was adorable and easy to talk to and I liked him immediately, but he had a girlfriend. I ran into him after they'd broken up and we clicked again as friends. Friends who dated on and off for years.

And now here he was e-mailing me after all this time. Did I remember him? Ha. I checked out his picture; to me, he looked exactly the same, right down to the scar I'd always loved because it somehow added a slightly rugged defiance to those almost-pretty features. He was always pleasant, easygoing, and fun. How I used to love his conspiratorial grin, the way he leaned in and sort of nudged me when we laughed, as if we alone got the joke. For years I'd found myself gravitating toward him again and again, drawn by his core of deep and solid kindness.

What I remembered most was the time he picked me up for a date and I asked him if he'd been to work that day. He answered no, that he'd only been mowing his neighbors' lawns. Wasn't that work, I asked? I still remember the way he said it. "Well, no—I mean, it's not like I'd charge them or anything," he shrugged. "They're old." As if that explained it. And it did. I believe I fell in love with him just a little bit at that moment.

Now here he was again, recently divorced, and although we'd both moved out of state, it just so happened we'd chosen the same one. He was only a few hours away. Would I like to get together? At first I panicked and stalled. I was thirty years older and twenty pounds heavier. What if he didn't like the middle-aged me? What if he did? I wasn't ready!

A couple of months went by, and I couldn't stop thinking about him. I also couldn't stop thinking how ridiculous it was to refuse to see an old friend just because I was scared. And worse, I was using the excuse that I wasn't ready to date someone new. Technically it didn't have to be a date, and he really wasn't someone new, was he?

So I picked up the phone and dialed the number he'd told me to call if I ever changed my mind.

All the while I couldn't help but hear my mother's voice in my head about never calling boys. Good thing he was no longer a boy! We were, after all, old friends, and we talked for ages, finally agreeing to meet in the middle for a simple, casual, easy day. When I started to panic about that upcoming date, it calmed me to remind myself that it really wasn't a first date at all. "Don't worry," my smart friend Mary comforted me. "He'll see you as he did back then. People do."

And guess what? I believe she was right. I know he looked the same to me. He was still cute. He still had the same walk, the same smile, the same gestures. The same conspiratorial grin, the same nudge. His gray hair still somehow looked brown to me. How easy it was, how simple, how natural, that we fell right back to feeling like we used to. When it was time to leave, before there was a chance for any awkwardness, he drew me in just as he'd always done and gave me such a sweet kiss, thirty years melted away under the warm summer sky. I giggled all the way home.

But what surprised me the most was the way all those years of living had made him even dearer to me. I'd forgotten how nice it was to be with someone who understood so much about where I'd come from. We'd both made some painful decisions at times, and we'd suffered some profound changes and losses, but we had eventually found our way to a better place. His core of goodness was as solid as ever. He had experienced his own struggles, and they'd given him depth and character. Wisdom.

Once again, I was drawn to his scars. I believe I fell in love with him just a little bit, all over again.

~T'Mara Goodsell

57

Short Distance Romance

Never think that God's delays are God's denials. Hold on; hold fast; hold out.
Patience is genius.
~Georges-Louis Leclerc

I was single and in my early forties. I'd been living in Boston for seven years, after leaving a career that allowed little time for dating. Building a social life was still difficult. The few dates I went on were draining. "Why do you read so much?" and, "Why are you so quiet?" were typical questions men asked me.

I was further discouraged by a shift in the way men I didn't know reacted to me. I noticed it one day as I was getting out of my car at the gym. Across the parking lot, about thirty yards away, a guy who appeared to be about twenty years younger than me paused at the gym's front door, looked me up and down, and grinned. But as I got closer, his grin turned deadpan and his eyes got wide, as if he was witnessing two trains about to collide. He grabbed the door handle and rushed into the gym.

The most stunning encounter came at my adult Sunday school class. A guy who looked to be about my age sat by himself three pews behind me. I noticed that whenever I turned around to hear what someone in the very back of the room had to say and met eyes with him, he had a pained expression on his face. I assumed that he must be younger than me and was put off by the idea of an older woman making eye contact with him.

As the months passed I would naturally meet eyes with the guy three pews back when he was in my line of sight. Each time I would regret that I had turned around. He was usually scowling. I promised myself that I would never turn in his direction again.

I told a co-worker about my Sunday school encounter. She told me to forget about the sourpuss and focus on going places where I could find someone before I aged out of the market. She told me that her sister, who'd turned fifty, joined an online dating site and got few responses, most likely because of her age. Panicking, I joined a site and rolled my age back by four years. I spent weeks communicating by e-mail with potential connections but never went further. I realized that I couldn't meet a man that way. I needed to see a potential date in person.

I joined an online site that organized group events, hoping to meet a number of prospects without the pressure of a one-on-one date. I enrolled in swing dance lessons, which were offered at a church hall near a university. After I paid my entrance fee I realized that most of the participants were college age. I stuck with it anyway. But one day I missed a cue and turned one way while my partner turned the other. The pain in my knee was so severe I had to quit.

I hobbled back to adult Sunday school a few days later. Without meaning to, I met eyes with the man three pews behind me as I folded my coat over the seat. He was grimacing. I became angry. I wanted to ask him what his problem was. But I didn't. I became more determined to get back out there and meet someone.

A girlfriend and I bought tickets to a Boston Celtics game. We made plans to hang out at a sports bar before the game, figuring there'd be lots of men there. However, we got stuck in traffic. By the time we got to the bar it was empty. Everyone was at the game.

I was exhausted. I decided to take a break from my man search. I became president of a literary association and organized events. I had a short story published in a creative writing journal. I sent a copy to my Sunday school instructor who'd read some of my earlier writings. The following Sunday he complimented me on the piece in front of the class. I heard about an open mike night at one of my favorite bookstores and decided to participate, reading a poem about my beloved deceased cat.

Then months later at the end of adult Sunday school, I heard someone behind me call my name. I turned around. He extended his hand and introduced himself. It was the guy three pews away. He told me he'd seen a picture of me posted online from the open mike night, that he knew I had signed up online for group gatherings. He was thinking about joining one himself—for divorced men. He said he knew I was a writer because he was there when the Sunday school instructor complimented my story. He told me that he was a former journalist, like me, and was writing a book.

I felt as if a statue had come to life. It was the first time I had heard his voice or seen him smile. This was the same guy who had sat behind me for years looking mad whenever our eyes met. Or was that just my interpretation?

Over the next several weeks we exchanged e-mails about our writing projects, our childhoods, our respective challenges with shyness. We agreed to meet for our first date on a blustery winter evening at a burger place across the street from an author event I wanted to attend. When I finally got to the restaurant he didn't seem to mind that I was late. We laughed when we placed our orders. The menu offered a variety of delectable-sounding burgers, but we both wanted the Cobb Salad. Six months later he told me he wanted to marry me. The following year we got engaged.

I've asked my fiancé why he took three years to approach me. He said when he began attending the Sunday school class, he had just gotten divorced. When he felt ready to start dating, he hesitated. He was afraid I wouldn't be interested. To find out more about me he turned to the Internet and discovered that we had similar interests. Ironically, my joining activities partly in reaction to what I thought was his rejection of me provided him with the details he needed to feel comfortable enough to introduce himself.

One day, as we discussed our wedding plans, I told him how

hurtful it was to look back in class and see him scowling. He said he didn't realize he looked unpleasant. I told him how for years I'd sit in church blinking back tears, wishing I had someone to share my life with, like the couples and families that surrounded me. My fiancé gave me one of his rare but radiant smiles, put his arm around me and said, "All you had to do was look back and say hello. I was only three pews away."

~Lisa Braxton

58

I Don't Date

Well, it was a million tiny little things that, when you added them all up, they
meant we were supposed to be together... and I knew it.
~Nora Ephron's Sleepless in Seattle

H
e pulled up to the curb in a red VW bug all smiles, obviously unaware that I was not dating. I clenched my jaw and knew instantly what was happening. A blind date (or as I now call it: a deaf, dumb, and blind date) set up by my well-meaning friends, without my permission.

"It's just dinner, Lori," my girlfriend whispered. "It will be fun and you could use some fun." She continued out loud now: "Everyone, this is Bob."

Well, I was not in the mood for any fun. Recently divorced, a single mom to a sick two-year-old and working two jobs left me little time or energy to go out with friends, much less date. I was tired and bitter. The last thing I wanted right now was to spend time with this happy stranger in the red VW.

Halfway through the evening Bob leaned over and asked, "Do you want me to give you a ride home? I know that you don't really want to be here."

"It's not personal," I replied. "I just don't date right now. I live more than an hour from here and my girlfriend is supposed to take me home."

"Grab your purse," he smiled. "Let's go."

Bob and I talked and laughed all the way home. I shared my

story so easily with him. The details came out so naturally it surprised me. I explained my failed marriage as well as my daughter Missy's illness. At one point I choked up as I shared the pain that I felt and how scared I was to do this all on my own now. Bob was so easy to talk to. Before I knew it we pulled up to my curb.

As I got out of the red VW Bob said, "Hey, maybe I could take you and your daughter to SeaWorld sometime." He laughed, "It doesn't look right for a grown man to go without a kid or something. It wouldn't be a date," he reasoned. "Just SeaWorld."

I hesitated. "Maybe. Can I think about it?"

The truth was there was no way that I could afford to take my daughter to SeaWorld. I was working as a dental assistant in the daytime and waited tables at night. The bills were piling up and I was barely making it.

"Yeah, maybe." I nodded. "That might be fun and thank you so much for the ride."

Over the next six months, Bob, Missy, and I went to every theme park imaginable. We shared meals that always included a toy. He would spend hours on my living room floor playing with Missy and the little neighborhood girls. The kids would giggle as they called Bob "Ken," grabbed their Barbies, and dressed them for adventure.

One afternoon I pulled into my driveway and noticed the red VW at the curb. I walked around the house and there was Bob mowing my lawn with that that big wide smile.

"I hope you don't mind but I noticed your grass could use a trim the last time that I was here." He went on. "Maybe some water too. I hope it's okay with you."

"It's okay, thanks," I replied. My hardened heart was starting to soften.

One evening as I cleaned my kitchen I caught a glimpse of Bob and Missy in the living room. They were walking around with pillows on their heads. I laughed, "What in the world are you doing?"

The pillow fell off his head. Missy shouted, "Bob and I are models! We are practicing walking with pillows on our heads." Bob's face turned bright red.

That evening, before Bob went home, I asked him if he would like to go out for a real meal, one that didn't come with a toy.

"What will Missy do?" he asked.

"I just thought maybe my mom could watch her sometime and we could go to dinner, maybe a movie too," I replied. "You and me."

"Wait a minute. I thought you didn't date!" he teased. "That sounds like a date to me!"

The happy stranger in the red VW won my daughter's heart, and then he won mine.

Happy 25th anniversary, Bob!

~Lori Bryant

59

My Favorite Dance Partner

Sometimes the very thing you're looking for is the one thing you can't see.
~Vanessa Williams

"How you doing?" I heard as I passed a pack of four guys. They all burst into laughter, then quickly followed my friend Julie and I across the bar.

"Hey, what's your name?" one shouted over the music.

We spent the next hour laughing and talking with this very entertaining group. Little did I know my life would never be the same.

Julie looked at the cute, dark haired guy directly across from me and whispered in my ear "dibs."

Dibs, AKA Joe, didn't talk much. He spent his time dancing in place. He started out slowly swaying with the beat, until he could hardly contain himself. Finally he grabbed my arm and said, "Come on!" Laughing at his lack of containment, I followed him to the dance floor. We talked, joked around, and danced for what seemed like hours.

I already knew that my newfound dance partner was not to be. Julie had dibs. But I couldn't kick the feeling that maybe I shouldn't have let him go so easily. Did I just miss my chance with this great guy?

Ultimately, Julie never dated him. But Joe and I had a connection. We quickly became friends. Really, he became my best friend. We talked on the phone daily. We went dancing every weekend. But mostly we spent our evenings talking about some crazy guy I liked or some silly girl he liked.

I thought many times about dating my favorite dance partner. The timing was just never right. It seemed like one of us was always dating someone else. As the years passed we both found serious relationships. Our friendship faded. Joe moved out of state. Eventually I heard he was married. I was devastated. I had always envisioned that Joe and I would end up together.

My own relationships didn't last long. By the age of thirty-two, I struggled with dating and the men in my life. I knew Joe was married and living out of state. I thought of him often. I thought about all the "what ifs." What if we had a chance? What if the timing was right just once throughout the years? What if Julie never called dibs? But now, our chance had passed.

One night I came home after a long day at work. I threw my grocery bags on the counter and checked my messages. I had three missed calls. Two were from friends and then, a voice I had not heard in a very long time.

"Hey, I'm home. I was just wondering if... maybe... you'd like to hang out sometime?"

I don't think my feet touched the floor as I flew over to listen to his message again.

Joe?

I could have played it cool and waited to call him. But I instantly picked up the phone and dialed his number.

"Joe."

"Yeah."

"When you say home, where is home?"

"Home, home. Washington."

I felt my stomach tighten. Goosebumps covered my entire body.

He was here.

The next day he came over with a pepperoni pizza and a bottle of wine. We spent the next eight hours talking about where we went wrong in our past relationships. We laughed about the good old days. We talked about the great friendship we had all those years ago. And how we seemed to have picked up right where we left off.

Both of us fell silent. Just then I noticed how dark the room had become. The only light was from the stereo playing our favorite songs. The wine bottle was just about empty and the pizza box was hanging halfway off the coffee table.

I looked back to Joe. Almost as if he were in slow motion he leaned in and kissed me. The whole room faded away. I don't remember the song playing or what he said right before he kissed me. But I will never forget the way that kiss felt.

After all those years. After all the missed opportunities. Finally, our chance had come.

~Diana Lynn

60

First Love Rekindled

Trip over love, you can get up. Fall in love and you fall forever.
~Author Unknown

Clutching a soft beige purse, wearing a print dress and the only hat in the crowd, an elderly lady sat alone and apart. I was attending a friend's wedding — her second — a country affair in a casual setting in her garden. "I'm a friend of the groom's mother," the woman offered when I asked, and she explained she had traveled some distance from a town I knew. "Oh," I blurted out. "My first love was from your home town." My blurt led to telling who he was. It happened that this lovely octogenarian was my former beau's mother's best friend. We chatted for some time and I sent my best wishes to her friend, his mother, and moved on to gossip with other guests.

Several months later, I was sitting in the kitchen with my two adult daughters when the phone rang.

"Kit?"

He always had a way of saying my nickname that caused the nerves to zing along my hairline and down my spine. They did again.

"I'm in town. I'd love to see you."

There was more conversation, something about his mother mentioning where I was and finding my phone number, but all I could understand was that after thirty-three years I was going to see my first love again.

My girls pumped me with questions, eager to learn all about a secret part of me. It hadn't been hidden; it had simply never been brought up in conversation. I delved into my photo box to find his picture. In it he stood in the water at the beach where we met. He was the lifeguard; I was the playground supervisor. At first I rejected his attention; he was too perfect, bronzed, tall, blond, and too sure of himself. I liked intellectuals. It turned out he was that too. I was smitten. I told my girls that we had planned to marry but for various reasons hadn't.

Two days later, blushing at the memory of a muscular fair-haired Nordic boy who'd been my sole reason for breathing for nearly three years, I was seventeen all over again. The hall mirror told me otherwise. Grey threads meandered through my dulled black hair and the corners of my eyes wrinkled when I smiled. I pulled the slackened skin up from my chin and let it sag back. I'd aged, but not too terribly. Nodding at my image, I assured myself I was acceptable. He was no longer the same young man. The years had surely aged him too.

The doorbell rang. My heart leapt. I fussed with my skirt, put a forced smile on my face, and opened the door. A familiar face—older but the same, with a stylish goatee—smiled at me. Over dinner we caught up on each other's lives, learned about families and careers. By the time the evening drew to a close we both knew the passion of old was smoldering again. The next few days were spent visiting galleries, taking in a play, and just walking together. We laughed, held hands, and let love take its course. The years apart disappeared and we fell into a rhythm that was both familiar and new at the same time. We felt the pull of love.

I showed him my city. He invited me to his. His life there was different from mine. We had travelled different paths, had become different people influenced by the direction our lives had taken. Yet, we both still felt the pull of intense physical and emotional attraction and wanted to see if there was any way to continue. Months went by when I traveled west and he traveled east. They were delicious months. We shared each other with our family and friends, talked, cuddled, and explored.

As our relationship grew, so did our knowledge of each other. We hashed over the reason we had broken apart when we were young and discovered that the cause was still a major factor. We still couldn't resolve it. We parted as friends and vowed to care about each other for the rest of our lives.

Today, another twenty years later, I look back on this precious interval in my life, aware of what a gift it was, and reflect on how life evolves as we grow older but nothing really changes. I will always love him, my first love—we just can't grow old together.

~Molly O'Connor

61

Out of Practice

Dating is like using the treadmill. If you don't do it often enough,
you might as well not do it at all.
~Beverly Grossman, Women Who Date Too Much

I was about to go on my first date after the end of my twenty-four-year marriage, and I was terrified. I had met Joe at a wedding three months earlier, so at least it wasn't a blind date. Nevertheless, my jittery nerves caused me to get ready way too early. I ended up all dressed up with no place to go for fifty minutes. I paced around the house going crazy. My hands were sweaty; my heart rate increased and my entire body quivered. At this rate, I would need a change of clothes or to call 911.

I stopped running around and sat down. This definitely wasn't the time to start an exercise program. I took a few deep breaths and tried to relax. After a few moments, which seemed like an eternity, I popped up just like bread out of a toaster, on the move again. I walked back to the bathroom and fussed with my hair for the umpteenth time.

Then my mind started whirling. One of my divorce after-effects, as I call them, was an aversion to feeling trapped, physically or emotionally. I continue to work on this because sometimes it puts me in a panic, as it did then. I started thinking of every possible bad thing that could happen.

Even though I knew Joe, I had decided to drive myself, just in case the evening went badly. But my car key was in my purse. What if I lost my purse? I'd be trapped! So I pinned a car key inside my bra. What if something happened to my car, stolen perhaps? Trapped! I ran to my desk and started rifling through the drawers searching for the business card of a nice cab driver who told me I could call her any time. She would come and get me. Where did I put this card? My bra. Then, just for good measure I also took a twenty-dollar bill and—you guessed it—put that in my bra too. Not only was I prepared for anything but my figure was looking better.

The seconds ticked by and finally it was time to go. I inhaled, filling my lungs with air, then released it, shaking my arms like a swimmer before diving in the pool. I said, "I can do this, and here I go."

I arrived a few minutes early, hoping to spot Joe before he went inside. I'd never walked into a bar or nightclub by myself and I didn't intend to start now. However, there was no sign of him. I took another deep breath and pushed open my car door. I leaped out before I lost my courage.

A man was checking IDs at the door. Not that he asked for mine—those days were long over. I stood there frozen. The old fear returned. What if Joe had changed his mind? What would I do in this place alone? I heard my flannel nightgown calling me home to safety. Although tempting, I'd come this far and wasn't going to let fear win.

The cool night air made me shiver. The man at the door said to me, "Why don't you go in?"

I said, "I'm meeting someone."

He pointed, saying, "Look, there's a seat at the bar just inside the door. If anyone gives you trouble just let me know."

I peered inside. It wasn't crowded yet, there was a seat and I was cold. All I had to do was walk six feet. It seemed more like six hundred miles. With all the courage I could muster, I placed my foot inside the door and made that long walk to the barstool.

The man sitting next to me was nice and bought me a drink. I was trying to be so cool, as if I did this sort of thing all the time. I didn't want it known I was in uncharted waters. I thought, well even if Joe stands me up, I've made a lot of progress tonight.

Then I spotted him at the other end of the bar. Well, I thought it was him. In the nightclub darkness I wasn't sure.

Did I have the courage to get off the stool and walk over? No! I took a safer route. I pointed at the man I thought was Joe and asked the bartender, "Would you please do me a favor and ask him if he's waiting for Tena?" As he walked to the other end of the bar my heart almost jumped out of my chest. What if that wasn't him?

Thankfully, as soon as the bartender asked the question, Joe whirled around and ran to my side. He said, "I was afraid you changed your mind." He took my hand and led me to a table across the room.

The date couldn't have gone better and quite frankly, it's a bit of a blur. I felt intoxicated being with someone attentive who actually listened when I talked. I realized the last several years of my marriage I'd always been alone. I think the loneliest feeling in the world is having someone sitting two inches away from you, who might as well be on the moon.

This was a new and welcomed experience. The best part was feeling like a normal person: talking, laughing, dancing and having fun. All of the pain, hurt and worries melted away for a while. I felt terrific.

It's good I didn't go crazy that night. There we would have been, in the heat of passion, with keys and cards and money tumbling out of my bra. It might have been worth it, just to see the look on his face.

Facing my fears away ignited my courage to embrace new experiences. I broke out of my comfort zone that night. I was so glad that I left my flannel nightgown in the drawer, where it belonged.

~Tena Beth Thompson

62

Memories

It takes a long time to grow an old friend.
~John Leonard

O ne of the advantages of growing up with an older brother was the chance to hang around all of his good-looking friends. Now, while most of these teenaged lotharios either ignored or tormented me, one — Bill — treated me with respect and kindness.

My parents approved of Bill. His hair was always combed, his clothes were presentable but never flashy, he always said "please" and "thank you," and because he knew the difference between a dinner fork and salad fork and never dropped food on the floor, he was a frequent guest at our family dinners. Even though Bill had no chance of ever becoming a valedictorian, his grades always exceeded those of my brother, thereby giving my parents even more reason to like him.

I was twelve or thirteen when I first met Bill and I immediately fell in love with him. He had a beautiful smile, great sense of humor and, most importantly, he was accessible. Unfortunately, my father issued an edict of "no dating before sixteen" so my attraction was deemed "puppy love" and discouraged, if not emphatically forbidden. Nevertheless, I tagged along whenever Bill and my brother went bike riding, fishing, bowling or ice-skating. I was even allowed to go to the movies with them once. Any time spent in Bill's presence was like a slice of heaven.

Just before I turned sixteen, my brother and Bill enlisted in the army. Devastated, I cried for a week, vowed I would never marry, and began writing letters and mailing home-baked cookies to my one true love. At first, I penned two or three letters and shipped at least one batch of cookies per week. By the time Bill finished boot camp, I was down to one letter a week and cookies only for the holidays. When he and my brother shipped off to Alaska, the cookies and letters stopped completely. I moved on, Bill moved on, and our would-be romance became little more than a fond memory.

Fast forward forty-five years and I'm on an interstate headed north to Colorado Springs to reunite with Bill. Although he and my brother had drifted apart after the army, my brother had acquired Bill's e-mail address and sent it to me suggesting I might like to rekindle an old flame. Never one to turn down a challenge, I took my brother's not-so-subtle suggestion and started exchanging e-mails with Bill. Why not? We were both retired, we were both single, and we shared a history.

After several months of e-mails progressing from prim and proper to downright hilarious, we agreed that a reunion was definitely in order. Since Bill lived in an area where my family and I often vacationed when I was young, driving to his location meant not only getting to see him but also having the opportunity to revisit some of my favorite haunts. It was a win-win situation. Two weeks later, I loaded my SUV with camping gear, made my dog comfortable in the cargo area, stuck a Peter, Paul & Mary CD into the car stereo and pointed the car north.

With more than 350 miles ahead of me, I had a lot of time to think and second-guess myself. Was I doing the right thing? What would we find to talk about? Should I just turn around and go back home? I stopped at every rest area I came to on the pretext that the dog needed to be walked. I filled up with gas when the tank was only half-empty. I stopped for lunch and ordered enough food to feed an army. If I was going to do this thing, I had to be well fortified.

It was late afternoon when I finally arrived in Colorado Springs. After I got set up in the campground, I called Bill and gave him directions on how to find me. "I'm driving an orange SUV... if you can't find it, look for an old lady with a silver ponytail and beige dog." Thirty minutes later, Bill, his daughter, and her two children arrived at the campground. Evidently, Bill had needed some fortification as well.

The first few minutes were awkward. With all the wrinkles, gray hair, and extra pounds that the past forty-five years had added, neither one of us was recognizable to the other. Acting like two middle schoolers attending their first boy-girl dance, we shuffled our feet and avoided eye contact as Bill's daughter introduced her children. Once that was over and done with, she scowled at Bill and me and asked, "Well... are you two just gonna stand there?" Taking that as our cue, Bill and I opened our arms and hugged as if there were no tomorrow.

Having had the foresight to include some old photo albums in my gear, I pulled them out and set them on a picnic table. Bill and I spent the next two hours gazing at pictures, sharing laughs and resurrecting memories. There were pictures of my dad: "I loved his pipe." There were pictures of my mom: "I loved her cooking." There were pictures of my brother: "Did he ever tell you about the time...?" And of course, there were lots of pictures of me in grade school, high school, before and after my marriage and all the exotic and not-so-exotic places I had been over the years. At one point, Bill stopped paging through the albums and turned to me. "Remember that high school graduation picture you sent me?" Of course I did. "Well, I carried it around in my wallet for years. I would still have it but I got mugged a couple of years ago and my wallet never showed up." Not knowing how to respond to such a revelation, I looked around, hoping for inspiration.

Without our noticing, the campground had begun to fill up and several families were firing up grills for dinner. I asked Bill if he and his family wanted to share my hotdog dinner but Bill replied that they had to get back for his granddaughter's soccer game. "Maybe we could get together tomorrow?" he asked.

"Of course," I replied. I'll count the moments, I thought.

After a mostly sleepless night, I met Bill the following morning and we set out on a day of sightseeing, reminiscing, and laughing. We toured Old Colorado City, drove past the road leading up to Pikes Peak (I'd never had the nerve to go up there... and still don't), found the remains of the dude ranch my family often visited in Woodland Park, and made our way up to Cripple Creek, a one time gold mining camp turned casino mecca. We took pictures, walked my dog, and never ran out of things to talk about. It was as if we had never been apart.

Now this is the part where some writers might say, "Once again together, they rode off into the sunset." However, life doesn't always work out like a drugstore novel. And while it might be true that some people find romance late in life, that wasn't something either Bill or I were searching for. Separately, each of us had our own home, our own family and our own life. Together, we shared wonderful memories, which as Elvis once sang, had been "sweetened through the ages just like wine." What more could anyone ask?

Nothing much has changed since that eventful meeting. I still think of Bill as one of the kindest, sweetest men I ever met and I remember all of our times together with much love in my heart. Of course, Bill and I continue to exchange e-mails and Christmas cards and who knows... maybe one of these days I'll start baking him cookies again. Maybe I'll even get a new photograph taken.

~Margaret M. Nava

The Dating Game

Happily Ever Laughter

*At the height of laughter, the universe is flung
into a kaleidoscope of new possibilities.*

~Jean Houston

63

The Best Tip Ever

Don't refuse to go on an occasional wild goose chase—
that's what wild geese are for.
~Author Unknown

The sun shone brightly through the large windows of the busy bakery and bistro where I was working one summer as a waitress. Each day, around 11:30, the crowd would filter through the door, group by group, filling every patio and dining room table by noon. Tan slim college girls in thin tank tops, short skirts and oversized sunglasses, clusters of professionals sporting suits, and groups of retirees in tennis attire or polo shirts all enjoying our gourmet salads, sandwiches and soups. The lunch "rush" was just that—a fast-paced two hours that left little time for deep conversations with customers as we skittered in and out of the kitchen grabbing food orders and sides of salad dressing.

This particular July afternoon was no different than any other; a slow morning start with orders of coffee and fresh bread giving way to the frenetic lunch shift. I moved quickly and chatted casually with many of the regulars. As the crowd began to wind down I noticed a new foursome grouped at one of my tables along the wall-side banquette, close to the front windows.

As I approached the table, two darker haired men in their early forties and two younger ones, with dirty blond hair, greeted me with smiles. One of the older men was particularly chatty and flirtatious.

He started by asking standard questions about the menu and moved smoothly into an inquisition about my dating status.

I smirked at his efforts, answered his questions with a smile and little detail, and rolled my eyes as I made my way into the kitchen to place their order.

Ugh. Couldn't these guys just stick to questions about the turkey sage sandwich and mixed greens salad?

As I returned to the table with water glasses in hand, Mr. Chatty started up again. "So, do you have a boyfriend?"

"You're persistent, huh?"

"Well?" he said, tilting his head inquisitively.

I looked around at the other six eyes staring back at me, smiling apologetically for their colleague's cross-examination.

"As a matter of fact, I don't," I said. The truth was I had recently ended a pretty tumultuous relationship—one that had been on and off again for months and which I had finally put a permanent end to several weeks earlier.

"Ahhh!" he said, obviously happy with my answer. As it turns out Mr. Chatty was married, but was enjoying the opportunity to play matchmaker for his younger colleagues, who, I might add, had been incredibly polite and quiet.

They were also, admittedly, both very handsome—tanned faces in starched white button downs and ties, bright blue eyes and their blond hair, one thick and wavy, the other shorter had caught my eye. As it turned out, they were identical twins.

Over the next twenty minutes, as I brought out food and filled water glasses, the chatty matchmaker threw out attempts to acquire my phone number to pass on to the quieter brothers. After turning down his request several times he threw out one last-ditch effort.

"You see my friends here, they're brothers who are working for me this summer and sharing a cell phone. What if I gave you their phone number? That way, if you feel like it, you could call the cell phone and let fate decide to see who answers."

Smooth, I thought.

I looked at the two brothers and smiled. They shook their heads in amused embarrassment. I put the bill on the table and walked away, smiling as each of the brothers said, "Nice to meet you."

"Nice to meet you too," I said, rolling my eyes in the direction of their boss. I never did answer his last question.

As they got up to leave they all looked in my direction and waved goodbye. Once I was sure that they were gone I made my way over to clear off their table, one of my last for the afternoon.

"Ha!" I said as I opened the checkbook to grab their receipt and tip money. There it was, a small slip of paper with scribbles in ink, "Scott + Mark" with a phone number.

I didn't call the phone number right away, but was curious enough that I hung onto the slip of paper in a small pocket of my wallet for several weeks.

Over those next two weeks both Scott and Mark wandered back into the bistro on separate occasions. Mark ordered lunch at the bar one afternoon, greeting me with a warm hello and chatting casually as he ate. Scott came in to order a coffee one morning and did the same.

One late afternoon, several weeks after that lunch shift, a group of my girlfriends invited me to go out to a local downtown bar with an outdoor, upstairs patio. It was a casual invitation, in a large group setting, and a great way to enjoy a hot summer night.

I agreed to join them and decided to call the cell phone number. What did I have to lose?

I dialed. The phone rang once, twice, three times... "Hello."

"Uh, hi. This is Lisa, the waitress from LeMetro."

"Oh! Hey! This is Scott. How are you?"

"I'm great, thank you."

Pause.

"Well, you see, the reason I'm calling is that a group of my friends and I are going downtown tonight and I thought I'd call to see if you or your brother wanted to meet us?"

"Sure," he said. "We'd love to. I'm glad you called."

Scott, Mark, and a female friend of Mark's joined us that night.

Scott and I sat on outdoor barstools and talked for hours. We paid little attention to anyone else in our group as we talked about our families, childhoods, career dreams, and plans to finish college. At one point, during the conversation, a very clear and direct thought passed through my mind, catching me off guard: You're going to marry this guy someday.

I laughed at the ridiculousness of such a thought and dismissed it as naiveté and youthful romantic giddiness. In retrospect, perhaps those who say, "you just know" when you meet Mr. Right were right after all.

The rest, as they say, is history.

Three years after that night downtown we were married and will be celebrating our tenth wedding anniversary this year. Scott and I are now parents to three beautiful daughters whom he swears are NEVER allowed to date!

He still likes to remind me that I forgot his coffee creamer that day we first met.

I still like to tease him that he is the biggest tip I ever received.

And, if I must confess, I suppose I'm glad their boss asked about more than turkey sandwiches that day.

~Lisa Littlewood

64

Dance Lessons

There is a bit of insanity in dancing that does everybody a great deal of good.
~Edwin Denby

Dating was the last thing on my mind. I had little appetite for food and even less money to eat out. My kids were grown, and I ate a lot of individual microwave dinners. Still, my three girlfriends asked me to join them one Saturday night for happy hour at a neighborhood bar and grill. We each pitched in two dollars and bought a bottomless pitcher of soda. We noshed on free veggie sticks and chicken wings until the band started up. We began to dance in our chairs. "Do you want to stay and listen for a while?" the youngest of our group asked.

"I'm not dancing. I'm not interested in meeting men. I'm only here to listen to music," I stated. "Same here!" said one of the other women. When the music began, she and I, the official purse watchers, leaned back and watched others. When a slow song came on and men prowled for partners, we would dart to the ladies room with two purses each under our arms. Occasionally we women all free-style danced together, but usually two of us danced and two of us observed.

The tap on my shoulder was gentle. I turned around. "My name's Bill. Would you care to dance the next fast dance with me?"

I didn't say what I was thinking: "Not interested, buddy, so don't try your lines on me!" Instead, I smiled politely at the tall, jolly-faced fellow and said, "No, thank you. I don't really know how."

"I'd be glad to give you a quick lesson, the steps are simple. I can lead you through it."

Nobody was leading me anywhere anymore. I was a free woman. "Maybe later." I dismissed him.

"I can give you a lesson during the band's break."

I watched him dance all evening with any woman who would accept a dance. Bill laughed joyously, didn't appear to be flirtatious, and seemed to really enjoy dancing. I noticed that he always walked the women (all ages and sizes) back to their chairs and thanked them. I was more impressed with his stamina than his prowess. That night I didn't receive his dance lesson. I chided myself for feeling slighted. Hadn't I learned my lesson yet about men? As my girlfriends and I left that evening, we vowed to go back the next weekend for cheap food, good music, and exercise.

That next Saturday at 11:00 p.m. when the band took a break, my friends and I left. I opened the door and walked right into the big dancing guy. He peered down at me and smiled.

"I beg your pardon. I know you from somewhere. Have we met some place?"

"Yes, we met last week, and you told me you would teach me to dance." Why did I say such a thing, and in such a snappy tone?

Bill continued, "Will you come back in and let me teach you? I'd be glad to give you a quick lesson."

I apologized and said, "Sorry, maybe next week. We really have to leave now."

The next week, I noticed that Bill wasn't a drinker. He ordered orange juice. I accepted a quick lesson and stepped all over his feet. He laughed and joked and made me feel at ease. I became one of his many dance partners, and we became fast friends.

Bill asked me to walk the park with him. "Not a date," we both agreed, "just as friends."

Our friendship developed and my appetite increased. As Bill put on the charm, I put on the pounds. He took me to a variety of restaurants. We had so much in common. I'd never laughed so much or eaten so well.

On one of our first dates we drove two hours to a famous restaurant where the waiters throw giant rolls, warm from the oven, to the patrons. I dodged the first and blushed. With Bill's encouragement, I began to relax and reach for the tossed rolls. The portion sizes were more than one person could eat, but in addition to my meal, I ate two hot buttered rolls. When I got into the car, I was so stuffed, I asked with embarrassment, "Do you mind if I unzip my jeans so I can breathe?"

Bill laughed and said, "I've never seen a happier eater in my life. You were rocking in your seat like the first night I met you."

Our next date, we pushed our tray down the cafeteria line, ordering a la carte. Bill left the table to go back for something he had forgotten and when he returned, he searched the side dishes on the table. "Did you see a little bowl sitting here? Did the server take it?"

"Oh, you mean that soup? I tasted it and it was so delicious, so I ate it."

"All of it?" He frowned.

"Yes, why?" I worried.

"It wasn't soup; it was brown gravy for my beef."

I wanted to slink under the table, but I wouldn't fit.

Meeting Bill was the beginning of the end of my thin days. Over the course of three years I gained fifteen pounds. But they were happy pounds. Soon, we began preparing our own meals at home, and the rest is history. The nice guy and I have been dining and dancing together ever since.

~Linda O'Connell

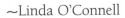

Still Dishing It Out

Anyone can be passionate, but it takes real lovers to be silly.
~Rose Franken

I was making less than minimum wage at our neighborhood eatery, because the tips I earned were supposed to supplement my hourly pay. That was assuming the diners were generous and could calculate fifteen percent of their bill. It was also assuming I was an efficient and talented waitress. I wasn't.

A personable server, I was. Hardworking, too. But able to line up four plates of food along my arm and get them across the dining room gracefully? No way. So there were times when I took too long getting orders to my customers, or sometimes I got orders mixed up and I didn't deserve an over-the-top tip. Most of the time, however, I deserved an adequate amount of money being left on the table, and sometimes all I got was a couple of quarters. And quarters couldn't pay my daughter's preschool bill.

As a divorced woman and mother of a four-year-old, I wasn't working for weekend "party" money. I wasn't working to make money to put gas in my daddy's car. I was working to support my daughter. With that mission in mind, I had tunnel vision. When a male customer flirted with me, I deftly sidestepped him. I kept my mind on my work and didn't even consider that I might possibly find a boyfriend during the breakfast and lunch rush; the only thing I thought about was putting groceries on the table.

However, my eyes eventually strayed from the salt and pepper shakers to a guy: Michael, the assistant manager. He was funny. He wasn't afraid to pitch in with bussing the tables or dropping off orders when the restaurant got crazy busy. And the two of us began to flirt—in a really weird way.

When the managers had a lunch meeting and I got stuck waiting on them, Michael would throw me a curve: he wanted a side of onion rings, but only small ones. I would have to shiver in the walk-in freezer and root around in the bag of frozen onion rings, picking out the little ones for the cook to fry up. Or he'd request whipped cream on his pie. I'd bring it out, and he'd say, "I'd like a little more." I'd squirt some more on, take it out and again he'd say, "A bit more, please."

Always willing to step in and help, when the dining room would fill up and the cook's grill was crammed with orders, Michael would lend a hand on the line. A great restaurant cook will help the servers by keeping a steady pace with the food output. An order comes up, they ring the bell and turn on the light that indicates which waitress's order is ready. Then they wait a few minutes before they put up an order for the same server.

But when Michael was working the griddle, he'd slam me. He'd get a glint in his eye and try to bury me with pancakes and sausage. The whole warmer would be full of my orders—a bunch of tables all at once—and he'd ring the bell, over and over, turn on my light and call, "Hurry. Your food's up and it's getting cold."

And what did I do in this bizarre dance of flirtation? I'd drag him out of the office, claiming there was an angry customer, and he'd sweat his way across the dining room, nervous about the barrage of complaints he was about to encounter. Once at the table, he'd find not an irate diner but instead a little old lady who wanted to speak to management so she could compliment the service. Even though I wasn't very efficient, I was the epitome of accommodation. If a senior citizen could not afford a short stack of pancakes, nor could they eat two pancakes, I'd offer to cut the order in half.

When we were both standing there and the blue-haired grandma started in on her accolades, I'd catch Michael's eye... and wink. And then I'd run off to continue my work.

Sending him to the dishwasher was another one of my tricks. Our ancient dishwashing contraption would sometimes have a conniption, and then the manager would have to make some adjustments. However, the guy who manned the machine was infamous for his fondness for trivia. Once anyone got trapped in a conversation with him, it was difficult to escape — this guy would go on and on, stringing together unimportant bits of information without stopping to take a breath. Michael avoided him by hiding in his back-of-the-restaurant lair whenever possible, but if I tricked him, saying, "The dishwasher's acting up," he'd have no choice. And again, when he was trapped by a filibuster of facts, I'd wink... and then scurry away.

After several months of joking with each other, one night he suggested an ice cream sundae once our shift was over. It was supposed to be a small group, but it ended up being just the two of us. Over spoonfuls of hot fudge, we talked. His brother and sisters, my daughter, his love of photography, my college classes — we got to know each other and fell into like, which soon turned to love.

Now, he's still my short order cook and I still serve him up a dish of trouble — every now and then...

~Sioux Roslawski

Meeting Mom

He that would the daughter win, must with the mother first begin.

~English Proverb

M y mom arrived in town for a visit. It was time for the Big Moment. "Why don't I take you and Geno out to dinner, somewhere nice, so that I can finally meet him?" she suggested.

Geno, my latest boyfriend, and I didn't get out to dinner much—and we never went anywhere "nice." When we dined together, it was usually on simple pasta or black beans with rice. When we felt like splurging, we went to a cheap neighborhood sushi place in Pacific Beach. Our total bill, including a couple of beers, was a whole twenty-five dollars.

The night that Geno met my mom, we went to the Chart House, an upscale seafood chain in downtown La Jolla. Over dinner, we covered all the basics in my mother's eyes, starting with Geno's education and career plans. There were no issues there—he was working on a doctorate in mechanical engineering and was interested in becoming a university professor.

We also discussed his family—two younger sisters who he adored, his mother who had died in her early forties of breast cancer, and a father who had remarried and now lived in Wisconsin. Finally, we discussed his childhood growing up in the Panama Canal Zone, with an American father and Panamanian mother.

Even at the young age of twenty-six, Geno had led an interesting life and had some engaging stories. An excellent conversationalist, he was very charming with his Latino good looks and friendly smile. There weren't any awkward lulls during the evening, so I was feeling very pleased at how things were going. More importantly, Mom was clearly taken with him.

The restaurant was quite busy that night, and the service a bit slow. It didn't matter, as we weren't in a hurry. As we waited for dessert, I mentioned that I still had recurring nightmares about the times when I used to waitress—scenes of demanding customers, all my table's orders coming out of the kitchen at the same exact time, the hostess managing to seat my entire section simultaneously, getting stiffed on a tip. That opened the door on the subject of recurring dreams in general.

I'd had quite a lot of them during various periods of my life. I spared them both the one about the ex-boyfriend with Mafia connections following me around in a dark car, but did describe some others. I recounted the one about when "they" kidnapped my little brother, tossed him into a clothes dryer, then collected his earwax. I'd had a lot of ear problems as a kid, though I'm not sure why my brother was involved, or why I'd had this dream repeatedly.

Mom mentioned that her dreams were a bit more traditional—for instance, showing up to a classroom for a lecture, only to find out that there was an exam that day for which she was completely unprepared.

"I've had that one, too!" Geno exclaimed. He paused, with a mischievous twinkle in his eye. He lowered his voice and leaned forward, conspiratorially, and continued.

"Only in my dream—well, the thing is, I'm naked."

Our eyes met. Mine narrowed, but his were still sparkling.

Then we both looked at Mom—a question mark hanging over that pivotal moment. Mom must have already decided that she approved of Geno, because she burst out laughing and the evening continued.

~Lisa Pawlak

"That does sound like an interesting dream.
I, however, prefer to keep my dreams to myself,
for proprietary reasons."

Reprinted by permission of
Marc Tyler Nobleman ©2013

Head Over Heels

Our wedding was many years ago. The celebration continues to this day.
~Gene Perret

I watched the chairlift scoop up skiers for the long ride up the hill. A shiver ran through me, more out of fear than from the cold. How did I get myself into this? I'd never skied before. I just wanted my boyfriend to think I was bold and courageous—the kind of fun-loving girl who was always up for an adventure. Who was I kidding?

Curt and I stood in the loading area, waiting for the chairlift to circle behind us. It smacked the back of my legs and plopped me onto the chair. The cable above us creaked as it carried us over the glittering snow. As we neared the top, Curt prepared me for my approaching dismount. He lifted the safety bar.

"Okay, ready?" He leaned forward and straightened his skis. I scooted up. Then he stood to his feet and promptly glided down a small mound of snow. Oops! I missed it! A safety bar whacked my leg and the chairlift stopped. Curt glanced back at me still perched on the edge of my seat.

"You were supposed to get off." He grinned, obviously more amused than the long line of skiers dangling behind me.

Even with the cool temperatures, I felt heat rise in my cheeks. "Sorry, I wasn't ready." I scrambled off the chair and inched my way toward Curt. I struggled to maneuver the long, awkward skis. So much for impressing him, I thought. I looked like a toddler learning to walk.

A steep hill stretched out before us. "Wow," I said, catching my breath. "It's a long way down. Shouldn't I start with a bunny hill?"

Curt's face was sympathetic. "This is the bunny hill."

I knew this adventure thing was a bad idea.

We started with the ever-popular snowplow technique. Curt demonstrated how to angle my skis inward as we edged our way down the hill. I spent more time lying in the snow than skiing.

First I fell backwards, the skis dragging me down the hill on my bottom. Then I fell sideways. Apparently I had leaned too far forward. Finally, just when I thought I was getting the hang of it, my skis crossed and I crashed again.

Curt raced to my side. "You okay?"

I wiped the snow off my face. "Oh sure, I'm good." I wondered if it was possible to look cute while tumbling face first into a pile of snow.

Curt smiled—a bright, charming smile—and reached his gloved hand toward me. "You're doing fine," he said, helping me up. "It just takes practice and patience." I gazed into his kind eyes. He certainly has patience, I thought. If I were him, I'd be back in the lodge sipping hot chocolate by now.

However, Curt stayed by my side. And he was right. Before long, I had mastered snowplowing and was ready to move on. On my next trip down, I turned my skis parallel ever-so-slightly.

"That's it, you're getting it." Curt skied alongside, cheering me on. "Lean forward a little and bend your knees."

"I'm doing it! I'm skiing!" I shifted my weight, enjoying the cool breeze and exhilarating joy of sweet success.

But within an instant that thrilling rush of adrenaline switched to pure panic. Too fast, too fast! I thought, hurtling out of control. I dragged my poles through the snow, trying to slow down and regain control. Finally, I crashed in a jumbled mess of legs, skis and poles. As the snow settled, I lay flat on the ground in utter frustration.

That's it, I thought. Enough is enough. My legs were twisted in opposite directions. My body ached. But my wounded pride hurt the most. Why would Curt want to ski with me anyway? He could handle any trail here; instead, he was stuck on the bunny hill with me.

Curt plopped down in the snow next to me. He handed me my wayward pole that had gone skidding halfway down the hill.

"I think you may have dropped this," he said, expressionless. Suddenly, two young children zipped past us, smiling. I looked at Curt and shook my head.

A slight grin tugged at Curt's pink cheeks. Suddenly he erupted in laughter—silly, yet delightful and contagious laughter. Curt's joy pulled me in—no matter how hard I tried to resist it. Even in my most awkward moments, he could make me laugh.

Though I had aching legs and painful bruises, that date turned out to be one of my best. Not because I learned to ski, but because I realized that Curt was the kind of man I wanted in my life. The kind of man I could marry.

A couple years later, I did marry him. Even today, I still appreciate those same qualities Curt had during our dating days. He is patient and kind, he makes me smile, and when life gets me down, he encourages me to get back up and try again.

After twenty years of marriage, I still can't ski well. Curt knows I'm not the most bold or courageous girl, but that's okay. He makes sure my life is full of adventure, or at least full of laughter.

~Sheri Zeck

Falling for Her

Gravitation is not responsible for people falling in love.
~Albert Einstein

I love it when puzzle pieces fall in place! I was on a temporary work assignment in Tampa, Florida, when Amy called me totally out of the blue. She said that she was flying down to Orlando to run a marathon on the upcoming Sunday, and then spending the following week with her friend, Andrea, in Gainesville. Amy and I hadn't seen each other in a year, and made arrangements to meet on the Thursday after the marathon. Woo hoo!

Amy was a goddess. I knew her as a friend for three years when I lived in Alexandria, Virginia. She was a flight attendant for American Airlines, and I silently worshipped her from afar with an undying crush. Fun, intelligent, athletic — how could a girl be so cool and so hot at the same time?

First a week and then Monday... Tuesday... Wednesday... the days dragged by.

On Thursday, I bolted from work early and drove over to Andrea's house. I'll never forget the rush that I felt inside when Amy opened the door and said "Hello, John." She had such a killer smile.

We both wanted to see the Universal Studios theme park in Orlando, so the game plan was to drive down, stay at the Westin — as friends — and then go to the park on Friday. Amy and I hopped into my car, and the two-hour drive to Orlando was nothing but a massive gabfest as we got reacquainted.

Then we checked into the Westin and continued the talk-a-thon over two cold beers in the Westin's bar.

After that, we walked to eat dinner at a place called Pebbles. The only thing better than our meals was the continuing conversation.

Upon returning to the Westin, I decided it was quicker to get to our room by cutting through the pool area. So I opened the glass door for Amy, and then followed her through. Upon catching up with her, I stepped to her side and promptly tripped over the pool's raised edge — falling into the water!

I've never seen Amy laugh so hard.

The next day, Amy and I completely covered Universal Studios, and I got her to the airport in time to get back to Alexandria.

Then we went from friends to dating.

~John M. Scanlan

Dinner for My Boyfriend

As a child my family's menu consisted of two choices: take it or leave it.
--Buddy Hackett

Bringing a boyfriend home to meet my mom could be cause for concern. Even after I was grown and living on my own, I still worried how someone I brought home would react to Mom's eccentric ideas. She was unlike other mothers, and not everyone understood or appreciated her unconventional ways.

Reared by parents who emigrated from Transylvania, she was greatly influenced by the customs they brought from their homeland. Growing up dirt poor during the depression, in the Yuma desert, Mom learned the value of hard work and frugal living. Her old fashioned ways were many and she was determined to hang onto them whether we liked it or not.

A fan of organic gardening, long before it was popular, Mom grew fruits and vegetables in a large plot behind our house on our five-acre farm. No insecticide or pesticide ever touched her plants. She didn't believe in being wasteful, either. Wormy and bird-pecked fruits and vegetables, that others might not find so appetizing, made it into the kitchen. She insisted that they could be salvaged, no matter how much had to be cut off to make them fit to consume.

Mom also raised animals for us to eat. While the men in the

family butchered the larger animals, Mom had no trouble dealing with the chickens. All she needed was a stump and a hatchet. One chop and it was all over. Then the real work began.

The chickens were dunked in a pot of scalding water. Then we'd pluck the steaming hot feathers. The worst part for me was singeing the pinfeathers over crumpled newspaper. The smell was horrible and it seemed to take forever to get rid of the odor on my clothes.

Every part of the chicken that could be eaten was used. Gizzards, liver, and heart were either fried or cooked in soups. Chicken feet were considered a delicacy to our mom, no doubt a tradition brought over by her parents from the old country. She was the only one in our family who ate them, and after many years of adamantly refusing to take even a taste, she knew better than to try to give me one. Looking back, I'm sure she enjoyed my explosive reaction to her teasing, since it was obvious that she wanted to keep them all for herself. I can still envision her holding a chicken foot over her plate and gnawing on it.

A great cook, Mom made everything from scratch. She baked cakes and pies that always drew raves. Mom was also known for serving a variety of meats that some friends and family had never eaten before—and never planned to. Besides traditional meats most people were accustomed to eating, guinea, peacock, rabbit and goat meat were regularly on the menu at our house while squab, burro, and beef tongue and brains were served on occasion. No animal was completely safe on our farm.

Mom didn't feel it necessary to tell her guests what she was serving unless they asked. She couldn't wait to see the horrified expression on someone's face when she offered them food they had never imagined eating. Returning guests with a squeamish stomach or sensitive conscience would not eat any meat Mom prepared, until it had been positively identified. When some unsuspecting newcomer came for dinner, they were sometimes unhappily surprised when they were told what they had already eaten.

So, when I took my new boyfriend to dinner at Mom's house for the first time, I worried about what she would be serving. I could only hope that she had prepared something he would recognize and was willing to eat. When we got to the house, I was relieved to find out we were having chicken soup. Who doesn't like chicken soup?

With the pot of hot soup already on the dining room table, we sat down to eat and Mom began serving the soup. True to her upbringing, Mom made certain her guest was served first and she poured a large ladle of soup into his bowl. Then... oh, no! Before I knew what was happening or could stop her, she added a special treat to his bowl. A chicken foot! Though my boyfriend was completely shocked and disgusted by the chicken foot in his soup, he did not say a word about it. But he didn't eat much soup, either!

I sometimes wonder if the chicken foot in my boyfriend's bowl was really just a test to find out what my boyfriend was made of, to determine if he would be able to adjust to our unique family traditions.

That boyfriend eventually became my husband, with no help from my mom. Over the years I've made countless pots of homemade chicken soup, just like my mom did, except I used chickens purchased from the grocery store, chickens with the feet already removed. But my husband was so traumatized by the chicken foot that, for twenty-eight years he refused to eat chicken soup, unless he knew for certain it came out of a can.

~RoseAnn Faulkner

Take a Chance

Truth only reveals itself when one gives up all preconceived ideas.
~Shoseki

"I'll most likely end up living alone in a townhouse with 100 cats," I told my friend. She was writing a Valentine's Day column for our college newspaper and wanted to get a snapshot of what students thought about their romantic future.

It's not that I hated Valentine's Day. I actually enjoyed being reminded that love existed, and daydreamed that my prince was just taking a scenic route while I ate heart shaped chocolates from my mum.

While most of my friends were paired up, and those who weren't appeared close, I seemed to be walking a separate path: one that led directly to the nunnery.

So I did what any self-respecting woman destined to be a forever cat-lady would do: lived my life, all the while keeping one eye open for Prince Charming.

I volunteered as a dog walker for the S.P.C.A., learned how to golf, and hopped a plane bound for Costa Rica where I backpacked the country with my girlfriends.

Back from vacation, and with Charming still in hiding, I resumed working as a lifeguard and swim instructor and prepared to have a fabulous summer with my friends.

"The problem is I have too many guy friends," I wrote in my journal.

It was true: I did have a lot of guy friends. Some were taken, and some were single, but all were off limits because of their co-worker status.

Over the last six years of working in what could be considered an extension of hormonal high school, that life lesson was ingrained in my head.

On the other hand, that line of thinking had brought me to this point: dateless. Maybe the saying was true: Guys and girls can't be friends. Who coined that? Maybe I should pick a guy friend and give it a whirl.

My brain was spinning. When you don't have a boyfriend, or even the possibility of one, the situation begins to feel desperate.

Even if you're sure of yourself at school and work, and proud of the life you're creating, when everyone else seems to be grabbing a partner, and you're still holding up the wall, the questions begin: What am I doing wrong? Should I be more sassy? Breezy? Flirty? Am I wearing the wrong bra?

My friend Mike broke up with his girlfriend before I went to Costa Rica. This was a good thing, as far as I was concerned. Together they were wet blankets, never wanting to join us after work for movies or adventures. They never had anything nice to say, and Mike had a tendency to be extremely black and white with his opinions, something I couldn't wrap my head around.

Subsequently, for the first six years of our work life, Mike and I were like oil and water. I sarcastically called him "Happy Time," and our paths barely crossed.

However, once he broke up with his girlfriend, he began to shed his cloak of darkness. By the time I returned from Costa Rica, he had started coming to Cheap Movie Tuesdays and Wings Wednesdays with everyone, and, it turns out he was a really interesting guy with a wicked sense of humor.

One day while we were working, Mike's parents arrived. They had come to Victoria for a visit and were checking in with him before heading to the house. A crowd formed around them at the side door of the pool deck as they showed off their newest addition: a puppy.

Even though I'd never met them before, and had zero designs on their son, I felt like I'd known them forever.

In December things started to shift. "Have you ever noticed that

Mike has a nice back?" my friend asked as we switched places on the pool deck.

"No," I said, squinting across the pool to where Mike stood, trying to see what she saw. Sure there were muscles but it was just a back. Nothing we hadn't seen in the thousands of swimmers who came through our doors each year.

Something in that moment resonated, and altered my view of him just a sliver. But, I pushed the moment aside, and rationalized that whatever-that-was happened because my co-worker was noticing him. If she wanted to go after him, she could. I wasn't his gatekeeper.

Determined to keep Mike securely in the friend category, I continued to pester him during hockey games, beat him at car racing, and steal bites of his chocolate torte when he wasn't looking.

Then early on New Year's morning it happened. He kissed me.

Just like in the movies, I backed away; convinced this was a giant mistake. I'd never had a guy friend like him, and now our friendship was ruined, or on the path to ruin, and I had no one to blame but myself and my dumb need to have a boyfriend.

"I've wondered since August why no one's snatched you up," he said. "Take a chance."

After years of bellyaching about a lackluster love life, I couldn't believe I was hesitating. But there was too much at stake.

We talked until 7:30 in the morning. Even after all that discussion, I still wasn't convinced that whatever this was, it was worth ruining our friendship over. But I trusted Mike, and blindly jumped, letting go of all doubt and reason.

Mike and I have been working together for eighteen years, and married for ten. We have three adventurous daughters ages six, four, and two and a dog. Turns out, Prince Charming was hiding in plain sight. I just had to open my eyes.

~Alison Gunn

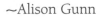

I Like You

*You have to walk carefully in the beginning of love; the running
across fields into your lover's arms can only come later when you're sure
they won't laugh if you trip.*
~Jonathan Carroll

We had been friends for almost four years. But it had only been a few months since my interest in Travis had grown to more than friendship. When we got back from Christmas break our senior year of college, Travis asked me to go to dinner with him. After a year of us joking about going to Red Lobster together, Travis and I finally had our first date there. I was nervous and excited and anxious. I thought up topics to talk about in case the conversation slowed and things got awkward. I picked out a nice outfit, did my hair, and waited for his car to pull up.

When Travis arrived, I ran downstairs from my apartment to his car. I didn't want him coming up to my door in case that was awkward. During the drive there, we talked about our experiences as camp counselors one summer. During dinner, we talked about our families, our hobbies, our first jobs, and all kinds of things. The conversation never died, and we learned we had a lot in common.

As Travis drove me back to my apartment, I could feel the nerves building. I'm not one to kiss on the first date, and I was so nervous Travis would try to kiss me. I liked him and didn't want to reject him if he tried, but I also didn't want to compromise my own dating rules.

As he turned onto the road I lived on, a plan formed in my mind: Don't give him the chance to kiss you!

As Travis pulled up to my apartment, I quickly said, "You don't have to walk me to the door. I had a good time. Thanks, bye!" I pulled the seatbelt off and was out of the car in a flash. I waved goodbye and ran upstairs to my apartment without looking back.

I walked into my bedroom with the biggest smile on my face. It was such a great date. I had a fantastic time and knew without a doubt that I really liked Travis. I changed into my pajamas—a T-shirt and sweatpants—when my phone beeped. A text message... from Travis! I opened the message with excitement.

"Can I talk to you?"

I didn't know if he meant he wanted to call me or if he was still downstairs in his car.

I replied: "Sure. Do you mean call me or in person?"

"Can you come back downstairs?"

I couldn't believe he was still there. What did he want? I was already in my pajamas!

"Okay, but I already changed into my PJs just so you know."

I ran downstairs and stepped outside. I didn't see his car, so I walked further into the parking lot. He came jogging toward me. We met in the middle of the parking lot.

"Sorry I made you come back down... it's just, well, um..."

For a second I thought he wanted to kiss me and my plan had backfired. But the more he struggled to say whatever it was he wanted to say, the more I realized he wouldn't have the guts to kiss me yet. What was he trying to get out?

"Well, I just wanted to tell you that, um, well... I like you."

"Well, I kind of figured since you took me on a date." I said, relieved. "I like you too Travis... so you can ask me out again."

"Okay, good," he said with a big smile. We hugged goodbye, and I walked up to my room with an even bigger smile than before.

It turns out Travis had wanted to tell me he liked me but I jumped out of the car so fast he didn't have time. As he drove away, he realized he couldn't leave without telling me. He turned around and came back to meet me in the middle of a parking lot in my pajamas. Just to say, "I like you" in person. It's something he's still telling me today—as my husband.

~Tiffany Stroud

The Dating Game

Meant to Be

*Fate, Chance, God's Will—we all try to account for our lives somehow.
What are the chances that two raindrops, flung from the heavens, will
merge on a windowpane? Gotta be Fate.*

~Robert Brault, www.robertbrault.com

Danger, the Ultimate Aphrodisiac

True love stories never have endings.

--Richard Bach

The driver stepped out and put on his black leather jacket. He rose to his full height, wearing stonewashed jeans, cowboy boots, and an open neck dress shirt. A revolver latched onto his left side in a cross-draw fashion I'd never seen before. The dark hair, stout shoulders, and trim waist caught my eye. I guessed his age to be around forty, but the close-cut beard made it hard to tell. Could be older. He walked toward me with a laid-back air and an expressionless face. More a Texas Ranger than a James Bond, more sour mash whiskey than a dry martini. The government's eclectic taste in agents surpassed my expectations.

He reached the steps of my front porch where I'd been waiting for him, broom in hand, sweeping pine needles into the flowerbeds. He flipped open his wallet credentials, and sunlight glinted off the badge. "Hello, I'm Special Agent Clark."

We were both federal employees. I was a federal loan officer, who'd been offered a bribe two days before. I'd called the powers-that-be for guidance, and they sent me my own federal agent.

His Georgia drawl eased off his tongue natural, comfortable. I gave his credentials a cursory glance and drew back. He put the black leather bi-fold back in his pocket with his left hand, no wedding band. But I didn't trust him.

No federal employee wants an agent around. The bribe was offered to me by a sleazy client who had loans with our agency. How was that my fault? But I'd also heard rumors. Federal workers knew agents reputedly transferred the scrutiny onto employees. Sure, I knew I had no skeletons in my closet, but nobody likes her motives being questioned.

Thirty minutes passed as he asked his questions. Common sense dictated he had to know me to work with me. Still, I felt like I was sitting for a high-powered job interview, with all the wrong qualifications. I couldn't read him.

After three hours of straight-faced interrogation, he told me he'd be at my office the next day, with his partner, pretending to be auditors. And I could tell nobody who they were. I had no choice but to cooperate as they pursued the case.

For two weeks, Clark and his partner had me schedule meetings with the client, attempting to set him up for a sting. They hoped he'd come forward with the money in exchange for me cutting all the government red tape. But the guy proved dodgy. We arranged meetings he never showed for. He began to get cocky, insinuating that we could become more than "partners" after this exchange was over. We could "hook up," he said. And still, I had to pretend I was on board with his offer, in hopes he'd finally appear with the money.

Hidden recorders, a camera disguised in a briefcase, scripted conversation, and sleepless nights ensued. In the midst of it all, I filed for divorce from my estranged husband. The client started making threats. My boss, who was not allowed to know about the investigation, wondered about auditors that he had no warning about. My staff began to sense these guys were more than accountants checking files.

Agent Clark's job was to keep me on task and focused on the investigation. When my world was spinning off its axis, he remained steady, bringing me water, helping me keep my head when meeting the client, assisting me in keeping up the façade, following me when taking back roads home to avoid the culprit if he was tailing me. And during that month-long period, during some intense stress he had to talk me through, we became friends.

The client never coughed up the money, even after numerous promises to deliver. The federal government wouldn't prosecute him just for making the offer. Unfortunately, or fortunately, depending upon the perspective, people noticed that the agent tended to my needs more than normal. We went to dinner to discuss the case, only to chat about each other's lives. He dragged out the investigation, in hopes of convincing the client to follow through on his bribe offer... maybe to avoid leaving me.

Suddenly, we were a scandal. Our sincere efforts to make a bribery investigation and take a seedy man off the street were ignored. Threats were still being delivered to me via the client's friends and neighbors, yet authorities no longer took me seriously. But Agent Clark and I had become close, and people noticed the glances, the smiles, the occasional brush of sleeves as one of us entered a doorway and the other exited. The mint on my desk. Knowing how each other liked his or her coffee.

They say danger is an aphrodisiac, misplaced adrenaline prompting an attraction. The danger scared me to death and romance was the furthest thing from my mind... in the beginning. But in the end, the gentleman turned into the white knight, the only person I could trust in a world where bosses and co-workers turned against me. We'd fought so hard to snare a culprit who'd ultimately turned dangerous, and as more and more people failed to care about the case, we became two souls anchored by what we knew we'd tried to do. We hadn't expected our respect for each other's work ethic to turn into something more. Something we felt too important to throw away.

I requested a transfer to another office to distance myself from the client, who was still angry I'd tried to have him arrested. Three months after the case closed, Agent Clark and I went on our first formal date. He also transferred to another state... mine. And a year later we married, the romance continuing stronger than ever, long after the aphrodisiac of danger had drifted away. Other scandals replaced ours as time went on, but our story remained ours... how a bribe brought a federal agent and a cooperating individual together, and made them a dynamic duo.

~C. Hope Clark

When One Door Closes

A door that seems to stand open must be a man's size,
or it is not the door that Providence means for him.
~Henry Ward Beecher

I sat beside my friends Penny and Brad in our pew with a view of the sanctuary entrance. I felt as if I had the cartoons of a good angel and a bad devil on each shoulder.

Penny, wearing the imaginary wings and halo, said, "Give him a chance. He's busy you know. Besides, he's probably just running late."

Brad, playing the part of the pessimistic devil chimed in, "If he's not respectful enough to do what he says he'll do, you need to ditch him. Men don't change. I know. I'm a man."

I, feeling conflicted over my boyfriend's unfortunate behaviors, said, "How about this: If he's not the next person to walk through that door, I'm done with him." And then the three of us waited and watched as the organist started our worship service by playing "In His Time."

And we watched.

My boyfriend and I had been dating for six months or so, and during those six months, I could count on one hand the number of times he had actually shown up to an event or picked me up for a date on time. And in recent times, he'd actually been skipping out on dates all together.

And we watched.

I'd discussed with my possibly-ex-boyfriend how disrespectful it was for him to say he'd be someplace at a certain time and then have him show up an hour later or not at all. Every time we'd talk about this, he'd promise to be more considerate, kiss me gently and then completely put it out of his mind. His behavior had grown worse instead of better.

And we watched.

I became more and more embarrassed and frustrated, yet I also felt determined that our days as a couple were numbered. On this particular Sunday, he said he'd be at church for the ten a.m. worship time. He said he'd stay after for our potluck supper, and he said he'd bring a big crock pot full of his famous baked beans so that I wouldn't have to bring anything to the luncheon myself. I brought a casserole just in case.

And we watched. As the organist hit the final chord and the door opened, a man walked into the sanctuary.

He was not my boyfriend.

Brad leaned over and said, "There's your answer."

Penny leaned over and said, "I'm so sorry."

I leaned into them both and said, "I know that guy."

Brian, the man who just walked into my church, and I had taken courses together at Northeastern State in Tahlequah. Last I knew, however, he didn't live in my town, yet here he was.

After worship services, I found him and reintroduced myself. I discovered that he had recently moved to Bartlesville and had decided to visit my church. He stayed for the potluck lunch and even complimented my casserole.

Within a few weeks, my church became our church.

And nine months later, it was where we hosted our wedding reception.

Yes, when one door closes, another one opens. I'm so thankful Brian opened that door.

~Heather Davis

I Found Him

Courage is being afraid but going on anyhow.
~Dan Rather

I sat at a table, untouched drink in hand, near an exit sign in case I needed to make a speedy getaway. I had come to hear a man I'd recently met play in a band. Actually, this was the sixth time I had showed up some place where he was playing, hoping that we might actually go out on a date. I was fifty-six and he was sixty.

When mutual friends introduced us at one of his gigs, I showed up prepared to get his attention. Our friends had asked me if I'd like to meet a very nice guy—retired library director and jazz musician—and I said sure. (They had not asked him if he wanted to meet me. They thought that might have scared him off.)

I had been told, "He doesn't talk. He's very shy." So I'd thought of at least ten good questions for conversation starters: How long have you played the clarinet? Do you play other instruments? Do you play in other places? My question strategy worked, and he did talk to me.

"Do you know much about jazz?" he asked.

"No," I replied, truthfully. "But I'd like to learn."

Smiling, he said, "I think I can help with that."

Since he had answered my question about where else he played, I told him I'd try to catch the band at one of those places. He seemed pleased. So, I started showing up at his various gigs. He would always come to my table during his breaks. After the usual, "How are you?" we began to get acquainted. He actually seemed interested in learning more about me, asking about my childhood, my career, my interests.

He was very easy to talk to, and as the weeks went by, he seemed to relax and be more comfortable with our conversations. I learned that he had advanced degrees, including a PhD in French literature, so one evening I blurted out, "My daughter has a PhD in biological sciences from Carnegie Mellon."

"Oh," he said, grinning. "She's a REAL doctor."

After about a month of this I thought it was time we had a date. I couldn't just keep stalking him in bars and restaurants. I knew he had not dated since his wife died three years earlier, and I had not dated since moving to Chicago the year before. Nor the year before that, nor the one before that, to be totally honest. Finding a husband wasn't important to me—I was quite happy with my life—but I did think it would be nice to have a little romance in my life.

As the band went into their "break" tune, I started to get nervous. I slugged down a little of my drink, steadied my shaking hands, and told myself I could do this. I knew I'd have to be the one to broach the daunting subject of dating. If it goes badly, I thought, I'm near an exit and I can just shoot out of here.

Sure enough, when the guys put their instruments down to begin their break, he walked over to my table. Holding his usual glass of water (I felt a bit depraved with my vodka drink), he sat down. He'd brought me a CD his son had given him that he was sure I'd like. It was Norah Jones's first album. I was pleased at his choice.

We talked a while as usual before I decided it was now or never. I said to him, "Does your band play every night?" knowing full well that they didn't.

He said, "No, not every night."

I plunged ahead. "Do you eat dinner every night?"

He looked a bit puzzled but said slowly, "Yes..."

I took a deep breath and asked, "So on one of those nights that you're not playing but you are eating dinner, do you think we might have dinner together?"

Holding my breath, I was prepared to bolt. Before I could even break into a sweat, he reached into his pocket and whipped out his PDA, looked up and said, "I'm free Monday, Tuesday, and Wednesday next week. Which night's best for you?"

This nerve-wracking evening was ten years ago. We've now been happily married for nine years. Oh, and last year for our anniversary, he wrote a song for me. He called it, "She Found Me."

~Alice Wiethoff Blegen

Really Looking

A man falls in love through his eyes, a woman through her ears.
~Woodrow Wyatt

I met my Prince Charming in a dingy college apartment that radiated beer from its very pores, between walls filled with *The Simpsons* posters and calendars of swimsuit-clad women. My chariot? A sagging futon with several questionable stains. Glass slipper? Didn't really matter, as long as you weren't barefoot on that carpet.

Did I mention Prince Charming blatantly ignored me the night of the ball? It was fireworks-on-the-beach, champagne-and-strawberries, weak-in-the-knees, butterflies-in-the-stomach love at first... snub.

One of my friends had a crush and had dragged me to this dirty apartment. My prince was a study in contrasts compared to the din of the party. While the other boys jostled for the attention of the girls and played drinking games, he was quiet, standing behind the homemade bar and bobbing his head to the music as the world rolled by.

I was a shy journalism student more comfortable with a book than a crowd, so I saw him as a quiet cove amidst the choppy seas.

I took a deep breath and dove in. I flipped my hair over my shoulder, straightened my top, and sashayed across the room toward him, looking my cutest and repeating my girl-power mantra to myself.

"Hi," I said, casually leaning against the front of the bar and coyly avoiding his gaze. "I'm Caitlin."

He was silent. I tucked my tail between my legs and prepared to slink back to my spot on the futon.

"Chris, turn around, she's talking to you," a friend helpfully bellowed to him from across the room. My face turned a shade of crimson just in time for him to finally look my way.

"Hi," he timidly offered, his voice quiet but piercing blue eyes steadfastly holding my gaze. "What's your name?"

Eight years, three apartments, one house, and a marriage after that fateful night, I still occasionally forget.

"Honey, can you grab me the olive oil?" I ask, without looking up from the shrimp sautéing in the pan and the spaghetti bubbling in front of me.

"Olive oil," I repeat, gesturing.

Alas, no olive oil appears.... Men.

I turn around, exasperated. He's still sitting at the kitchen table. The olive oil is still sitting in the pantry.

And he's still smiling away at me.

"Honey, olive oil," I demand again, losing patience.

He springs into action. "You just have to ask!"

My Prince Charming has a number of check marks on the "soul mate" list—tall, blond, blue eyes, artistic, kind, likes photography and reading.

But I never thought my Prince Charming would be deaf.

Robbed of the majority of his hearing when he was a small child, he finds his way through the world reading lips. The fateful night at the college apartment, I had failed to see his hearing aids, partially obscured by his hair.

Today, that refrain that first got his attention has become the chorus to my life.

"Turn around," he tells me when I'm mumbling away while cooking.

"Turn around," I tell him as I tap his shoulder before regaling him with a story.

"Turn around," he told me one sunny April day as I stood under an arbor gazing out over the horizon of the park. I turned around to see him on one knee, holding out a ring and sporting his heart on his sleeve and tears in his eyes.

It's music to my ears now. And to his eyes.

The connection forged through absolute necessity has only strengthened our relationship. How often does the communication between spouses devolve into shouting across the house? How often do we actually gaze into (or even glance at) a face we've long ago memorized?

We don't have the luxury of carrying on conversations through walls. We're cursed with the blessing of being forced to look into each other's eyes every time we want to talk.

It may not ever be easy. "Turn around" is heard just as often as, "What'd you say?" and, "Hey, you!" and I still struggle to hold back a smile when I ask, "What do you want for dinner?" and hear "Good."

But how can you ever fall out of love when you're always looking right at it?

~Caitlin Q. Bailey O'Neill

Almost Synchronicity

Truth is a great flirt.

~Franz Liszt

Two years after my divorce from Jim, my brain was saying, "Stay single. You—and the kids—are still recovering." My libido was saying, "desperate and dateless." I'd been asked out a few times, but declined, primarily because I was convinced that no man would want, or be good to, my children.

On a Friday evening, because I'd worked late, and was working Saturday, my mother took my children to her house for the weekend. I was surprised when my ex-husband's brother, Jerry, phoned at eight that evening.

"I want to talk to you about some things Jim told me," Jerry said.

"Sure. Ask me anything," I said.

"In person. I'm picking up Mary Jo when she gets off work at eleven. Can I come now?"

"Sure."

I put on a pot of coffee. Jerry and I talked about some family matters. At 9:30 Jerry flipped through the TV channels. "Nothing on—why don't we go have a drink—then I'll pick up Mary Jo."

I shook my head. I had never gone anywhere with Jerry.

He frowned. "C'mon, it'll do you good. It's almost ten. We'll go over to Pat's. I only have time for a couple—my wife doesn't like to wait so..."

I shrugged. "Okay, but only one. I have to get up early,"

Jerry glanced at his watch. "Five minutes—I'll meet you at Pat's Bar."

All the tables were full, so Jerry and I sat at the bar. After a couple sips of his beer, Jerry leaned toward me and pointed to a man standing behind him. "This fella just asked me to play pool. Okay?"

"Sure, I'm leaving anyway. I'm due at work by six tomorrow morning," I said.

Jerry nodded and walked toward the pool table. I phoned my mother to check on the children. I didn't notice someone took Jerry's seat until he spoke to me.

"Okay if I sit here?"

Still talking to my mother, I nodded.

He ordered drinks for both of us. I shook my head. "No, don't. I'm leaving."

He shrugged, took a drink and stared straight ahead. I finished talking on the phone. He extended his hand toward me. "Name's Butch. Butch Stanfield."

I smiled, told him a fake name, shook his hand, and looked toward the pool table.

"Come here often?" he asked.

I shook my head. "No. First time. I'm with my brother-in-law. He's over there—playing pool."

He smiled.

He asked me more questions—married? Kids? Job? Hobbies? And he told me about himself—worked out of town, was in town visiting friends this weekend, divorced, four kids, self-employed, loves the outdoors, especially hiking and camping.

I told him my parents and I camped all over the U.S. when I was a kid, that I loved to camp. He invited me to dinner the next day. I refused, explaining I had three children and two jobs—my free time belonged to the kids. He nodded.

"My hunting club's having a family picnic—one price includes me and my guests—up to six. Would you like to go?" he asked.

I shook my head. "Thanks but no. I don't—don't date."

"Well, it's not really a date—your kids'll have a good time. They have a swimming pool, games and prizes for kids. Not a date—just a nice Saturday afternoon."

I frowned.

"Your kids would like that, wouldn't they? You wouldn't want them to miss out on a good time, would you?"

He'd hit my soft spot—my children. I agreed to the picnic, gave him my phone number, told him my real name. He called every day—we dated for three months, then got married.

Twenty years later, during a large neighborhood block party, the conversation turned to telling how each of the married couples met. I took my turn.

"It was so unlikely that Butch and I would ever meet. Butch didn't live here at the time—he was visiting old school friends. I'd never been to Pat's Bar before or since. I've never gone anywhere with my ex-brother-in-law, except that one night. As far as I know, Jerry wasn't a pool player—and the place was full of people, but the guys needed a fourth. For some reason, they asked him to play. Butch sat down next to me, and we started talking. The rest is history."

My husband burst out laughing.

"That's how we met—isn't it?" I didn't see anything funny about my story.

"Those were my friends that invited him to play pool. I paid for their game—and the club didn't plan their picnic for a month," he said.

"Why'd you do that?" I stared at him.

"I wanted to meet you, so I had to get him out of the seat next to you."

~Alvena Stanfield

77

The New Guy

Using the power of decision gives you the capacity to get past any excuse to change any and every part of your life in an instant.
~Anthony Robbins

W as I really checking out the new guy standing at the reception desk? What was I thinking? I was engaged. The date was set. Plans were in place. My mother had found the perfect wedding gown.

It's not every day a guy like that walked into the office. Most men didn't wear a dress shirt and tie in our department. He was tall and slender. His dark curly hair was professionally styled. This guy was hot!

"Get a grip," I thought to myself. It was time to refocus on my work. I lined up my ruler to the mechanical I was working on. I wondered what my fiancé was doing. He was a navy man stationed in Beirut. Not a safe place to be in 1987. I had just received his letter the previous day. His voice sounded content on the cassette he sent to me. I could tell he was missing home. It would be another six months before I would see him again.

Later that day my boss Joe introduced me to the new guy.

"This is Kevin, our new illustrator," Joe said. "Tammy is one of our graphic artists."

"Nice to meet you," I said. "If there is anything you need, just ask."

I worked in a cubical across the room from Kevin. Within a few weeks he began staying late on the same nights I had to stay. He was training on the new Macs stationed next to my desk. We shared the same interest in music, classic rock, and pop. Our friendship grew as we met up with co-workers after work.

One evening after work I went for a run with my friend Kate. We were training for a race held by the public school in my hometown.

"He is good looking, has a great sense of humor," I went on and on to her about Kevin. "You should meet him, Kate. Someone should snatch this guy up before it's too late."

"Tam, why don't you go out with him if he's so special?"

"Come on Kate, I'm engaged," I said.

I couldn't help but think that if things were different, I might consider it.

As time went on, Kevin and I became close friends. We had lunch together and went for walks around the track. We were just friends so I convinced myself it was okay.

A gang of us at work were invited on a hiking trip in upstate New York. I was a little surprised when Jeanne my co-worker suggested Kevin and I drive up together.

The drive from Pennsylvania to the Finger Lakes took about six hours. Conversation came naturally on the trip up. It was as if we had known each other forever.

We did everything together that weekend. We spotted deer. We checked out the local town. We admired the beautiful river alongside the cabin.

It was that weekend, lying in my bunk, that I realized I had feelings for this guy. I couldn't stop thinking about him. I had butterflies in my stomach every time I thought about him. Why was I in this impossible situation? Was I really in love with my fiancé? Had we really spent enough time together? I did travel with him from Pennsylvania to California to transport his car where he was stationed. I was out of a job and it seemed like a fun thing to do at the time. I stayed in Los Angeles at cheap hotels for a month getting to know him better. Then there was the week or two he came home on leave. There was the week I flew back to LA to see him.

Did we really know each other well enough to get married? I counted the weeks we actually spent with each other. Maybe he asked me to marry him on a whim. Maybe I should have thought longer before I said yes. I was just so excited when he popped the big question. I cringed at the thought of how many people I would disappoint if I were to call off the wedding. Besides, I wouldn't have the nerve to do such a thing.

One Friday night I went dancing with friends from work. After everyone had left, I sat down next to Kevin. I was practically out of breath from dancing.

"What are you doing to me?" he said.

"What are you doing to me?" I said with surprise.

That was all it took. It was out in the open. We both had feelings for each other. This wonderful friendship had turned into something more. I couldn't let him slip away. There was more than just a connection. I had to call off the engagement to my fiancé. I couldn't be of those girls to write a Dear John letter. I'd ease the idea in with small hints.

My fiancé finally came home. I arranged to meet him at a local diner. My hands were trembling beneath the table as I sat across from him. We made small talk. I had to get it over with.

"I think we should call off the wedding," I said. "We barely even know each other."

Even he agreed that we hadn't spent enough time to really know each other well enough. Sadly, we would have gone through with it had I not said anything. I knew this decision would disappoint our family and friends. I slid the ring across the table.

The evening finally came for Kevin to meet my parents. We were both a little nervous. I invited Kevin into our living room and introduced him to my father. My brother-in-law Greg was sitting next to Dad discussing plans for a hunting trip. They were comparing a 30/30 to a 7mm.

"What do you prefer, Kevin?" my brother-in-law asked.

"Twenty-seven, twenty-eight, whatever it takes." Kevin always had a quick comeback.

Laughter broke the tension. It was obvious Kevin didn't know the first thing about guns. But I'm sure the discussion made him a bit a nervous, especially meeting my father for the first time.

It wasn't long before Kevin fit right in with my family. Calling off the wedding was one of the scariest things I ever had to do. I have never regretted the decision I made twenty-four years ago. After all, I met my best friend and my soul mate the day that new guy walked into the office.

~Tammy Pfaff

"The relationship you have referenced, Maxine and Steve, has been changed. The new relationship is Maxine and Paul. Please make a note of it."

78

No More Keep Away

The meeting of two personalities is like the contact of two chemical
substances; if there is any reaction, both are transformed.
~Carl Gustav Jung

Unforgettable! That's one way to describe that Sunday in July, a sweltering 101-degree day. Imagine me standing outside a friend's house with Matt playing his newly invented game: throw-the-ball-on-the-roof-and-see-who-can-catch-it-wherever-it-falls. For a Southern girl, I was almost perspiring. Okay, I was sweating. Yet, I was trying hard to appease my nine-year-old son. Matt had been a good sport all weekend, playing alone while I gabbed away with my best friend Nina.

It had been a year since Nina and Steve had moved an hour away. For me, it had been one whole school year teaching high school art and English as a single mom without my best buddy for encouragement. Nina is that friend every woman needs, not only when she's going through a divorce, but afterwards, when all of her other married friends have abandoned her.

It was Nina who affirmed, "Ann, you've been a great wife and mother. It was his choice and now his loss." Throughout those days I needed to be reminded I was a person of worth when all I felt was rejection.

And it was Nina who had appointed herself to be my official matchmaker.

"I have just the one for you, my brother... my mechanic... the choir director... Steve has a colleague..." Nina believed there was a knight in shining armor for me when I couldn't.

And so it was for that weekend too. Once Nina had arranged my visit and knew I would be able to help her with moving their college-aged daughter into this rental house, she also arranged for some man to bring his truck and help.

"Bill's perfect for you, Ann. He's new to town, recently divorced, and a great father who has custody of his two sons."

I kept my distance, of course, as a standard rule of caution I had established by others' unsportsmanlike behavior. And just when Bill and I were starting a conversation in the kitchen, Matt ran in breathless.

"Mom, come play ball with me."

I smiled and excused myself.

So, imagine my surprise—and delight—when Bill walked out the front door beside me and playfully grabbed the ball as it dropped from the roof. Matt sprang into action, stealing the ball from Bill, I supposed because that's what guys do. I paused to wonder why Bill didn't leave by going out the back door to his truck. I still didn't get it.

"Mom, you move into the middle," Matt said. "Then try to get the ball from one of us." He tosses it over my head to Bill. "It's called 'keep away.'"

"I know how to play keep away, silly," I said, noting to myself how good I'd gotten at it lately.

What should have been an easy game with Matt and this stranger developed into an unexplainable event for me. Something strange happened each time I caught the ball and Bill rushed towards me. His blue eyes focused on my mine, and I had to gasp from the fluttering in my chest. "I have a heart?" I thought. "I have a heart!"

"How long have you and Nina been friends?" Bill asked, propelling the ball over my head to Matt.

I leaped up. My hands curled over the ball, barely catching it, placing Bill in the middle.

"Four years."

Bill advanced closer just as I pitched the ball over his head.

"How long have you been divorced?" he asked.

His question struck me with its boldness, making me question if he was snooping, actually interested in me or just plain rude. Matt's return ball thrust into my chest. "Three years." I regrouped, hurling the ball back into the air.

At that point, I might have quit this game of keep away. Except that with Bill, I suddenly wanted to get caught. Bill's boyish yet masculine good looks were captivating. And he approached me with such strength and confidence. Yet, he had a gentle, humble demeanor.

This time when Bill rushed towards me, and my insides rotated, he casually cast out another question. "Date much?"

Several minutes passed while I decided my halfhearted attempts had to end. I jumped-up, easily grabbing Bill's slow, low ball meant for my taking. As he passed me to get in the middle, I replied, "Yes and no."

I caught his smile.

I thought about Bill during that hour drive home and much of the rest of the evening. Finally, standing next to my kitchen pantry, worn out by my thoughts, I offered my prayer, or, maybe more of a compromise.

"Okay, Lord, I can't think about him anymore! I'm giving him to you. If You want him in my life, You bring him back."

I gave an exasperated sigh, one God would surely understand.

"But, Lord, if he's not the one... well, could You give me someone just like him? I've never felt like this before."

For the next three months I continued on with my life and the busyness of beginning a new school year. I was also in the midst of developing an educational seminar for high-school students on documentary films.

Then one quiet night, the phone rang and it was Bill. And with that ring, Bill and I began the most extraordinary game of our lives. The air was intoxicating, infused with new life and love. And our most devoted fans cheered us on.

We dated long distance the first year, seeing each other every weekend, spending weeknights on the phone. Throughout those weeks I often paused at the kitchen sink or wherever I was when the thought overwhelmed me, whispering, "I love you, Bill Robertson."

I had to say it out loud, for it was far too big to hold inside me.

One night Bill confessed: "Do you know after that Sunday we met, I thought of you every single day. I figured that surely if I gave it a few months thinking about you would go away. Maybe I'd see other women and think of them, too." He shook his head. "I only thought about you."

I laughed, remembering my prayer.

We tried to be wise throughout those two years we dated, easily recognizing our differences: I'm all art and English, drawing words and lines into creative expressions, seeing the world lopsided. Bill's all math and science, carving cancers out of body parts where they don't belong, a constant symmetry kind of guy. His pristine white coat is ironed with heavy starch; mine is splattered with paint.

Yet, for seventeen years, what has kept us steady throughout our death-do-us-part marriage is that we meet each other in the middle on the issues that matter, like work ethic, family values, and most of all, our faith in God. We play by the rules, wholeheartedly.

No more "keep away" for us.

~Ann Elizabeth Robertson

79

Love for Rent

You know you're in love when you don't want to fall asleep because reality is finally better than your dreams.
~Dr. Seuss

is name is Nick. He has dirty blond hair, owns a lot of soft sweatshirts and plays guitar. You're going to be obsessed with him." I laughed in response to my best friend Anna as she described the guy who, in her mind, was going to be my future husband. Anna had a tendency to exaggerate.

I laughed until I laid eyes on him mere weeks later, his dirty blond hair draped partially over his piercing blue eyes, his voice when he said "hello" as soft as the aforementioned sweatshirts. If there is such a thing as love at first sight, this was it. Time to break out the champagne and write "Chase & Nick 4ever" all over a math notebook. But wait, not so fast! Of course there had to be a twist. A twist worthy of a classic romantic comedy starring Julia Roberts opposite someone British.....

Nick was my new roommate.

It was my last year of college at Boston University and we had a vacancy in our six-person home. Enter Nick, a friend of a friend.

Nick was unassuming, and when he spoke, it was worth listening to. I loved that and quickly began to love everything about him. The way he laughed when watching TV late at night, and the gentle strumming of his guitar as the music drifted up from underneath his door. I loved it all, so naturally I avoided him. The end. Just kidding.

November 29th rolled around. Nick and I had lived under the same roof for almost four months with minimal interaction and yet the electricity between us, this silent yet palpable understanding, had never been stronger. The days grew colder, our hearts grew warmer, and on that fateful night, after a romantic game of darts, we kissed.

It was the kind of kiss fairy tales and movies are made of, the kind of kiss where nothing exists except that moment. The best part? No walk of shame home.

Imagine being a little kid and living at Disneyland and every day you get to see Mickey and Snow White and all your other favorite Disney characters. That's what dating your roommate is like. My house became the happiest place on earth because Nick was there, and he was my favorite (next to Tinkerbell of course).

On our first date he picked me up at eight on the dot. He climbed the ten or so stairs leading from his room to mine, his knock barely audible. He was nervous, as was I. We left our home together and walked to a cozy Italian restaurant just a few blocks away.

I noticed the collared shirt he had put on under his pullover sweater and smiled. I suppose the soft sweatshirts hadn't made the cut. We ordered what would come to be our usuals, cheese ravioli for me and chicken Parmesan for him. That was the thing with us; we were never putting on airs, never trying to change the other. We were who we were and liked what we liked, and we were perfect for each other, imperfections and all.

After dinner we walked home through the sharp Massachusetts cold. There was no question of "can I come in?" or "would you like to come in for a drink?" We were both going in regardless of how the date went. He walked me up the ten or so stairs to my bedroom like a gentleman, then murmured, "I had a great time." He kissed me on the cheek and walked downstairs to his room.

That night I fell asleep to the sweet strumming of his guitar from the room below me. For the next two and a half years after that, I fell asleep with him.

~Chase Bernstein

Waiting
Is the Hardest Part

Who, being loved, is poor?
~Oscar Wilde

I'll admit it. I was a wee bit excited when I became single again after my divorce from Jason, who I had been with since the ninth grade. He was a mamma's baby and our relationship just couldn't develop past the fact we were just dumb kids. I dreamt of dating real men — rustic, maybe. What I wanted most was a feeling of protection — from the man, not his parents. I wanted a cowboy.

I was still young, only twenty-four, and many men had told me that I was pretty. But my rude awakening came when the phone didn't ring.

I called my mom crying. Trying to help, she set me up with some "really nice guy," not knowing he was gay. It was awkward.

Then, I got so desperate for some male attention that I let my ex-husband set me up with a friend of his. Only twenty-four, he was still living with his ex-wife and two kids and was so bald on the top of his head that he had a comb over like an old man. What was I thinking?

I had just gotten good at pretending that I didn't care about dating when my boss, Tim, started trying to get my attention. He was gorgeous, had his own home, and a good career. I couldn't believe he was flirting with me? Could he be my cowboy?

We had fun flirting at work and we talked a lot, but we were complete opposites. He was an atheist and I was a Christian. He was a mountain biker and a risk taker; I was a writer and a thinker. It would never work.

I prayed to God for patience and to help me find somebody in an unlikely place so that we would know it was fate. What I didn't know was that I wasn't going to have to wait much longer.

As luck would have it, my truck broke down at the gas pump. Some young boys helped me get it running enough to get me home, and I went in to pay for my gas.

"You don't know anybody who works on cars, do you?" I asked the cashier.

"Yes, I do and he's been wanting me to give you his number for months. He would have done it himself, but he was afraid you would think he's a stalker. He's a good guy, I think he's kind of cute, and he's not dangerous or anything. In fact, he took my friend on a date once just as friends and even let her bring her little girl. He lives in a house right behind your apartment complex and he's a mechanic. Here's his number."

I remembered a man who had waved at me and smiled. Could he be the one? When I finally got up the courage to call his number, he admitted it was him. The next day, he worked on my car and patted it in a sweet way as it left his driveway. Still, there was no asking for a date. He said he would have to wait until he caught up on some payments first before he could take me out. With my self-esteem in the gutter, I took that to mean he wasn't interested. But, I was wrong. Instead of asking me out, he became my friend, cooking supper for me and bringing lunch to me at work.

Now, of course, Tim saw a big change in me and he couldn't stand it. "I think we should take it to the next level."

I tried to ignore him, but he was persistent. He said he wanted to spend money on me, buy me new outfits, and take me to expensive restaurants. A year had passed and I still had not been taken on a romantic date. I decided I would just go out with Tim.

I explained it to Steve the next day. I owed him that much.

"Given what you've told me about Tim, I don't think he'll be what you're hoping for," Steve said. "When he breaks your heart and you're afraid you'll lose your job because of him, you know where I live. You can knock on my door anytime, even if it's in the middle of the night." I was confused. Why was he being so sweet to me?

My relationship with Tim seemed to be moving in the right direction until one night at a restaurant, for no reason at all, he started giving me the silent treatment. When we got back to his house that night, his phone rang. He answered and talked briefly. Then, he hung up and said, "You can go home now. I've got some guys coming over in a few minutes to hang out." I left, completely let down, knowing he had replaced me with another woman.

On the way home, Steve's words kept echoing: "You can knock on my door even if it's in the middle of the night." Well, it was bedtime when I reached Steve's house, and he was not awakened by my rather quiet knocks or by my calls to his cell. Maybe he had decided not to see me anymore, even as a friend. I couldn't blame him. So I took my tear-stained face to my apartment to try to sleep, but I couldn't. I was worried about how my relationship with Tim would affect my job.

Like a good friend, Steve came by my house at eleven the next day. I told him I had not slept all night and that I had tried to wake him up the night before. He apologized for not hearing me and said, "Would it help you sleep if I was here? How 'bout you turn on some music and lay your head in my lap, while I watch you sleep."

From that day forward, Steve and I were a couple. I learned he had been laid off from his factory job and had two children to support. But dates involving fancy restaurants and new clothes weren't important to me anymore. He did everything he could to make me happy. When I told him I didn't want him drinking around my ten-year-old son, he poured his beer down the sink. When I told him he couldn't stay in my bed, he made himself a pallet on the floor, just to be near me. And when I needed a friend, he was always there. I had found my cowboy.

~Melisa Kraft

81

Finding Mr. Write

Living involves tearing up one rough draft after another.
~Author Unknown

I waited for Michael's response to my manuscript with all the jitters of a schoolgirl at a middle school mixer. As the newest member of the writers' group, I'd taken a lashing in previous weeks from other group members, and Michael had offered me the support to keep pecking away at the keyboard. While driving to the writers' group that evening, I imagined his critique. "I love your juxtaposition," he would say, "and your array of literary devices is quite masterful." Or perhaps he'd whisper one word: "Bestseller." I'd be coy and act as though I might take his opinion into consideration when revising my novel if I felt generous. But that fantasy ended as I watched him carelessly flip the pages of my manuscript, now littered with his red ink.

I choked back the urge to yell, "Be careful with that. Do you know how long it took me to write those pages?" But of course he knew since he was a novelist himself. Then he let out an exaggerated sigh. Letting the pages fall back into place, he tapped his fingers atop the front page while gathering his thoughts. Never a good sign. Positive responses within the writers' group usually sprang forth, like great writing itself. No, he was gathering words that would get to the point without cutting too deeply: careful, deliberate words, holding no accidental flattery.

I shifted in my chair and braced for the critique that I no longer wanted. It's merely one person's opinion, I reminded myself. Maybe he wasn't my audience, I rationalized. Maybe he didn't know good writing when he saw it. Maybe he was grandstanding for the rest of the group. Oh, who was I kidding? Michael's critique would be honest and fair because he was brilliant. And insightful. And gorgeous.

He cocked his head, and I readied my pen to take notes on my copy of the manuscript, hoping to catch an accolade or two. "Have you considered dropping the first fifteen pages of your novel?" he asked. "The story actually starts with the second chapter. The first chapter is nothing but backstory that the reader neither needs nor cares about."

There. He said it. He didn't care. Wait. Worse yet, nobody cared. I nodded, and my pen made a big red "X" over the front page, proving to the group that I could take criticism like a professional. As he blathered about "sprinkling in backstory" and "dropping the reader into the middle of conflict," I silently planned my response to his critique. I would not only keep the first chapter, but I'd add more pages to prove my literary prowess. During the next group session, he'd see his error in judgment and apologize for his gross oversight. Then the word "boring" snapped me back into the moment, and my chest tightened. Whoa. Boring? Was that necessary? I jotted, "You're boring" on my copy and smiled at him while I drew a frowny face with his name underneath.

As others in the group took turns jabbing and poking the life out of my prose, Michael's comments still tumbled inside my head. Why did his opinion matter so much? Others had said far worse in the past. Perhaps it was because his writing was poetic, sensuous, and vivid. His words transported me to new places with their stunning imagery. And, on those special occasions when he read his work aloud, I closed my eyes and let the melodic words wash over me — refreshing and delightful. As a new writer, I wanted his admiration for my work because I so admired his. I needed his encouragement to keep writing since I doubted my ability. But it wouldn't come this evening.

After the meeting, I gathered my notes and scooted out the door as the others mingled.

"Cathi," a voice called from behind. I turned to find Michael walking toward me. "Aren't you joining us for dinner?"

I pointed to my car. "No, I think I'm going to head on home."

"I hope I didn't offend you with my comments tonight."

"Offend me?" I waved off his concern. "Not in the least. I need honest feedback to improve my writing." I wouldn't let him see my disappointment.

"Are you sure you can't come to dinner?"

"I'm sure."

"Oh, okay. Well, I'll see you next week then." Interestingly, he let his disappointment show.

I smiled. "Next week."

As I sat at home with his copy of my manuscript spread out on the desk, I pored over his comments in the margins, soaking up each "nice" and "insightful." He had, in fact, written plenty of compliments. Rereading the first chapter, I realized he was right. It was backstory that I needed to develop my protagonist, nothing more. I highlighted the chapter and hit delete, thankful for Michael's honesty.

Over the next several months, we continued to support one another's writing, and then we started dating. However, once romantically involved, the critiques became a little more personal. And as our love strengthened, I became less pleased with his brutal honesty.

"What do you mean my plot twist reeks of convenience?" I pressed him, thrusting my story in front of his face.

He laughed. "Just what I said. Try again." He failed to back down on account of hurting my feelings.

Yet another reason I loved him so after hating him for a few minutes.

The more time we spent together, the more I realized his gift of intellect. His vocabulary often proved challenging. As a fellow scribe, how could I admit that I didn't know the meaning of many of his highbrow words?

"Excuse me," I said, rising from the table at the restaurant. Then I squirreled myself away in the bathroom and whipped out the pocket dictionary from my purse, searching for the word "impecunious." Why did he have to be so smart?

I left the bathroom and slipped back into my seat. "I'm sorry, you were saying...?" And we'd pick up the topic with him none the wiser.

Soon, the fantasy versus reality questions surfaced. We wrote fiction, after all, and had been known to have a flexible relationship with the truth.

"You aren't lying, are you?" Michael asked with a raised brow.

"What? Of course not," I said.

"Exaggerating?"

"Well... maybe."

Next came the-character-in-your-story-is-me accusation.

"C'mon, honey," Michael said. "How can that be you when her name is Rachael?"

"Like we don't change names to protect the guilty?"

"Well... yes... but I swear she's not you."

The next week, he read a passage from his novel, portraying Rachael as sexy, strong, and superior.

The writers' group members left and I asked, "Are you sure I'm not Rachael?"

He smiled. "Well, not exactly," he said as he kissed me. "You're better."

I lingered in his arms, knowing I had found Mr. Write.

After ten years of marriage, four novels, and dozens of stories between us, we continue to delight in the written word. We can only hope to create a world better than the one we share.

~Cathi LaMarche

82

Love in the Sewer

*Love has no desire but to fulfill itself. To melt and be like a running brook
that sings its melody to the night. To wake at dawn with a winged heart and
give thanks for another day of loving.*

~Kahlil Gibran

O ffice romances never work. At least, that was my experience. Working with someone and dating him was
bound to lead to disaster. I watched co-workers attempt
it. It never lasted. As a single mother of two children, I
steered clear of romantic interests at work like they were the plague.

I spent my days as a Public Information Officer for a city sewer
rehab contract. My days could range from pleasant to downright
deplorable, all depending upon how the contractors performed their
day-to-day tasks and how many people they angered in the process.
My job focused on intense damage control.

Enter Travis. He served as the Field Superintendent for one of
the contractors working under this program. A soft-spoken, mild-
mannered man, from my experience, he had the ability to set homeowners into a frenzy of complaints and threats.

One morning, I was called out to the site to handle a homeowner
who was banging on the side of his house with a plunger, yelling at
the construction crew regarding the noise level. When I arrived on
site, I could tell the crew was taking pleasure in my situation. Travis
especially.

The work his crew performed elicited more complaints than any other. His was my nightmare crew. Loud pumps that ran all night, heavy equipment on property, and tons of digging to repair aging sewer lines had that effect on people. I spent two years running interference for that contract.

I dreaded answering the phone every time I saw his number, and couldn't wait until his crew shut down each day so I could finally relax. Day after day, I fielded complaints, sat on site, and sweet-talked homeowners into allowing the work to continue. I didn't hate him, but he drove me crazy. I believe to this day, he enjoyed watching me defuse explosive people.

As the work progressed, we spent more time together. I learned about his family and how tight-knit they are. A large and loving family was something we had in common. We shared stories of growing up in such an environment and how vital it was to who we became.

We shared quick coffee and lunch breaks and regrouped at the end of the day to discuss upcoming work. I learned about his childhood and how much trouble he got into anytime his mom was out of the house. For some reason, he only seemed to hurt himself while she was gone. The more defusing I did on his behalf, the more I got to know him and like him.

⁘ I never saw it coming, but somehow the guy who I used to dread hearing from was now the guy I couldn't wait to hear from. A million things could go wrong dating a guy I worked with, so I tried to ignore my feelings. I knew it would never work out. I told myself that I didn't care that the feelings were mutual and growing daily. I was convinced it was destined for failure.

Late one evening, after spending fourteen hours on site, it began to snow. A thick, white blanket covered the entire area. Living in Georgia, we don't see much snow. It was beautiful. As I sat with him in the truck waiting for it to ease up, we talked. In the middle of our conversation, he stepped out of the truck and gathered up enough snow to form a snowball. He tossed it right in the truck at me! Not one to allow this, I quickly began gathering my own snow and throwing it back. I felt like I was fourteen again. It was the most carefree moment I had experienced in much too long and it was wonderful.

He told me that he was pretty sure he loved me that evening and I stopped being able to rationalize why I couldn't date someone I worked with. Despite being convinced that an office romance was not for me, I entered into one with hopes of discovering I had been wrong.

I quickly found out that dating someone I worked with actually helped make the day better. I had someone else working with me, watching out for my wellbeing, and pitching in when I needed help. Not only did he understand what I did all day, he never found fault with my long hours or the demands of the job. I had a partner both at home and at work. It was amazing. All the preconceived notions that I once held faded away.

Five years later, I am happy to report that I still feel like I am fourteen when I am with him. We were married a little over two years ago, have three beautiful children now, and are still going strong. I never would have imagined finding love at work. I laugh when I think about how opposed I was to an office romance and now I am a firm believer in finding love where you least expect it. I found mine working amongst sewers.

~Shannon Scott Poteet

83

Beyond Expectations

There is no surprise more magical than the surprise of being loved.
It is God's finger on man's shoulder.
~Charles Morgan

I n all of my twenty years, I never imagined that one day I would be doing the very thing I had dreamt about since I was a little girl. Yet, there I was on the last day of summer: bags packed, tear-filled goodbyes spoken, plane ticket and passport in hand. I had joked about how much I needed to leave the country with classmates in the school cafeteria after every failed test, over dinner and dessert with my girlfriends, after every breakup, and with anyone who would listen on every dreary Ohio day. Now, it was finally becoming a reality. I was about to embark on a four-month journey of living, studying and traveling throughout Europe, and I had no idea what life-changing adventures would ensue.

After a long flight, two layovers, and one life-threatening taxi ride, I finally arrived at my apartment in Florence, Italy. My room-mates and I headed out that first evening for dinner and a night on the town in our new home away from home. Though my dating life the past summer had been less than riveting, I was feeling independent. I was twenty and in Europe, and oddly okay with being single. I had seen the romantic comedies and read the romance novels, so I knew the drill. You go to Europe to reinvent yourself, to check some things off your bucket list, and most importantly, to fall in love. That's what it seems you're supposed to do, and in case I forgot, my family and friends at home were there to remind me.

"Don't go falling in love with some boy while you're there! It happens more often than you think!" I was constantly warned. I would remind them of my subpar romantic history, assuring them, "I am definitely not the girl to be worried about. I don't want that to happen anyway." It's true, I didn't. When my roommates, captured by the exhilarating romance that fills the city, would go on and on about how wonderful it would be to fall in love in Florence, I would suppress laughter while trying not to roll my eyes. I was there to learn about myself, step outside of my Ohio-sized comfort zone, and open my eyes to all life had to offer. Besides, I wrote in my seventh grade journal that I was determined to meet the perfect guy in a coffee shop and still held firmly to that idea. He would have curly brown hair and a guitar casually slung over his shoulder. We would lock eyes, and the stars would align. I was not about to let just any boy intrude on everything I had planned.

Life, however, had its own plans. Exactly one month after I arrived in Florence, a brown-haired, blue-eyed artist from Boston introduced himself to me on the outdoor terrace above St. Mark's English Church. He had the facial hair of a seasoned world traveler and an amazing smile. He possessed charm and charisma that made me blush as soon as we shook hands. Vince had just arrived in Florence, and we conversed about how we both stumbled upon St. Mark's in search of a good, English-speaking church. We became friends right away. The more time we spent together, the more I realized what a brilliant person he was. He had a sense of humor that never failed to make me laugh, a love for God, and a passion for life that was contagious. I reminded myself of my desire to stay single during these next few months, but the more time we spent taking walks, visiting museums, and battling it out with shopping carts in the supermarket, I couldn't help the way I felt.

Let's get something straight. I am painfully shy and socially awkward. These things do not happen to me regularly. I don't just go to Italy, ride off into the sunset with an incredible guy, and live happily ever after. I'm the type of girl who misses her mouth with her fork on the first date—not just once, but every time and on every date. Let's face it: amazing guys date amazing girls—that is just a fact. Every remarkable guy I've known has a girlfriend who causes me to question my significance on this planet. Just once I wanted to be the girl who snagged the wonderful, handsome boy, but I had already picked out some names for my future cats, so chances were looking pretty slim.

As with other times when I am questioning something in my life, the one thing I always know to do is chat with God. This time, I found myself kneeling by the altar in an empty St. Mark's one evening. I really liked this boy. Instead of wanting him to feel the same, I just wanted my feelings to go away. I remember thinking that I could never be with him because I wasn't good enough, but I wanted someone like him.

However, I've heard people say that we often overvalue everything we aren't and undervalue everything we are. I realized that the only thing getting in my way was myself.

Little did I know that three months later, I would be kneeling by the very same altar on a snowy December morning, thanking God that the following day I would leave Florence with so much confidence in myself, unforgettable memories, and a few extra pounds (oops). Not to mention the beginning of an incredible relationship with Vince—the boy I insisted I wasn't good enough to have.

Six months after leaving Florence, we both still laugh about the unexpectedness of it all. Vince doesn't have curly brown hair or play the guitar, and we didn't meet in a coffee shop. But do you know what? Between traveling, studying and working, we never found ourselves at church again on the same Sunday while in Florence. If we hadn't met that first day on the terrace above St. Mark's, we never would have met at all. And I think that's a story worth rearranging my plans for.

~Elizabeth Blosfield

The Dating Game

Will You Marry Me?

I dreamed of a wedding of elaborate elegance,
A church filled with family and friends.
I asked him what kind of a wedding he wished for,
He said one that would make me his wife.

~Author Unknown

Lights, Camera, Action

The only thing better than singing is more singing.

~Ella Fitzgerald

"Hey I'm on 110," Travis said. "I only have about twenty minutes until I'm in Houston!"

"Okay, I'll see you soon," I said. "Oh, the gate code to the apartment is 2162."

I hung up the phone thinking, "I can't believe he drove his car all the way here from Michigan. Is he serious? And what did he do with his apartment?"

I ran up the stairs and fumbled in my make-up bag looking for my special lip gloss. A short time passed and just as I was fluffing the pillows on the couch the ringtone that made me smile so many times before made my heart drop. After all, we'd been friends for years, tried dating, and then I moved over 2,000 miles away. And now he was here. So many thoughts ran through my mind. Then my cell phone rang again.

"Guess what?" Travis said. I could see him smiling through the phone.

"What?"

"I'm here. Coming through the gate now."

"Okay, I'm coming out!"

Before I knew it I was skipping out the door. I saw his silver Mitsubishi Diamante. It seemed to have an entire apartment packed in it. I couldn't help thinking, "Is this real? Did he really drive twenty-one hours for me?"

When Travis saw me, he stopped the car, got out and hugged me so tightly that I could feel the love connecting his heart to mine. From that day, we picked up right where we left off; only this time it was so much deeper.

One day while cleaning, Travis began to sing the most beautiful high note that seemed to float in the air. I always knew he could sing. He sang opera, gospel, classical, you name it. Not to mention we sang together. But this was something special. It was so many things wrapped in one.

I remembered there was an audition in San Antonio for *America's Got Talent* the following week. Knowing his passion for singing, I felt this was my chance to support him as he had done for me so many times before. I just had to get him there!

Being the fun and spontaneous guy that he is, it was no problem getting him in the car, although he kept asking why I wanted to drive all of a sudden. I told him that we were going to San Antonio for date night to hang out with friends and I would drive since it was my idea. I still can't believe he fell for that one!

After two hours of laughing, singing, and telling jokes, we pulled up to the city's convention center. Travis said, "Honey Bunny, look at all these people. What are we doing here?"

I anxiously answered, "Well Babe, I have a confession. I brought you here to audition for *America's Got Talent!*"

We both laughed and he said, "You're serious? Okay, let's do it, I'm ready!"

I was so relieved. My plan had worked so far. Now all I had to do was get him to sing soprano and I knew that would not be easy.

Hours passed, as we waited in lines just to wait in more lines. We saw every act from dancing to sword swallowing. You name it, it was there—even other opera singers. That is when I turned to him and said, "Babe, if you want to get on this show you are going to have to sing like a soprano!"

Travis was shocked. "Like a woman? That's something I do

around the house for fun." I took his hand, looked this masculine, physically fit man straight in the eyes and said, "Babe, trust me, I promise you that if you do this, you will be on this show."

Praying he would trust me on this one, I continued, "People want something unique. You're it!" Finally, he agreed.

We waved to each other as he went in with his audition group to see the first set of judges. Two hours passed and finally he came into the waiting area. "Honey Bunny, you were right. They liked it! I'm going to be on the show!"

In the meantime, we were given details about the televised auditions. I was even more confident that the celebrity judges would love him as well.

I thought about the sacrifice it took for him to leave everything he built in Michigan to start over in Texas with me. It felt good to be chased by him and it felt even better to support him.

Finally, the celebrity auditions came, and I was wearing the black and white dress he loved to see me in. I was led to the front row in the auditorium. But before I left him backstage, he said with a certainty I've never heard before, "I've got this. Things are going to change for us."

"I know. You're a star!" I replied, imagining the audience response from the performance that was soon to take place.

After seeing several acts, a cameraman came and positioned himself right in front of me. I knew Travis would be next. He was so handsome as he walked out on stage.

He began singing, but this time it was even better than the times I had heard him playfully singing around his apartment. The crowd went wild and once the performance was over, everyone was on their feet. Travis told the judges I put him up to auditioning and he wanted me to come on the stage.

Now, imagine bright lights, a huge stage, cameras, and millions of viewers—including the audience—watching you. This was supposed to be all about Travis. Feeling nervous and excited at the same time, I stood on stage next to the man who drove over 2,000 miles to be with me. One of the judges told him I was a keeper and he thought it was wonderful that I got him to audition. Travis replied, "I know and I have something to say to her." Travis turned to me and said, "I have loved you from the first time I laid eyes on you...."

The audience started screaming, as I stood in disbelief as to what was actually happening. It was almost like everything else was muted and I could barely understand what was going on until he dropped on one knee and said, "Will you marry me?" Everyone was cheering, I was crying, and a judge said, "Well, what's your answer?"

"Yes!" I shouted, still trying to see if this was all real.

This marked the first time that a contestant had received five yeses! I had surprised him with an audition and he gave me an even bigger surprise in front of millions—an engagement ring!

~Elvira Van Horn

Editor's note: For a great treat, watch Travis Pratt's impromptu audition on this YouTube video. You'll see Elvira in her black-and-white dress getting her proposal too!
http://www.youtube.com/watch?v=FdG3KOO6joQ

Punt, Pass, Propose

Love — a wildly misunderstood although highly desirable malfunction of the heart which weakens the brain, causes eyes to sparkle, cheeks to glow, blood pressure to rise and the lips to pucker.

~Author Unknown

I didn't want to go. It wasn't that I was disinterested, more like disheartened. I was twenty-seven, single, and could see a pattern developing: Girl meets guy, girl gets to know guy, girl is introduced to guy's index of neurosis, girl remains single.

But being the hopeless (okay, relentless) romantic that I am, I truly wanted to believe that this evening would indeed be different. A week prior I had met a book publisher named Marian, who, during our chance encounter, had sworn that she knew the perfect guy for me after talking with me for no more than fifteen minutes. Marian, a self-professed yenta who unabashedly boasted that her first two matchmaking efforts had led to the altar, then produced a photo of her with two former NFL football players, one of whom was the very recognizable (and very married) Detroit Lions Hall of Fame running back Barry Sanders. The other was one of Marian's clients, who also happened to be one of Sander's offensive linemen.

"This is Scott," Marian said as she pointed to the tall (and, yes, handsome) gentleman on the right. "You guys will be good together." Marian spoke with both authority and compassion, as if I had no say in the matter, yet it would be for my own good. I gave a meek protest.

A pompous athlete was the last thing I needed, but Marian wouldn't hear of it.

"Hush," she interrupted. "He's different. His foundation is holding a strolling dinner next Friday to raise money for children's literacy. Put on a nice dress. Come. It'll be fun."

I didn't know how to decline.

A week later, I arrived at the entrance of Somerset Collection, a high-end shopping center that would serve as the site of the fundraiser. I rooted around in my purse for a tube of lip gloss, a blatant attempt at stalling. The party was in full swing and the cacophony of guests mingling amid the sounds of smooth jazz was audible from the sidewalk. I stalled some more and proceeded to check my cell phone for any text messages. Not that I was expecting any.

This was absurd. I'd ripped off Band-Aids faster than this. Realizing that I could stay out here until my toes froze or I could act like an adult and face the music—and my yenta, for that matter—I braced myself and went in.

Marian was the first person I laid eyes on, and she wasted no time getting to the nitty-gritty. "You're here," she said, lifting her glass of merlot. She wore a bright red dress and an even brighter smile. I tucked my purse under my armpit and ran my hands down the front of my white and gold gown. "C'mon," she said and grabbed my hand.

I saw Scott before he saw me. He was huddled (no pun intended) around a handful of gentlemen who were so tall and broad, they could have easily given the Pittsburgh Steelers' Steel Curtain a run for their money. One of them gave Scott a nudge, and Scott turned to face me. Clad in a perfectly tailored classic black tuxedo, he was even more beautiful than I had recalled from the photo, and for a split second, I was convinced that my knees had turned to Jell-O.

It all happened so fast: Scott's pals got lost, Marian formally introduced us, and then she disappeared, too. Out of nowhere, a waiter deposited a glass of white wine in my hand. I took a sip—much too dry—and set it down on a nearby end table. Scott and I engaged in polite, rudimentary chatter, the details of which danced over my head like clouds in the sky. The next thing I knew Scott and I had photographers in our face. "Mr. Conover, we'd like to get a photo of you and your girlfriend, please," said the lead photographer of one of Metro Detroit's premier lifestyle magazines.

Both immensely flattered and utterly embarrassed, I glanced up at Scott to gauge his reaction. He wrapped an arm around my shoulder and smiled for the camera. And then something totally unpredictable happened: I relaxed. The rest of the evening was a mix of effusive laughter, fine chocolate, and a sense of wonderment I had yet to experience on a first date.

At the end of the night, Scott summoned me into Mont Blanc pen boutique, an event sponsor. "Here, try this pen," he said with a coy smile. He handed me the Meisterstück he had received as a gift from the company. "Why don't you write down your phone number?"

And then it started. A real, genuine... wait for it... relationship. Scott had returned to his home state of New Jersey after retiring from the Lions, so we did the long distance thing for about three years. It was hardly stressful, I think, because we knew this was it. The real McCoy.

It's funny how things come full circle. That's precisely what happened nearly two years after we'd met. Scott flew in for a Sunday afternoon Detroit Lions charity luncheon that was to be held at a hotel half a mile down the road from Somerset Collection. While we were en route, I looked to my right and saw one of Scott's former teammates driving in the next lane.

"Look, it's George!" I said. "He must be on his way to the lunch, too." Scott's jaw tightened, and he hit the gas. Hard. That was my first inclination that something wasn't right. The second, in hindsight, was that George was not wearing a suit—or even a nice shirt—but an I've-been-working-in-the-yard-all-day-type tank top. The third was that Scott turned left at the light—the opposite direction of the hotel—and right into the parking lot of Somerset Collection. But this time Scott quelled my suspicion by stating that we were stopping by Mont Blanc before the luncheon so he could get his Meisterstück cleaned and ready to go for the autographs he'd sign at the lunch, which seemed plausible.

But it was all a ruse.

We entered the boutique hand in hand and walked right up to the counter. Scott then pulled the pen and a piece of paper from the inside pocket of his jacket. He handed the pen to the store's associate and the piece of paper to me. I stared at it in disbelief: It was the paper I had written my phone number on the night we met. I stepped away from the counter to look up at Scott, but he wasn't towering over me like usual because he was on bended knee.

"Courtney..." he began. "Will you marry me?"

Time stood still. I couldn't believe my ears, I couldn't believe that I didn't see this coming, and, most of all, I couldn't believe my good fortune.

I was unable to move, but, thankfully, I was able to say what I felt: "Yes."

Never before—and not since—has an impromptu trip to the mall been so exhilarating.

~Courtney Conover

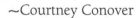

86

Finding Love After Breast Cancer

You block your dream when you allow your fear to grow bigger than your faith.

~Mary Manin Morrissey

We had been dating for three months when I was diagnosed with breast cancer. I could sense his internal dialogue. "I like being with her, but do I want to deal with a cancer patient?" We stayed together, but he never once visited me in the hospital or kept me company during my treatments. I knew he didn't love me, but I was scared to leave him because I was afraid no one else would ever want me. My surgeries had left me scarred on the outside and extremely vulnerable on the inside. After two years, we finally gave up on our relationship.

There I was, twenty-nine years old, back in the dating scene. It was terrifying. How could I tell someone, a male someone, that I only had one breast? When I finally did go out on a date, I panicked when he got a little too close to lifting my shirt while we were kissing. I had anxiety attacks about revealing my secret. Before our next date, I walked all over town thinking and crying because I was going to tell this guy about my breast cancer. The night of the date came, and I still didn't know how to bring it up. He never showed. After all my anxiety, I was stood up. I felt so upset. My friends were angry for me.

One friend told him to his face what a horrible person he was. He probably sensed my anxiety but had no clue what it was all about, so he ran for the hills.

When my sister first suggested I go out with the youth leader at our church, I laughed. This guy was really involved. He volunteered for the youth group, he sang at the contemporary service every Saturday night, and he played the trombone for church services every Christmas and Easter. I didn't think he'd be the right man for me.

But then, I started looking at Keith in a new way. He was kind of cute. Plus, we were both in our thirties and still single. Even though I lived over an hour away, I kept going to our family's church. I kept trying to ask Keith out after church on Sundays, but I either couldn't get up the nerve or he had to hurry off to teach Sunday school. (Honestly, he was a Sunday school teacher. Did I really want to date someone that good?) But still, I developed quite a crush on "church boy" as my friends called him. Mom got tired of me talking about him and not doing anything, so she stepped in. She got his e-mail address from a mutual friend. I asked him out for coffee after Sunday school. He replied, "Let's go out for pancakes!" and gave me his phone number.

I called him, wondering what I would say. I didn't even have a chance to worry about that. We chatted easily for an hour. Breakfast went even better and we both knew we would see each other again.

As I got to know him, I realized he wasn't the man I thought he was. I assumed he would listen to the contemporary Christian station; it wasn't even a preset on his car radio. I discovered his absolute favorite band was Def Leppard and he listened to bands I had never heard of, like Queensryche and Shaw-Blades. He was always singing along to the radio and getting me to sing along, too. He worked at a machine shop and he swore like a truck driver... but not around me. He could be friends with anyone. He talked to the little old ladies at church and he hung out with the guys from the shop. He was completely different than I thought he would be and I quickly fell in love.

Fortunately for me, Keith believed in going slow. He hugged me on the first date, kissed me on the cheek for the second, and didn't go for the lips until the third date. I was in no hurry to tell him my secret.

One weekend we went camping together. On our first night it was dark, it was romantic, and I was terribly nervous. My heart was pounding. But I trusted him. "I had breast cancer," I said.

"I know," he said. "I remember praying for you in church."

We talked long into the night about my breast cancer diagnosis and treatment and about our relationship. Keith told me a few weeks later that our camping trip was when he knew he loved me.

One weekend, Keith made reservations at our favorite restaurant on a Friday night. We decided to dress up a little, and have a night out on the town. I even wore heels, which was rare.

After dinner, Keith wanted to take a romantic walk around the lagoon by the university. It was a little nippy, but I was up for a walk.

We drove to the lagoon, only to find that a sky-high chain-link fence surrounded it. We got out of the car and stared at the mud. The lagoon was being dredged, and a fishy smell filled the air.

Keith urged me to walk around the lagoon anyway.

We walked slowly, holding hands. My feet started to hurt and I began to shiver. As we completed the walk around the lagoon and approached the parking lot, I headed for the car. "Let's walk around again," Keith said.

"Are you kidding?" It was the beginning of April, I was freezing, and those high heels seriously needed to come off.

"Come on!" Keith dragged me back to the path and we found a bench to sit on. I don't remember the exact words he said, but he did tell me this: he couldn't imagine life without me. He pulled out a little black box. He got down on one knee, opened the little box, and asked me to be his wife.

"Yes, yes, YES!" I cried as I flung my arms around his neck almost knocking him and that little black box right to the ground.

My doctor asked me once how I dealt with dating since I was such a young cancer patient. I said that you just know. You just know who to trust and when the time is right to tell someone. When I was single I didn't know how long I had to wait before I found the right person. Those four years between my mastectomy and the beginning of my romance with Keith were extremely long years. It was worth the wait.

~Christa M. Grabske

87

Chicken Soup for the Soul

The Boyfriend, The Boss, and Me

Show a little faith, there's magic in the night.
~Bruce Springsteen

I had always scoffed at people who got engaged at baseball games, or on national television, with their shrieking, weepy faces plastered on a giant screen while everyone applauded. What kind of person wants to share one of the most defining moments of her life with thousands of complete strangers?

For me, a little candlelight, some expensive wine, and, of course, a declaration of undying love seemed more appropriate.

Which is why I was completely floored by what happened to me in New York City a few years ago.

Although we came from completely different religious backgrounds, Martin and I were drawn together through music, especially live music. Music was the soundtrack to our life together in Montreal, whether it was vintage blues playing in the background as we cooked a romantic dinner at home, or guessing what song was being played live in front of us from the first few notes. (I usually won our "Name That Tune" contests.)

Our friends made fun of the fact that we'd often take spontaneous road trips to see an artist we both liked. We went anywhere that we could get to within a day's drive — Toronto, Philadelphia, Albany. I'd chart out the fastest way to get there via MapQuest, find a funky, reasonably priced hotel with free breakfast and parking, and off we'd go.

We especially loved Bruce Springsteen and the E Street Band. Throughout The Rising tour of 2002-2003, we caught six Springsteen shows in six cities, including the last night of the tour in October 2003, outdoors at New York's Shea Stadium. (Hey, some women buy expensive shoes, I invest in rock n' roll experiences!)

It was pouring rain throughout the whole seven-hour drive from Montreal to New York, and was freezing cold when we finally arrived. Our shoes and socks were soaked, my hair was frizzy and out of control, but we were thrilled to be in the Big Apple for the final night of The Boss's tour. Despite the horrible weather, the parking lot was jammed with tailgate parties featuring die-hard fans huddled in front of their cars or vans, trunks open, music blaring, barbecues fired up, makeshift tarps sheltering them from the rain.

Once inside the stadium, we begged (okay, bribed) a beer concession employee to part with two jumbo garbage bags, which we wore throughout the show, holding hands through the armholes Martin had hacked with his Swiss army knife.

The rain finally stopped to reveal a clear, starlit sky just as Springsteen began strumming the intro to his next song on his acoustic guitar. Famous for his intimate conversations with his audience, Springsteen spoke of commitment, of how fragile relationships can be, of how easy it is to lose one another if you're not completely invested in your love. As he started to sing, we were amazed to realize that neither of us die-hard fans had ever heard this song before. In fact, we later found out it was the first time he had played "Back in Your Arms" in concert.

The crowd sat in silent appreciation, and as the first verse ended, Martin leaned into me and whispered, "I'm sorry I didn't plan anything." Thinking he was referring to finding a hotel in New York on five minutes' notice, I shushed him. "I think we should get married," he announced, in front of the 60,000 people who sat, drenched, under the stars with us.

My hands started shaking, and I'm not sure if I was shivering from the damp, cold air or the growing warmth in my heart. I threw my arms around Martin's neck, and as the crowd cheered (for Bruce, not for us), I felt grateful for this perfect marriage proposal that was unlike anything I'd dreamed of. Instead of candlelight, we were bathed in bright, concert spotlights. Expensive wine? Nope, just warm American beer mixed with rainwater. A declaration of undying love? You bet.

Four months later, with "Back in Your Arms" as our first dance, we got married in a small civil ceremony with close family and friends. As he slipped the wedding band onto my finger, Martin said, "I promise to keep taking you to Springsteen shows as long as we can both still dance." And I knew he meant it.

~Wendy Helfenbaum

88

Hearts on Fire

Poetry spills from the cracks of a broken heart,
but flows from one which is loved.
~Christopher Paul Rubero

Stephen and Nina had a relationship that many of our friends envied. They were in love and they were best friends, soul mates. On the rare occasion when Nina visited our family without Stephen, everyone knew that Stephen and Nina would speak to each other on the phone frequently throughout the visit. However, after twenty years of dating, no one expected them to get married; they were perfectly happy just the way they were.

As a classical composer, Stephen spent his days composing music and nurturing the musical talent of his students in his small New York apartment. Nina's apartment was one floor above Stephen's. Their dogs played in Nina's apartment as she worked for an architectural firm. Steven was passionate about music and about his students, many of whom became a part of their lives. Even as a young boy Stephen loved writing music, composing his first major work at the age of eight years. After decades of quietly composing classical music and teaching, one of his students submitted one of Stephen's compositions to an international award committee. Nina and Stephen were thrilled when Stephen won the prestigious award. The award winning composition required a particularly talented violinist. Stephen found the right musicians in Vienna and they were anxious to meet Stephen and to perform his composition.

As Stephen and Nina packed for their trip to Vienna where the composition was to premier, Nina was more excited and proud than Stephen was about his award. They anticipated a magical week, rich with beautiful music in historic Vienna.

The trip turned out to be all that Stephen and Nina had hoped it would be. Stephen's composition received a standing ovation; they fell in love with the musicians and with Vienna. It was a perfect trip—until one terrifying moment.

On the night before their departure for home, everything changed. Stephen was suddenly pale and short of breath. He whispered that he felt as if there was a fire burning in his chest. Nina had never seen him so pale and weak. Nina was terrified as she called for a doctor to help. When the doctor arrived, he rolled his eyes muttering, "Yes, yes, yes..." in response to her concerns. The doctor was sure that it was a simple case of a tourist who had a bit too much to eat. He politely tried to calm Nina down by assuring her that nothing serious was wrong as they walked through the hotel. However, a brief examination of Stephen transformed the doctor's demeanor. His face changed as he announced, "This man is very sick. We must get him to a hospital right away." Suddenly their Viennese dream had become a nightmare.

The fire that Stephen felt in his chest was his failing heart. Within minutes Stephen was holding onto life—strapped to a stretcher in a strange hospital in a strange city. Nina stood at Stephen's side, helpless and afraid. In broken English, the doctors explained that Stephen would not survive the long trip home to New York without open-heart surgery. The hospital team suggested that Nina return to the hotel to get an hour or two of sleep before the surgery. Nina was reluctant to leave, but Stephen trusted the doctors, and he also urged Nina to try to get a bit of sleep. Sleep was out of the question, but Nina returned to the hotel as instructed, knowing the days ahead would not be easy. Squeezing Stephen's hand, she promised to return quickly.

Not long after arriving to her hotel room, Nina received a call from the hospital. She was asked to return to the hospital right away with her passport. Fearing the worst, Nina left immediately. At the hospital, Nina saw a group of doctors and nurses talking in hushed voices, gathered by the door to Stephen's room. Although it was early in the morning, the doctors and nurses from the night shift were still at the hospital by Stephen's side, now joined by a new group who had just arrived to work the day shift. They all seemed to be waiting for something or someone. Several of the nurses were crying, and others avoided eye contact as Nina walked toward them. Nina was numb with fear.

Stephen's doctor approached Nina and explained that Stephen refused to have the life-saving heart surgery. He smiled and said, "Stephen wishes to postpone the surgery until you are married."

"Married?" Nina replied.

"Yes—married!" the doctor explained, smiling, "And we don't have much time." Stephen's hospital team had been hard at work during the night. As Nina entered Stephen's room, she found the nurses in tears holding makeshift bouquets made of carefully folded hospital linens. Through a jungle of tubes and monitors Nina could see that Stephen clutched a wrinkled marriage license and a ring in his hands. The doctor, who was now transformed into Stephen's best man, stood smiling next to Stephen as he lay in the intensive care bed.

Nina reached through the tubes and machines to hold Stephen's hand. "Marry me?" Stephen whispered. Now speechless, Nina nodded yes. The local magistrate had all of the necessary papers as he stood at the end of the bed ready to perform the wedding ceremony. Despite his failing heart, Stephen beamed as they exchanged their vows.

Stephen's proposal was his most beautiful composition. The doctors allowed Nina to squeeze Stephen's hand one last time as he was wheeled into surgery. Nina waited for word as the hours passed. Finally, the doctor came from the operating room to tell Nina that Stephen had survived the surgery. In the weeks that followed,

Stephen's broken heart healed with the help of his doctors and their new friends in Vienna. The hospital staff and the musicians who performed Stephen's piece became part of the eclectic, extended family at Stephen's bedside. After a long recovery, the newlywed couple returned to New York where they are still enjoying love, life, and an occasional visit from their new family from Vienna.

~Robin Heydenberk

89

Message in a Bottle

Faith is a passionate intuition.
~William Wordsworth

My mom called to tell me that our home church in Pinedale, Wyoming, was finally getting a new pastor. The pastoral position had been vacant for months. Pastor Meadows was moving from Kansas, where he had led a small country church for several years. I had to smile at the name. Like a pastor, in the meadow, protecting his sheep.

I returned home for the Christmas holidays, excited to meet the man behind the name. A few days before Christmas, when I accompanied my mom to a music rehearsal at the church, I met Bryan, Pastor Meadows' son. He was standing in the back of the sanctuary, having come with his mom to the same rehearsal. He, too, was home for a holiday college break.

As the days passed, I kept thinking about Bryan. I was being silly. Bryan and I had only talked twice — that first night and briefly again at the Christmas service. He had appeal, but I had resolved not to date until I finished college. Besides, I would be spending the entire next semester in Peru to study art and literature. My flight was just weeks away.

A few days after Christmas, I still could not get Bryan off my mind. Tossing some clean clothes into my suitcase, I suddenly dropped to my knees, closed my eyes, and prayed: "Dear God, if it is Your will that this guy is supposed to have a purpose in my life, show me. If not, get him out of my head."

That afternoon, I returned home from the post office and realized I had forgotten to mail an important letter that had to go out immediately. I braved a blizzard and icy roads to return to the post office with that one envelope. It was on that second trip, as I was walking back out to my truck, that I bumped into Bryan, who happened to be on a walk with his mom. She ducked into the post office, and in the half-moment Bryan and I stood alone in the post office entrance, he asked me out.

Fast forward to a winter Friday night one year later at Gustavus Adolphus College in St. Peter, Minnesota. It was two days before my twenty-second birthday. I walked across campus thinking about dinner in the college cafeteria. Friday night meant cream cheese crab rangoons. I was starving. I would meet my roommate in our dorm room, and together we would trek up the hill to the cafeteria for dinner like we had done every other Friday for the past four years.

I walked into the room and dropped my flute on the grungy yellow couch. She was sitting at her desk. She was very still. Her expression—was she hiding something?

Then I noticed a small bottle on my desk, capped with a cork. Inside it, a note.

What?

I remembered the conversation well—how, months ago, on a spring afternoon with Bryan, I had told him how I had always dreamed of receiving a message in a bottle. Yes, I was one of those girls. I was a sap.

Now, here it was. A message in a bottle. For me.

I think I uttered a few incomprehensible syllables. I don't remember. But I do remember my roommate's stone face, the words she said while trying so hard not to crack a smile: "You need to change, for dinner. And you are not eating dinner with me tonight."

I had a million questions. Where was he? How did he get here? He went to school at Purdue in Northern Indiana, 500 miles away. Change clothes? What in the world would I wear?

The questions came out in shrieks, a stuttering of repeated sentences.

She remained a rock. "First, you get out of your jeans. Then, we look in your closet…."

I think she got me dressed. I think she chose some jewelry for me, and I think she uncorked the bottle and took out the note, reminding me I had to read it before I saw him.

My message in a bottle was written in pencil on two beige sheets of paper:

I am in love, but somehow it's more than just love. How strongly I felt about love when I told you "I love you" for the first time pales in comparison to how I feel about love now.

It's your smile that I can't get enough of. It's your support when all else in my life seems to be upside down. It's walking hand in hand along the Chicago waterfront. It's all these things and more. I could go on for pages and pages about all the things I love about Kate Neely, but no matter how much I write there still would be more. The problem is that there are no words for this "more." It's something that even in my wildest dreams I never would have thought possible to feel. It's love, but still it is something more.

The only thing that I can say or write is, I love you, Katie. I love you now, and I will love you forever. With that, there is only one thing I can give you for your birthday. Meet me at the front doors to the chapel. I'll be waiting for you.

I remember walking up the hill to the chapel alone. I remember shaking, taking deep breaths, uttering three- and four-word prayers while I coaxed myself to put one foot in front of the other.

I remember standing at the back door of the chapel. Wondering if he saw me before I saw him. Then, there he was, in the back of the church, coming toward me.

I don't remember what he said, except for those four all-important words: "Will you marry me?" I remember crumpling into his arms as soon as I saw a flash of a ring.

I didn't answer for a long time. Not because I didn't have an answer—I simply could not push it out of me. I cried. I shook. I kissed him over and over. Finally, he said quietly, "You haven't answered."

Yes. Yes and yes a thousand times over. This was the man I would spend the rest of my life with.

~Kate Meadows

90

My Love Is Like an Extension Cord

You have to leave the city of your comfort and go into the wilderness
of your intuition. What you'll discover will be wonderful.
What you'll discover is yourself.
~Alan Alda

After studying and working in Philadelphia for six years, I returned to my parents' house in Queens to figure out what my next step might be. Through a good friend, I met Tom. We were both from Queens, both had traveled abroad, both were successful young professionals who aspired to do something unique with our lives.

On the first night we really talked, Tom told me about backpacking through China and how he met Peace Corps volunteers along the way and what interesting lives they led. We discussed how amazing it would be to join the Peace Corps someday. We started dating and went to an information session for the U.S. Peace Corps. The speaker informed the group that the only way two people could serve together was if they were married. It had only been a few months, so we were not ready for that level of commitment.

Months went by and Tom and I fell more and more in love. We spent a lot of time in his apartment, and I was helping him make it more comfortable. One day, we needed an extension cord and I mentioned that, after clearing out my parents' basement, I had found several. He said he'd have to get some from me in the near future.

Days later, I left work feeling quite sick. Tom had promised to pick me up at the train station near his apartment since I was feeling so ill. But when I arrived he was nowhere to be found. I called and he said he had gone to my parents' house to get an extension cord from my father and was caught up there. It seemed strange to me, but I didn't say a word. I walked to the apartment fighting chills, drank some orange juice, and put myself to bed. He was gone for some time and finally returned. I was tired, cranky and, most of all, suspicious. I questioned whether he was really on an errand to get an extension cord. He pulled a long white cord out of his pocket and held it up for me to see. "Here it is," he said. "Why would I lie?" Hmph. I turned over and went back to sleep.

After 9/11, I decided to quit my job and make a radical change in my life. My last day at work was Monday, October 1st so that my health benefits would extend for another month. Tom announced he'd take me out to dinner to celebrate and we ended up at the Four Seasons in their lobby lounge. It was beautiful and fun. I was so happy and felt very free having just quit my job. Tom seemed anxious, getting up several times during the first part of the meal to use the bathroom. I sipped on some champagne and watched the celebrities like John and Joan Cusack eating dinner nearby.

Finally, Tom returned from his last bathroom visit.

"Are you okay?" I asked.

"Yeah. Well, there is something I want to ask you." He got down on one knee and I could no longer see. My eyes were filled with tears. He took something out of his pocket. I couldn't see what it was. Everything was a blur.

"What is that?" I asked.

"An extension cord."

Thankfully, it was not an extension cord. It was an engagement ring made out of the clustered diamond earring that belonged to my grandmother. He had gone to my parents' house that night, months before, to ask their permission for my hand in marriage and, of course, for the diamond earring that I had put aside to be made into an engagement ring for whomever was thoughtful enough to ask my parents' permission. My father was late getting home and Tom was stuck there, waiting to speak to him. I called and he got caught so he made up an excuse about an extension cord to try to make his reason for being there more plausible.

Kneeling there, Tom looked so sincere, so handsome, so warm and loving, so willing and wanting to make me happy. I, of course, said yes.

Five months after our wedding, our plane touched down in Kyiv as we began our commitment as Peace Corps volunteers. Everyone always thinks of Ukraine as being such a cold place but we lived in the beautiful western Ukrainian city of Lviv, learned the language almost fluently and made many friends, both American and Ukrainian. Despite its challenges, we found our lives there full of warmth and friendship from those around us as well as those back home who supported us with visits, phone calls, letters and cards.

Fourteen months after returning from Ukraine, our daughter was born.

Fourteen months after that we bought our first house.

About a week after moving in, I unpacked an extension cord from a box.

And I smiled.

~Cristina T. Lopez-O'Keeffe

91

Relationship Status

Isn't it cool when the days that are supposed to feel good, actually do?
~Jim Carrey

We had finally come to the last day of our cruise, which just happened to coincide with our two-year anniversary. As we snuggled and exchanged anniversary kisses, we turned on the ship's news channel just in time to hear the cruise director read a message that I had dedicated to Will, my "fiancé." We actually weren't engaged yet, but we had introduced each other that way on the cruise, since we knew that we would get a free bottle of champagne if our shout-out made it on the morning show.

That evening, feeling relaxed, sun kissed, and blissful, we headed to the Lido Deck for a champagne sunset that was the perfect setting for a proposal. I stared into his gorgeous blue eyes, and I knew that he was about to ask the question that I had been waiting for all my life. Every move he made, my heart beat a little faster, anticipating that he would reach into a pocket or get down on one knee. Only he never did, and my heart sank. As lovely as this celebration was, I was disappointed. If it didn't happen now, I knew it wasn't happening on the cruise. That was it, and our time was up.

After sunset, I tried to enjoy the rest of our evening, but not much could distract me. I had been selected to perform as Brittney Spears in the final night's show and even that didn't clear my mind. You would think donning an itchy wig with pigtails and a tartan skirt would do the trick, but not in this situation. Nevertheless, the show went off without a hitch and we adjourned to the main lobby to have our "photo op" for the 2,000 or so people there to see us.

The cruise director then announced that there was a guest with something important to say. I wasn't paying attention with all of the commotion going on, so when I heard Will's voice my heart jumped. Suddenly, I realized what he was saying — I had misinformed them of our relationship status and he was not my fiancé. Hold up, WHAT? For all I knew, he was breaking up with me in public... in front of 2,000 people. My mind was going a million miles a minute. That is, until he said, "Janna, I spoke to your father," pulled a little box out of his pocket, and got down on one knee.

You'd think that, after all the waiting, I would immediately have said yes. I was ready to say yes! But instead, without thinking, I threw myself into his arms and said "I love you, but I HATE you for proposing to me while I am dressed like Britney Spears!" Luckily, he knew that meant yes, and I am happy to say we have now been married for three years. There has never been a question of our relationship status since then, and there never will be again.

~Janna R. Bogert

The Dating Game

Lessons in Love

Life can only be understood backward, but it must be lived forward.

~Soren Kierkegaard

92

An Empty Dream House

Relationship is an art. The dream that two people create is more difficult to master than one.
~Don Miguel Ruiz

As a child I spent countless hours turning the pages of the *Sears, Roebuck* catalogue and dreaming about the fancy, spotless rooms and bright colors, so different from the worn browns of our farmhouse. Thirty years later it looked as if my dream house was finally within reach when my boyfriend Brian and I started discussing marriage. I thought it went without saying that we'd each sell our current residence and purchase a new place together. Brian assumed I'd move into his much-loved home.

The moment I walked into my boyfriend's house, I knew I could never live there. Facing north on the mossy slope of a hill, the downstairs was dark and the upstairs a labyrinth of small, leaky rooms. In my modern condominium, skylights brightened every space. I'd long admired the cool perfection of minimalist designs in *Architectural Digest*.

I stifled my own sobs, like a thwarted child, after we discussed permanent living arrangements. Our first major disagreement, the conflict blindsided me.

"You can redecorate if you want," Brian offered, a tempting carrot.

"I'm willing to sell my home, why can't you do the same?" I countered, optimistic that he'd come around to my point of view.

My parents welcomed Brian with relief, after my romantic false starts with an ardent hairstylist and a rock musician without a band. In November my mother invited him to throw his name into the hat for our holiday gift exchange. On Christmas day, one month shy of our first anniversary together, Brian gave me a necklace with a diamond pendant.

"It's the right stone, but in the wrong place," my father teased. Dad was closer to the truth than he knew: A future together dangled in sight, if only we could solve our housing problem.

As the months passed we each held fast to our dream and replayed our arguments like a warped record. We shelved our discussions of marriage.

When we weren't talking real estate our relationship flourished. We hiked the trails of Marin, laughed at Woody Allen movies, and vacationed in Mendocino and Santa Fe. Brian's two teenage daughters accepted me as I listened without parental judgment to their problems, and they eventually started calling me their bonus mom.

But our standoff escalated every time we discussed living arrangements.

"You're choosing your ugly house over me!" I cried, tears sliding down my cheeks.

"You're asking me to sell the place my daughters have considered home since my divorce. And for no good reason!" Brian crossed his arms over his chest.

Recklessly we raised the stakes—Brian refused to accompany me to open houses; I wouldn't set foot on his property.

After three years of dating, spending time with my family became increasingly awkward. Brian stayed at the John Jay Inn when we visited my old-fashioned parents, and we'd meet surreptitiously in his hotel room. We skipped a reunion at my rustic mountain cabin when my brother questioned our sleeping arrangements, hinting we'd be a bad influence on the niece and nephew I adored.

Still unmarried at the age of forty-two, I'd historically cut and run when conflict threatened a romance, and I considered that option now. Our housing deadlock seemed hopeless.

But the thought of leaving Brian made my stomach churn.

As a last resort I suggested couples therapy, believing a neutral third party would expose my boyfriend's unreasonable attitude. Dr. Brown's office was furnished like a cozy living room of childhood, the threads of the tweed sofa worn thin by decades of jittery clients. We settled together on his couch, holding hands, and I began describing how happy and compatible we were.

Prodded by the therapist, I outlined my rationale for buying a new house. Brian restlessly shifted his feet, anxious to plead his case. When it was his turn to speak, his voice rose with the emotional heat of his arguments, and I drifted to the sofa's side, hugging its padded arm like a life vest.

"Jan, you're adamant about purchasing a dream house together," the therapist said at the end of the session.

"And Brian, I hear you saying you're strongly attached to the home you've owned for twenty years." Brian nodded vigorously.

"Your attitudes toward your housing stalemate are very similar," Dr. Brown summarized.

"Wait a minute," I interrupted. "I'm willing to sell my house. All I'm asking is that he does the same," I said, contrasting my flexibility with Brian's stubbornness. I'd begun to regret agreeing to a male therapist, who'd missed the obvious inequity of our positions.

"You want to sell your condo, so that's not a sacrifice for you. If Brian sold his house, it would be an emotional loss. You're each asking the other to give up something important, but aren't prepared to meet halfway. Neither of you has been willing to compromise."

Several weeks into therapy I discussed our progress with an unmarried girlfriend.

"Compromise," she scoffed, "doesn't that mean not getting what you want?" Coming from a woman who ran from commitment, her quip opened my eyes to my single-minded focus; my viewpoint sounded petulant and selfish. The truth struck me head-on—by refusing to find middle ground, I risked losing the man I loved.

While Brian was at work I brought my metal tape gauge and graph paper to his house and reconfigured the rabbit warren. Eliminating one small room, I enlarged the two remaining bedrooms and created a new master suite. An architect improved my ideas, raising the roof and adding clerestory windows for sunlight.

Brian loved the plans transforming his house into a sunny, contemporary space, but he balked at the price tag. "When I said you could redecorate, I thought you'd paint a couple of rooms," he objected.

Eventually we met halfway. Brian consented to my improvements, and I agreed to live in his house.

Four years after our first date, we moved into our remodeled home.

I still page through home decor magazines, attracted to austere designs with a single white orchid on the coffee table. But I see what's missing in those empty rooms when my husband walks through our front door.

~Janice Westerling

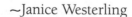

93

Love, Loss, and Cake

*After eating chocolate you feel godlike, as though you can conquer enemies,
lead armies, entice lovers.*
~Emily Luchetti

I used to be a baker. Not a good one, really. But I did bake. It was a good stress buster and I enjoyed the cakes, the brownies, the buckeyes, the cookies. I always enjoyed my concoctions, but I never really thought they were worth sharing. Not until I was with my boyfriend, Greg.

It was perfect when I was with Greg. Greg cooked. He concocted crazy pastas and delicious guacamole and risotto and it always tasted like it came from some fancy gourmet restaurant. I don't cook. But I presented him with dessert to follow our dinners. Lots and lots of cakes. My cakes were a joke, simply because there were so many.

"Want some cake?" I'd ask.

"What? Isn't it gone?" he'd laugh.

"There's a new one!" I'd grin, winking at him as I unveiled a new peanut butter or cinnamon or chocolate cake.

After we broke up, I didn't bake for an entire year. The last time I baked a cake was his birthday, and it was my famous "Darn Good Chocolate Cake" (name passed on from my mother). It was a joke all night with his friends. "When do we get to try Carrie's Darn Good Chocolate Cake?" Somehow, though, we ended up at a late showing of a movie and at one a.m., no one felt bad telling Greg they were going home and not up for trying my famous cake.

So I yawned as I lit his birthday candles, and sang "Happy Birthday" as I paraded it to the table in front of him. "It looks amazing, honey," he said. "I love you." And we devoured the chocolate cake together. Just the two of us. And then we passed out in a chocolate coma.

A month after his birthday, we broke up. Losing him, I lost the best friend I'd ever had. I lost the comfort that one can only receive from being in a loving and caring relationship. A comfort that can't be rivaled by anything — although a good chocolate cake comes pretty close to that comfort.

And so, for months and months and months, the thought of baking a cake sent me into tears, reminding me of the comfort and love I'd lost. I couldn't bake a cake and not share it with Greg. I couldn't look at my mixer and not think of Greg. I couldn't see the words "Darn Good Chocolate Cake" in that order. But then my mom mentioned her blueberry muffin cake. And I thought about how long it had been since I'd had it and how delicious it was. And so I set about making one.

It took me ten minutes to find the Bundt pan, because it was shoved behind every other kitchen item I own. Because it hadn't been used since Greg's birthday, twelve months earlier.

When the blueberry cake was done, I felt triumphant. It was like coming out of a cave and finding comfort again. Only this time I wasn't sharing it with anyone. I was okay with me, myself, and I... and a piece of delicious cake!

Not long after I started baking again, I found my true love, Dustin. Just last month, Dustin and I laughed with pure joy as we shoved wedding cake into each other's mouths. Perhaps I needed to be okay alone — just me and the cake — before I was ready to really move on.

~Carrie O'Maley Voliva

94

Uncomfortable

Be willing to be uncomfortable. Be comfortable being uncomfortable. It may get tough, but it's a small price to pay for living a dream.
~Peter McWilliams

I was at my boyfriend Richard's house over the weekend and his big, sweet cat came and plopped himself on me. He was stretched at an obviously awkward angle with his little head burrowed into my chest. Richard made some comment about how much Mittens loved me and I responded with, "No, I think Mittens just likes having a comfortable place to lie." Richard's response: "No way. Look at him. That doesn't look comfortable—that looks like love."

"That doesn't look comfortable—that looks like love."

Such a seemingly innocent, yet profound statement. I mean, think about it. How many times does this end up being the case? Love just really isn't always all that comfortable. You know?

I watched my cousin feeding my grandpa in the nursing home a few weeks ago. She stood there for a very long time, and I'm sure she got tired of all of that standing. I'm sure her legs were sore. I'm sure her arms got sore from the time it took to feed him. I'm sure it was hard trying to understand what he was telling her and what he was asking for through his incoherent rambling. I'm sure it was... well... uncomfortable.

That doesn't look comfortable—that looks like love.

I remember watching my daughter once serve as a capo for my boyfriend's guitar. No, really. He was using a capo-less guitar that didn't belong to him to play a requested song for my family at a holiday get-together. My daughter jumped up and offered to hold it for him so it would sound right. She stood there and pressed down on the strings as he played. It was just so darn cute. And afterwards? Bless her heart, she had grooves in her little fingers from where she had to press so hard. But she was so proud to have helped.

That doesn't look comfortable—that looks like love.

I watched my sister stand for hours beside the incubators of her newborn premature twin babies. I know she got tired standing there. I know it wasn't the most comfortable thing to stand there and hold a syringe up above the babies so that their milk could flow down through their feeding tube. I know that as a brand new mom it certainly wasn't comfortable trying to work around all of the wires and monitors to change a teeny tiny little squirming baby's diaper. I know it's not comfortable giving up hours and hours of her days traveling to and from the hospital that is close to two hours away while she continues to take care of them during the many weeks they remain in neonatal intensive care until they're big enough to go home. But she does it.

That doesn't look comfortable—that looks like love.

My boyfriend and I have been through some tough times. We both have had issues to rise above and move past. Sometimes we've given up temporarily, but we keep finding our way back. We sometimes find ourselves surrounded by reminders that take us back to things we're trying to forget. We sometimes have outside influences that, knowingly or not, chip away at what we're trying to build together. And sometimes our own selfishness and insecurities do the chipping without any help. No, love is definitely not always butterflies and rainbows. Sometimes it's just plain... uncomfortable. It hurts, it's hard, it takes work. But yet, we stay. Why do we do that? Why are we still here?

Well. You know.

That doesn't look comfortable—that looks like love.

~Melissa Halsey Caudill

95

The Gym Rat

If you doubt yourself, then indeed you stand on shaky ground.
~Henrik Ibsen

My previous relationship had lasted for four years. We had started out as best friends and there was never a typical "first date." It seemed as though my ex knew everything about me, as if through osmosis. Needless to say, when we broke up, I was lost in the dating world. Start again? Meet someone new? Impossible.

Months went by without a date in sight. I had almost given up hope when a girls' trip to the mountains came along. And there I met him. Tall and handsome, he stood out in the mountain town crowd. My friend spotted him first and moved in for the kill, only to discover that he was a principal back in the city. The inner matchmaker in her came to life as she said, "My friend is a first grade teacher; you have to meet her!"

The principal and I talked on the dance floor. The music was loud, the crowd wild, and he was beyond dreamy. Suddenly he was asking if I would like to go to dinner when we returned to the city. Dinner? As in a real and true first date? My jaw nearly dropped to the ground. I thought dates only occurred in movies, or on TV. My mind raced and I vaguely remember myself saying, "Sure, call me."

"He'll never call," I said to my girlfriends on the drive home. But just in case he did, we went to work. Google, Facebook, Twitter, Instagram, LinkedIn. You name it, we checked it. Each method of social media confirmed it: he was a catch. One day passed. Then two. On day three, low and behold, a voicemail.

Fast forward to Friday night. Fifty outfits later my roommate and I decided on a flowy top with black skinny pants. Perfect. (Dreamy later informed me that my shirt looked like a bag. Noted.)

Just like in the movies, he picked me up right on time. He came to my front door, opened the car door, pulled out my chair at dinner. Was I living in a fairy tale? As I began to hear wedding bells somewhere in the distance, my fantasy came to a crashing halt. He did something that I wasn't expecting, wasn't prepared for, and hadn't rehearsed! He looked at me over a glass of wine and inquired, "What do you do in your free time?"

I panicked. My mind went blank. I know, this sounds like an easy question to answer. But something was wrong; I was a blank canvas with no control over the English language. What do I like to do?

Before I knew it, the word vomit began. "Well, I love to run. Ski, hike, bike," I began to rattle off every athletic activity that came to mind. Several of which I had never even tried. "Can't forget yoga, Pilates, strength training, rock climbing, swimming..." Somewhere between kayaking, triathlons, and deep sea diving, reality set in. What was I saying? But it was too late. He was intrigued.

He began to ask questions about the marathons I had run, the oceans I swam across, and the personal trainers I had worked with. My mind raced. How could I admit to a white lie, okay a huge lie, on my first date? I frantically tried to change the subject.

As the weeks passed, he tried relentlessly to take our dates into the great outdoors. Rent a tandem road bike? Climb an early morning fourteener (14,000-foot peak)? Join him at his next bench press competition? At first I tried to deflect. I already worked out that day, my knee was bothering me, my friend had borrowed my bike. But my excuses started to wear thin, and so did his patience. As I was busy drowning in a sea of lies, my dream romance was fizzling.

Needless to say, fizzling turned to fizzled. My days as an avid exercise enthusiast were over, as was my fairytale romance. As I came to terms with being back at square one, I felt a subtle relief: pretending to be a gym rat was over. I could be me again! And me I was. I took the next months to rediscover myself as a single woman. What did I like to do without my ex? What drove me, what was I passionate about?

The journey of self-discovery was an incredible one, and establishing my independence felt good. Really good. And so today I say, bring on the first dates! I am ready to face the dating world again. But not without a small list of my hobbies in my pocket, and a slightly less flowy shirt.

~Kate Lynn

96

Not So Scandalous After All

To free us from the expectations of others, to give us back to ourselves —
there lies the great, singular power of self-respect.
~Joan Didion

I t all started in a coffee shop in Chicago. It was November 2012 and I had just returned from a business trip to find no work waiting for me back at the office. To help while away the empty hours, I retreated each morning to the coffee shop around the corner. Undercover-style, I would tuck my Kindle inside my winter coat, wedging it in my armpit, before I nonchalantly padded toward the elevators.

"Tall vanilla mocha," I'd say. My hand would dip into my coat and the Kindle would appear from the dark recesses. I couldn't help but notice that there was a ruggedly handsome young man whose daily routine also involved a roughly hour-long interlude with coffee and a book.

November and December blew through Chicago, and this man and I continued to get our caffeine fixes and work through our reading lists. I fancied sometimes that his eyes would glance my way as he passed near to get his sugar. I observed that he seemed well liked by the baristas; he was a friendly sort of guy. I noted that he was careful with his trash, and would even clean up after others; he was a courteous sort of guy. I knew I would never talk to him, but I thought that if I were a weaker woman, I just might do it and like it. But I was married, so he would always remain a mystery.

I went on a wonderful vacation with my husband from Christmas to the New Year. On vacation, we were perfect together. But the problem is, most of life takes place out in the real world. Out there, I was the camel and my husband was the straw-loader. I habitually shrugged it off, and was dealing well enough, until the day my parents held a sort of intervention for me. It all happened so fast. My dad had hired a private investigator. My mom and dad wanted to tell me together that my husband was a pathological liar and they had the proof in writing. It didn't hit me too hard then. It was a spacey feeling. My knee-jerk reaction was to fly to counseling and fix my husband's lying.

But in the wake of our first lying counseling session—during which the therapist advised my husband to do things that would upset me and then practice telling me the hard truth—I began to have my doubts. Suffice it to say that evening did not turn out well. That night it hit me that this camel had just had a log thrown on it. I was in some serious trouble.

The Monday after my intervention, I spoke to the coffee guy. "Is that the new Kindle Paperwhite?" It seemed scandalous and I felt guilty, but I was so hurt and angry and altogether felt like my mind was unraveling and my life was falling apart—I threw caution to the wind. Pure weakness.

Over the next few weeks we fell into a routine. We sat at the same table, me with my double-steel-walled mug and him with his Venti cardboard cup, and we talked about books. It was great. It was more than great—it was wonderful. He was smart and interesting, and he just seemed so very, very easy to be with.

Almost exactly a month after my intervention, unbeknownst to my husband, I finalized moving plans for him. It was such a wretched feeling. I felt like a crouching predator, a slinking spider in her web, waiting for the kill. Meanwhile, I imagined that Venti must be wondering what sort of cruel joke I was pulling on him. After all, I'd been wearing a wedding ring this entire time! And by the fourth week the innocent book talk had evolved into discussion of family, jobs, school, likes, dislikes... basically, it had begun to take on the feel of the longest first date ever. And all along I tried to avoid mentioning the obvious and I felt he tried to avoid asking questions that would result in me mentioning the obvious.

That was one of the worst weeks of my life, feeling like a lurking villain at home and a conniving adulterer at the coffee shop. I was despicable. How had I screwed things up so badly?

That second weekend of February, my husband moved out. Monday found me anxiously waiting at our table, wedding ring gone. Venti never showed. I didn't have his phone number or e-mail address—nothing. I was too late; he'd slipped through my fingers. I held my Kindle in my hand, but I just stared over it at the door, waiting.

My paranoia ended the very next day. I told Venti everything and the following evening we went on a date. That's right; we left the coffee shop. So wonderful, but so terrible too! I had a date for Valentine's Day the week after my husband moved out. It was wrong, wrong, wrong! I was so ashamed I didn't even tell my very best friend, with whom I typically share every last disgusting detail of my life. I waited many weeks to mention Venti to my family. It was a shock for them. I saw my book club in February and told all my friends that I was getting a divorce. Only a couple weeks later I met up with them all again and brought my new boyfriend. Scandalous!

And from there ensued a series of awkward incidences and conversations with friends, family, and co-workers. I hated that I had to be secretive and ashamed about my new relationship. I wanted to shout to the rooftops what good luck I'd had, to find such a wonderful man so quickly. I desperately wanted to be able to share those blissful feelings you have when you're flying through a whirlwind of a romance. But I found this incredibly indecent. I felt weighed down by guilt. It was a mental game to let myself be happy. If I could've changed things and met him at a more respectable date in the future—would I? Should I? Was I horrible for answering no?

And finally it clicked. My friends, my family—none of them

were judging me. They were only worried about me. I was the one judging me. All of my closest and dearest family and friends, the ones I really cared about—never once did I feel their judgment. They understood because they know me. Trust in your family and friends; you may find they are kinder to you than you are to yourself. Through them, I am able to accept that it's okay for me to think of my tale as a love story, instead of a scandal.

~Maggie Anderson

97

Breaking Up
Is Hard to Do

*In the end there doesn't have to be anyone who understands you.
There just has to be someone who wants to.*
~Robert Brault, www.robertbrault.com

Her long dark hair shone as she came toward us in the low light of the bar, and I thought how young and lovely she was. Did we know her? She was coming right for us. Suddenly she knelt down next to the little marble table where our drinks stood, and said, "I'm sorry to bother you. I just wanted to tell you that you two really give me hope. You've obviously been together a long time. Maybe love can work."

Wayne and I looked at each other. "Oh, thank you," I said, and smiled at her in what I hoped was an encouraging way.

"Of course love can work," Wayne said. "Don't give up."

She stood up and smiled. "Well, thanks so much," she said. "Maybe it will work out for me too." She turned and walked out the door into the night.

We were silent. A few moments before, we had decided that being together was too difficult and that we'd be better off apart. We had just broken up. We had come in to this bar for one last drink together, and then we were going to call it quits.

Now we had given a young person hope. Maybe it was because we were holding hands.

Although it may have looked that way, Wayne and I had not been together for a long time. At that point our relationship was less than a year old, and it was rocky. Each of us had come to it with issues we needed to work on. After all, we were both in our sixties and you don't get to that age, single, divorced, or otherwise available, without some issues. That's where we were, and it was a hard and uncomfortable place to be.

"I told her not to give up," Wayne said. "Maybe I should listen to myself."

"I know. I thought about that too."

"Do you think we should have told her we had just broken up?"

"No," I said. "That would have been mean. She really needed to believe in us."

"Well, then. Maybe we shouldn't break up. Maybe we should keep trying."

"Maybe you're right." I didn't know whether I was relieved or not. Our relationship was a lot of work.

We sputtered along. A few months later, Wayne enrolled in a master's degree program in counseling psychology at a local college. He did it because he thought it would help him "figure me out." I didn't think I needed to be figured out. I was fine. He was the one who was obsessive and afraid of relationships. But I was glad he enrolled, because I thought it would take his mind off me, and trying to control me and define me. That was hard to take.

I liked him though. In addition to being obsessive and afraid, he was smart. He knew a lot about various sciences, he had a special relationship with machines—he could fix almost anything—and he loved to dance. Most important, he was willing to talk about his feelings. I had never known a man who could talk. A part of me really wanted to make it work.

As part of his curriculum, Wayne was required to do fifty hours of personal therapy. He chose a male therapist in the city he lived in, and started seeing him once a week. He told me he talked about me in those sessions.

One day the therapist said to him, "When are you going to start talking about yourself? It sounds to me like you are going to have to find a way to get comfortable with uncertainty if you want to keep this relationship." Well, that was the issue, wasn't it?

Uncertainty was hard for Wayne—it was something he'd brought from his childhood and it caused him major anxiety. For my part, I had learned never to be predictable as a way of coping with my own upbringing. It was easy to see why we had conflict.

After a few more months we decided, once again, that it was too difficult to be together. Although we had a lot in common, we also had opposite styles and neither one of us felt we could or would change to accommodate the other. Bravely, we decided to let each other go so we could each be happy some other way. Wayne wanted me to go with him to see his therapist. The therapist would help us part with no hard feelings.

I went with him. The therapist held a parting ceremony with us, where we named the things we liked about each other and where we also named the reasons we were parting. Wayne and I both cried. In the end we vowed to respect each other and our decision, and then we turned to leave.

We had hardly gotten out the door before we were in each other's arms, both saying we were too sad to part. Maybe we'd each have to change in order to make things work. Breaking up really was hard to do too.

Wayne and I have been together nearly ten years now. He no longer worries about me or tries to control me, and I try to speak openly to him about the way I think. I have exposed my system of coping, something I never thought I'd do. Wayne was able to get to this place by facing down his anxiety—not an easy thing to do. He decided to trust me, even though I couldn't be pinned down to anything resembling "predictable." He has shown great courage.

We both made difficult concessions in order to realize our goal, which was to have a happy relationship that was fun for both of us. Even after all this time, we still get comments from people young enough to be our grandchildren when we go out.

"You two are so cute," whispered a pretty young girl who was standing behind me as I waited to pick up my drink from the bar at a club. Wayne and I had been dancing, easily the oldest patrons there. "When I grow up, I want to be just like you."

I smiled happily. "Thank you," I whispered back. "Never stop having fun and you'll always be that way." I thought back to the dark-haired girl who said we had given her hope so many years ago, and was glad we hadn't given up too soon, even though we'd certainly tried to.

~Dana Hill

98

Thicker than Blood

Nobody has ever measured, even poets, how much a heart can hold.
~Zelda Fitzgerald

"He's ten years older than me!" I said to my friend, Kathy, as she tried talking me into meeting her husband's best friend.

"You don't have to marry him; just go out with him. I hate seeing two of my closest friends hurting the way you are and thought you'd be good company for each other."

Recently widowed at the age of thirty-two, I was anxious to be married again. Bill, on the other hand, was separated, with no plans to ever have another wife. Yet, once I agreed to meet him, we clicked and started spending all our available time together.

With four daughters between us, alone time was a precious commodity. We spent hours on the phone, talking late into the night. With each passing month, we grew closer and closer. Yet, we still had opposite marriage goals for our lives.

It wasn't long before I was, as they say, head over heels in love with Bill. He'd walk into a room and take my breath away. However, my feelings made him uncomfortable. After all, he was still in love with his wife, and wanted nothing more than to work things out with her. While I agreed that would be the best thing for him and for their two daughters, it was apparent the family was not going to reunite.

He admitted his struggle one night as we sat listening to The Moody Blues. "I don't know what to do," he said. "I have strong feelings for you and can't imagine my life without you, but I still love her."

"Of course, you do," I empathized. "I'm not asking you to stop loving her. Loving me doesn't preclude how you feel about her."

"I don't understand. How could I possibly love both of you? It just isn't right."

"Who says it isn't? Don't you think I still love Jim?"

"That's different. Your husband is dead."

I paused, trying to put my thoughts into words. "Do you remember how you felt about April when she was born?"

"I loved her with everything in me. What does that have to do with anything?"

"Well, when you found out you were going to have another baby, didn't you wonder how you could possibly love a second child the way you loved the first?"

Still confused, he answered me. "I guess so."

"So, when Mindy was born, did you have to take some of your love away from April in order to love her?"

"Of course not. I just loved her... as much as I loved her sister."

"Exactly," I said, confident my point was made, "you didn't have to split that love in two to share it. Your heart simply grew."

"That's a good way of putting it. But I still don't understand what that has to do with us," questioned Bill.

"Well, I'm not asking you to stop loving your first wife. She's the mother of your children and you were with her for over twenty years. Love like that doesn't go away. But that doesn't mean you can't love me, too. You just have to give your heart permission to grow."

Over the next few days, he thought about what I said. And then, it happened. Not only did he allow his heart to grow, but he also gave himself permission to say the words I desperately wanted to hear.

"I love you, Hana," he said gently, tears filling his eyes. "I really love you."

A few months later, sitting across the table from me at the restaurant where we'd had our first date, he asked me to marry him. Naturally, I said yes.

We've been married for over twenty years now. My children, who were only nine and seven when we wed, were blessed with the best daddy they could have hoped for. Now, with children of their own, Grandpap is the heart of the family.

"You'll never find anyone who will love Bethany and Jessica as much as Jim did," a relative told me the week after my husband's death.

She was wrong. Bill loves my girls, our girls, as much as he ever loved his own two daughters. Blood is thicker than water? Maybe. But love is much thicker than blood.

~Hana Haatainen Caye

99

Learning to Be a Grown-Up

Everyone is the age of their heart.
~Guatemalan Proverb

In a whirlwind six weeks, I graduated from college, moved back in with my parents, launched my career as a full-time freelance writer, and began dating a great guy named Paul. For as long as I could remember, my life had been as structured as a chess game — every piece in its place, every next move planned. I thrive on a sense of routine. When you're juggling classes, homework, a part-time job, and some semblance of a social life, you need to micro-organize your time to fit everything in.

But when I began dating Paul, I was feeling a little lost, still settling into a new routine of wide-open days without any imposed structure. My daily life was suddenly confusing, messy, uncertain. The world around me seemed fluid, at times even unstable. My checklist of "next steps" had vanished. I had the urge to stop people on the street and announce my new grown-up status. "Ta da! I am living on my own! I am part of the Real World! I am a Grown-Up!"

But I did not feel like a grown-up.

"When will I?" I wondered. I kept waiting for a ticket to the Secret World of Grown-Ups to drop into my lap. Adulthood seemed like an exclusive club I couldn't find the entrance to, no matter how diligently I searched and searched.

I met Paul at a young leaders mixer in my hometown. He was a writer for the local newspaper, and as a writer myself, we hit it off immediately. We talked all through the mixer; afterwards, he walked me to my car, and we continued talking and talking—neither of us wanted to say goodbye. My cheeks hurt from smiling. He was tall and handsome, with close-cropped dark hair and a boyish twinkle in his eyes, and he looked at me with such sincere interest. I couldn't remember the last time I felt so attractive and captivating. When he finally asked for my phone number, my hand shook as I wrote it down on the back of an old receipt. He gave me his business card, and I thought, "What a grown-up! He even has business cards!" As I drove home, a giddy smile on my face, I realized he made me feel like a grown-up, too.

If you had asked me then, I would have guessed Paul's age to be late twenties. He later admitted he would have guessed my age to be mid-twenties. On our first official date—a real grown-up date, where Paul cooked me dinner at his house and we drank nice bottled wine in real wineglasses—we discovered the true extent of our age gap: ten years. I was twenty-two; Paul was thirty-two.

"Well," Paul asked me. "How do you feel about this?"

Staring into his kind brown eyes, I thought back on the evening: a delicious homemade pasta dinner, three hours of easy conversation, a stroll through the darkened neighborhood streets, when I laced my arm through his and felt the inside of my stomach explode in butterflies. I knew how I felt about Paul, the person. Paul, the environmentalist who had a compost bin in his kitchen, read quirky science fiction, and often pedaled his bike to the pier to watch the sun set over the Pacific Ocean.

But how did I feel about Paul the thirty-two-year-old? Should it matter that he was thirty-two, as opposed to twenty-six, as opposed to twenty-two?

"I like you," I told Paul. "I feel a connection between us. But here's the thing: you're a grown-up. You have a job, a car, a house. You have your life together." I sighed. "My life is not together. I'm living with my parents. I'm driving the family car. I never know where my next writing assignment will come from. I feel like I'm trying to put together a puzzle without a picture on the box."

Paul laughed, lacing his hand through mine and squeezing it gently. "My life is exactly the same way," he said. "It may seem 'together' from the outside, but from the inside, it's an unpredictable mess. I hate to break it to you, but if I'm a grown-up, then you are, too."

At a family dinner a few weeks ago, my dad, the super-glue who holds our family together, mentioned that while his outer self has aged, inside he still feels like the sixteen-year-old high school tennis standout he once was, the world an unfurled map of opportunity and excitement spread out before him. My mother, who has a master's degree, manages her department at work, and keeps our household running, said she still feels at times like her anxiety-ridden twenty-one-year-old self, working at the campus dining hall, trying to figure out what to do with her life. My grandpa—who lived through the Great Depression, fought in World War II, saved countless lives during his career as a general surgeon, raised four children, and lost my grandma, the love of his life, eighteen years ago to a heart attack—confessed that he sometimes closes his eyes and becomes a fourteen-year-old boy again, fishing for trout and playing baseball on empty lots and learning to drive his father's Buick in the small farm town of his childhood.

Dating Paul helped me discover that I was approaching "adulthood" all wrong. He taught me that real adulthood is about embracing life's uncertainties rather than knowing everything. From him I learned that being a grown-up means that sometimes, behind the façade of thorough knowledge and preparation, you are actually flying by the seat of your pants. Paul and I only dated a few months—we ended up caring about each other more as friends than romantically—but I will always look back fondly on my time with him. I am grateful for our ten-year age gap, because it taught me that age truly is just a number. I now know that real life, regardless of your outer or inner age, is simply about trying your best, day by day by month by year, to be the best self you can be, to be open to the newness that life throws your way, and to love those around you as unselfishly and authentically as you can.

~Dallas Woodburn

100

No Middle Man Needed

Even when the future's not certain, our hearts can still be certain—
of love and happiness and all that's good.
~Terri Guillemets

I almost didn't do it. The nerves in my stomach had generated an icy chill that was working its way from my gut to my heart and into my throat. On this otherwise balmy spring day, I was freezing.

It had taken several weeks to gather what little courage I had, and if I didn't take action soon it would be too late. Besides, my courage was ready to run for the hills, and this anxiety was wearing me out. With the urgency of "now or never" pushing me forward, I did something I had never done before. I asked a guy for a date.

As the manager of the guys' varsity basketball team for most of my high school career, I went to all of the games and hung around the gym after practice. I developed strong friendships with many of the players. I loved it.

Gabe was one of them. Although he was a junior, he was also in my sociology class, so I knew him better than most of the other players. With his sandy brown hair, easy gait, and eyes that were continually seeking the best in people, Gabe looked like a younger version of Ashton Kutcher. He was humble, kind, and funny too. I was always up for a laugh, and over time, we had become good friends.

Because I routinely hung out at the gym, Gabe didn't hesitate when I asked to speak to him outside afterward. The gym opened to another outdoor basketball court that doubled as a student hangout, and that afternoon the usual teenagers were chatting, doing homework, and on their way home after club meetings, play practice, band, and volleyball.

Once we were in a quiet corner, I started the conversation. Believe me, I wasn't the world's best communicator in that moment. Even though I had been rehearsing my lines in my head for weeks, prepared "speeches" sailed out the window. Also, I remained shy and awkward and somewhat lacking in social graces, all made immeasurably worse by my icy nerves. After a gulp that could have drained a large Slurpee in a single swallow, our interaction began something like this: "Gabe, do you happen to have any plans for the third Saturday in May?" My exhale came out in a rush.

My friend did his best to hide a grin. "Gee," he replied, "is that the date of the prom?"

"Why yes, yes it is, Gabe. The prom does happen to be on that day. Would you consider going with me?" It was technically a question, but in reality it came out in a series of long squeaks.

This moment stretched into the stratosphere. I couldn't feel anything in my arms or legs. Was I starting to float? Beam me up, Scotty! I thought I might die.

Without the slightest hesitation, he responded, "I would love to go with you." He said, "The only thing that would stop me is if I have to work. I promise to keep you posted." Then Gabe knelt down beside my wheelchair and gave me one of the sweetest hugs I have ever known. "Thank you so much for asking me."

As it turned out, Gabe did have to work on prom night, so we never attended. But that is only part of the story. Several months later, I went to college. Choosing to attend a university hundreds of miles away created obstacles I hadn't anticipated. With no familiar faces to fall back on, I was forced to make new friends, and I desperately wanted everyone to like me.

Somehow, I fell into a pattern of doing a certain kind of favor for the people I hung out with, even though it made me uncomfortable. When people I knew were attracted to each other, they would often use me as a go-between. More specifically, a guy would ask me to check in with a girl to see if she liked him. The girls would ask me to relay the message that she did or didn't. Many a relationship started between two of my friends with me as the "middle man."

It didn't seem like a big deal at first. I wanted to fit in, and if I could play a role in the happiness of some friends, I was happy to help. For a while. But the situation began to take its toll. As my freshman year unfolded and I was surrounded by more and more couples, I started to wonder about my own future.

Would a nice guy ever find me attractive? Would anyone be able to look beyond my disability and focus on the person inside? Would anyone want to get to know me enough to think about sharing his life with me? Would I ever be loved like that?

These questions left me feeling lonely and scared. Then, after a particularly difficult day when — count them — three sets of friends asked me about each other, discouragement began to get the better of me. On a whim, I called Gabe.

He was still a senior in high school, biding his time, it seemed, until graduation. I, on the other hand, was somewhat overwhelmed and stuck, and couldn't move on until I got an issue clarified.

After catching up a bit, I summoned the courage to ask another question.

"Gabe, did it ever bother you that a girl in a wheelchair asked you to prom?"

Without skipping a beat, he said, "Well, there was some concern that you couldn't do the twist."

Once my laughter subsided, he continued.

"Seriously, though. A girl in a wheelchair didn't ask me to prom. You asked me to prom. I never saw it any other way."

Flooded with relief, I hung up the phone with new resolve and better boundaries.

I will find the right guy someday. I just have to wait. When we meet, we will talk often and get to know each other. Like Gabe, over time he will be able to see all the good things that make up who I am.

We won't even need a "middle man."

~Lorraine Cannistra

Finding Lovetown

You must love yourself before you love another. By accepting yourself and fully being what you are, your simple presence can make others happy.

~Author Unknown

There's a saying that you can't love someone else until you love yourself first. I found that out the hard way—on national TV.

In the summer of 2012, I participated in the filming of a reality show for the Oprah Winfrey Network called *Lovetown, USA*. I was invited to be one of the "Singles" on the show, set in Kingsland, Georgia, with Paul Brunson and Kailen Rosenburg as our "Love Coaches."

I arrived raring to go, ready to find love in a jewel of a town. I was battling cancer for the third time but that didn't matter to me. I was strong. Empowered. I had big earrings. Nothing was going to stop me!

Yep. My dates were a disaster.

See, I was so focused on love as something to check off a list, that I came across as aggressive and unbending. I couldn't get out of my own way. As a cancer survivor and entrepreneur, I'd learned the power of action, of going after goals and conquering them. But bringing this attitude to *Lovetown* was a mistake. From my first mixers to my first dates, I was ill at ease, too determined to complete my "dating tasks." It was like I was on a job interview, not joyfully seeking out love.

Paul and Kailen were supportive and kind, reminding me that I needed to slow down and allow myself to be approachable. My own drive to survive my cancer had made me incredibly single-minded, yet they suspected that what I needed to do right then was not seek out a man to love me, but to love and appreciate myself, and share that with others.

Their words hit me hard. They were right. I'd spent four years fighting pancreatic cancer. I didn't need to find love. I needed to give it! So Paul and Kailen gave me an extraordinary chance—to stay with the show without the stress of dating, as a "love ambassador" to the town, sharing fun, love, and kindness. I immediately consented.

It was wonderful. I wrote anonymous notes of love for townspeople who needed a smile. I worked with local kids and adults in need. I emceed games and events to bring the town together. It was terrific to be able to focus outward, to forget my illness and drive, to just give and accept love in the largest most beautiful sense.

I carried that sense of love and self-acceptance into my life after the show. My mind wasn't racing to the next goal. Despite my cancer, I didn't need to be on the fast track 24/7—and neither did the men I dated. I could simply pause, and listen—to their voices, and to my heart.

Returning home, I attempted to put some of the lessons I'd learned into practice. I worked hard, as always, on my careers as an entrepreneur and model, and also continued to fight my cancer. But I also made sure to focus outward, and, thinking of Paul and Kailen, I became a public speaker, hoping to empower others to fight for health, happiness, success, and love.

I also joined a major dating website for fun, and went on some dates. I didn't repeat my *Lovetown* mistakes of snap judgments, instead trying for multiple dates to really assess potential connections. There were no deadlines. I knew love was out there sometime.

As it turned out, I'd already met him.

During this whole time period, I had also been interacting with friends and acquaintances on social media. Among these, I'd been talking with Andres, a kind, funny guy who had actually lived in my hometown of Jacksonville for over a year and a half (but who'd been too shy to talk to me). He'd just moved back up to New Jersey, but we found ourselves bantering on the same things. I thought, "I really like this guy. I wish I could spend time with him, and get to know him better."

Finally, shyly, we took the leap and (a little embarrassed at meeting via social media) exchanged phone numbers. And the universe rewarded us, as we got to meet not even one week later, as I was headed to D.C. for the Pancreatic Cancer Action Network's Annual Advocacy Day, and Andres had some free time in his schedule to drive down to meet me. He even offered to drive all the way down Jersey to pick me up from the airport.

I experienced a moment of understandable panic. The thought crossed my mind at lightning speed: Was I crazy? I'd only spoken to this man on the phone for the past week! Granted, it had become hours of conversation but this was America in 2013 and serial killers did exist... yet our conversations had given me so much of what I'd been seeking! So after praying and thinking about it, I decided to take the leap.

I landed in D.C. After the long walk to baggage claim, there he was, as handsome as his picture, and looking as shy and nervous as me. We made the required serial killer jokes, but within seconds, our shyness dissipated and we were both relaxed and smiling, realizing our connection was as strong as ever.

Our first date lasted six hours. We talked and talked, pouring out our hopes and dreams as we strolled through one of the most beautiful cities on earth, surrounded by the monuments of men who had dreamed of the best in mankind. I didn't feel driven or insecure, on a timetable to meet expectations. I just felt joy that it could be this easy. We spent that week talking as much as possible, and after two more weeks of conversations and texts from afar, he visited me in Florida for four days. We'd both fallen head over heels.

The next weeks flew by in a flurry of phone calls, texts, and video calls (thankfully, modern technology allowed us to see and hear each other from afar). Then it was my turn to visit, and I flew up to

New York City, where Andres and I spent that time laughing, talking, holding one another, and dreaming of the future.

It's been a year since *Lovetown*, and I have what I'd been seeking—a loving and exciting relationship that has given me wings. We talk, communicate and share openly and joyfully, and without fear. We both know we've found something special.

I think back to one year ago, when I'd wanted love so badly I'd pursued it on national TV like a hunter. Yet in listening to Paul and Kailen, I'd learned that in sending love outward, we draw love back to us exponentially.

And now I'm reaping the benefits, with a man who sees and supports my dreams, and whose dreams I encourage with prayers and ribbons of hope.

I may have gone to *Lovetown*, but the place where I truly found love was within myself all along.

~Alicia Bertine

The
Dating Game

Meet Our Contributors
Meet Our Authors
Thank You
About Chicken Soup for the Soul

Meet Our Contributors

Maggie Anderson received her M.S. degree from the Johns Hopkins University and works as a biologist in Chicago, IL. Away from work, Maggie enjoys reading and writing fantasy stories. Her first short story was recently published in the anthology, *When the Hero Comes Home 2*. E-mail her at margaret.g.anderson@gmail.com.

Karen Bauer lived in North Vancouver, British Columbia for twenty-three years and now resides in Ontario. She has worked with the elderly as a Personal Support Worker for seventeen years. Karen enjoys walking her dogs, baking and quilting. She plans to volunteer in Palliative Care in the future.

With a journalism degree from Boston University, **Chase Bernstein** is a twice-published author in the *Chicken Soup for the Soul* series. She currently lives in Los Angeles where she performs stand-up comedy.

A three-time pancreatic cancer survivor from Atlantic Beach, FL, **Alicia Bertine** is a model, businesswoman and motivational speaker. In 2012, she was honored as the Pancreatic Cancer Action Network's "Champion of Hope," and she inspired viewers each week on the OWN TV show *Lovetown, USA*. Contact Alicia at AliciaBertine.com.

Debbie Best has been working with Esther Hershenhorn, a writing coach out of Chicago. She completed an online screenwriting class from Gotham out of New York and is passionate when writing for any age group. She's currently writing a story about her friend who lost her battle with cancer. E-mail her at oceanbluewriter7@peoplepc. com.

Alice Wiethoff Blegen is retired from her career with JCPenney at the company's corporate headquarters in Plano, TX. She has recently returned to her hometown of Kansas City, MO with her husband, John. Alice wrote and edited numerous business articles during her career. She is now documenting her memoirs.

Elizabeth Blosfield is studying broadcast journalism at Kent State University. She has been writing all her life, and her favorite subjects to write about are love, nature and art. She is also a dancer and loves anything involving ballet or the color pink. Read her blog at elizabethblosfield.blogspot.com.

Janna Bogert is a happy military spouse living in Colorado. She has a bachelor's degree from FAU, and now writes for the blog www.perceptioniseverything.blogspot.com. Janna enjoys traveling, the outdoors, cherishes friends and family, and any time that she can get with her soldier. You can contact via her blog or Twitter at Janna_Renee.

Grand prizewinner in the Coast Weekend's serial mystery chapter contest, **Jan Bono** is writing a cozy mystery series set on the southwest Washington coast. She has written four humorous short story collections, numerous one-act plays, two poetry chapbooks and over 750 blog entries. Check out her work at www.JanBonoBooks.com.

Lisa Braxton earned her Master of Fine Arts degree in creative writing from Southern New Hampshire University. She is immediate past president of the Women's National Book Association/Boston Chapter and an award-winning journalist. She is completing her first novel. You can read her blog on writing at www.lisabraxton.com/blog.

Lori Bryant is an author, speaker, storyteller, and writes poetry for

Art with a Voice. Lori has contributed to *Zoe Life* devotionals and Chicken Soup for the Soul. Her passion is helping people live life to the fullest! Contact Lori at www.Loribryantsstories.com, or on Facebook at Lori Bryant's Stories or Art with a Voice.

Maureen Buckley lives in Eugene, OR with her two dogs. She gets her greatest pleasures from her family, friends, and exploring the great Northwest. She enjoys writing short stories, poetry and essays focusing on issues facing women in transition. Read her blog "Girl, I Got Your Back" at msmaureenbuckley.com.

John P. Buentello writes fiction, nonfiction, essays, and poetry for a variety of magazines and journals. He is the co-author of the novel *Reproduction Rights* and the fiction collections *Binary Tales* and *The Night Rose of the Mountain*. E-mail him at jakkhakk@yahoo.com.

Lorraine Cannistra received her Bachelor of Science degree in English and Master of Science degree in Rehabilitation Counseling from Emporia State University. She enjoys advocating, cooking, reading, writing and motivational speaking. Her passion is wheelchair ballroom dance. Read her blog at healthonwheels.wordpress.com and e-mail her at lcannistra@yahoo.com.

Liane Kupferberg Carter is a journalist whose articles and essays have appeared in many publications, including *The New York Times*, the *Chicago Tribune*, and *The Huffington Post*. She writes a monthly column for *Autism After 16*, and is currently completing a family memoir. Contact her at www.facebook.com/LianeKupferbergCarter.

Melissa Halsey Caudill is a real estate paralegal, two-time cancer survivor, and proud mother of two. Her hobbies include acting, running, and writing. She just recently started a public blog, and is honored to have her first story published in the *Chicken Soup for the Soul* series. E-mail her at caudillmelissa78@yahoo.com.

Hana Haatainen Caye, speaker and writing instructor, has a copywriting, editing, and voice-over business in Pittsburgh. With over thirty children's books published, she has won awards for her poetry, short stories, and blog (www.greengrandma.org), and is author of the nonfiction book, *Vinegar Fridays*. Learn more at www.wordsinyourmouth.com.

C. Hope Clark lives in rural South Carolina on a beautiful lake where she maintains a writer's website and blog by day and writes *The Carolina Slade Mystery* series by night. Many of the stories were spawned from hers and her personal agent's escapades with the Federal government. Learn more at www.chopeclark.com and www.fundsforwriters.com.

Courtney Conover and her ex-football player husband are the parents of two young children under the age of three and enjoying a happily imperfect life in suburban Detroit. This is her tenth story published in the *Chicken Soup for the Soul* series. You can find her online at courtneyconover.com and contact her at courtneyconover@yahoo.com.

Laura Dailey-Pelle received her master's degree in Healthcare Administration from Central Michigan University. She works at a hospital in southeast Michigan as the Director of Radiation Oncology and Healing Arts. Laura enjoys walking, reading, writing and spending time with her family. E-mail her at ldpelle@gmail.com.

Heather Davis is a momma, an author and a humorist. *TMI Mom: Oversharing My Life* and *TMI Mom: Getting Lucky* are collections of humorous essays that Davis has penned. She and her family live in Oklahoma where she chronicles her life at www.Minivan-Momma.com. E-mail her at Minivan.Momma.2@gmail.com.

Laura J. Davis is an award-winning author and avid reader. She owns www.interviewsandreviews.com, a website where Christian authors and readers can connect. She is a previous contributor to *Chicken Soup for the Soul* books. Her greatest inspiration is her husband of thirty-one years. E-mail her at lauradavis@laurajdavis.com.

Ginny Dubose is living out her dreams in central Florida with her husband Ray and her two sons, Dan and Alex. A Florida Southern College graduate, she lives with joy and faith each and every day!

Kristen Duvall is a writer of tales both real and make-believe. In addition to nonfiction, she also writes young adult, science fiction, fantasy, and speculative fiction. She lives in Southern California with her boyfriend and two furbabies. Contact her at www.facebook.com/kristenduvallwriter.

Sue Fairchild is an insurance agent 9 to 5 and a writer every other moment. She enjoys spending time with her husband doing just about anything, but mostly traveling, kayaking, cooking and laughing. Sue has been published primarily as a devotional writer. E-mail her at suemidd48@yahoo.com.

RoseAnn Faulkner is a retired teacher from Yuma, AZ. She enjoys documenting family history through her stories. Her mother Dorothy Faulkner, the inspiration for this story, passed away in 2005. RoseAnn and her husband, Stan Smith, have been married for thirty-two years. E-mail her at roseannfaulkner@gmail.com.

T'Mara Goodsell is an award-winning multi-genre writer and teacher who lives near St. Louis, MO. She has written for various anthologies, newspapers and publications and is currently working on a book for young adults.

Christa M. Grabske and her husband, Keith, have two beautiful daughters. She teaches preschool and enjoys singing and dancing with her students. Christa and her family have traveled to many national parks across the United States. They love spending time outdoors. She blogs as Ginny Marie at www.lemondroppie.com.

Alison Gunn is a writer living in Victoria, BC with her soul mate, Michael, their three adventurous girlies, and faithful hound. She lives in a pink world and blogs about it at cautiousmum.wordpress.com. E-mail her at alisheehan@yahoo.com.

Tina Haapala eventually found love online and now lives with her husband in Wichita Falls, TX. Tina's fifth contribution to the *Chicken Soup for the Soul* series is close to her heart because she is currently writing a memoir about the ups and downs of her romantic journey. E-mail her at tinahaapala@gmail.com.

Jesse Hayworth (also writing as Jessica Andersen) is the bestselling, award-winning author of more than fifty novels of romantic fiction, including the critically acclaimed contemporary Western romance, *Summer at Mustang Ridge*. She and her husband live in Connecticut, and always hold hands.

Ruth Heil writes from Green Lane, PA, where she encourages readers to follow their instincts. Passionate about conservation and simplification, she helps people preserve and communicate their stories through her freelance service, The Write Beat. She is working on a book about nature and the benefits of spending time outside.

Montreal-based writer and television producer **Wendy Helfenbaum** has explored everything from the elite world of Olympic diving to combining home renovations and parenting without losing your mind. Her stories have been published worldwide, and she also does content marketing for corporations and non-profits. Visit her at www.taketwoproductions.ca.

Robin Heydenberk is a university professor whose research encompasses conflict resolution, peace building and the role of the arts in education.

Camille Hill is an animal communicator and storyteller living in Canada. Camille enjoys working with animals, spends her free time writing and creating works of art with her beading, feathers and leather items. She is a frequent contributor to the *Chicken Soup for the Soul* anthology. E-mail her at camille@bluewolfspeaks.com.

Dana Hill lives in Oakland, CA. After a long career in the airline industry, she is now a bartender at a resort hotel. She shares her passion for cooking on the "Two for Dinner" blog at www.danasdinnerfortwo. blogspot.com and enjoys family, friends, writing, reading, gardening, dancing, and listening to vinyl.

Carlton Hughes is a communications professor at Southeast Kentucky Community College and is a children's pastor at Lynch Church of God. His works have been featured in numerous publications, including the book *Simple Little Words*. He and his wife Kathy have two sons, Noah and Ethan, and reside in Cumberland, KY.

Amy Schoenfeld Hunt is a freelance writer for newspapers and magazines, the author of three published books, and a past contributor to the *Chicken Soup for the Soul* series. She's also a costumed historical interpreter at Old World Wisconsin, a museum that depicts life in the 1800s. E-mail her at Shaynamy@aol.com.

Daniel James lives and works in the Denver area and besides spending time with those he loves, also writes and photographs the great outdoors.

Along with her writing and speaking career, award-winner **Bethany Jett** is a Florida State fan, cheerleading coach, wannabe chef, wife, and mother of three adorable little boys. Find her dating book,

The Cinderella Rule: A Young Woman's Guide to Happily Ever After, in bookstores everywhere.

Fifteen years ago **Christy Johnson** and her husband John were married at the same ice rink where they had their first date. As a dynamic speaker, life coach and author of *Love Junkies, Seven Steps for Breaking the Toxic Relationship Cycle*, Christy is passionate about inspiring hope. Learn more at www.christyjohnson.org.

Janice Johnson completed a three-year voyage aboard a schooner as first mate and has written about her experience in an e-book, *Stumbling Aboard: A Reluctant First Mate Travels Through 20 Countries*, available on Amazon.

Vallory Jones, author and cancer survivor, founded Victorious Val & the Breast Cancer Crusaders, a Facebook community of encouragement for survivors and supporters. She's also the "Survivor Driver" for the charity Rally Cross racing team, Pink, Fast 'n' Dirty. Visit www.victoriousval.com, www.thebreastcancercrusaders.com, and pinkfastndirty.org. E-mail her at victoriousval2011@gmail.com.

Shannon Kaiser is a travel writer, inspirational speaker, life coach, and author of *Find Your Happy: An Inspirational Guide to Loving Life to Its Fullest*. To connect with her, visit her award-winning website Playwiththeworld.com. She lives in Portland, OR, with her adventure buddy, her dog Tucker.

Rebecca Kaplan graduated from Purchase College in 2013 with a Bachelor of Arts degree in creative writing and journalism. She currently lives in Brooklyn, NY, where she spends her time reading, writing, and making short films. Visit her website at rebeccakaplan.weebly.com.

April Knight is a freelance writer. She spends her free time riding her horse *Gypsy Wind*. Her most recent novels are titled *Sweet Dreams* and *Nobody Dies in Kansas*. E-mail her at aknightscribe@gmail.com.

Writing legal opinions as a Circuit Judge in Broward County, FL was too narrow a scope to hold **Miette Korda's** attention for long. Her interests range from sky to sea, as a licensed pilot and a certified SCUBA diver. She is married with two children and five grandchildren.

Melisa Kraft lives with her husband, Steve, and her two sons and two dogs in Benton, KY. Reading and writing have become very important to her as she deals with the symptoms of MS. She attends church and spends much of her time encouraging friends with similar health-related problems.

Cathi LaMarche has contributed to over twenty anthologies, including *Chicken Soup for the Soul*, *Cup of Comfort*, and the *Not Your Mother's Book* series. As a composition teacher, a novelist, and a writing coach, she spends most days immersed in the written word. Cathi is currently working on her second novel.

Ginny Layton received her Bachelor of Arts degree from Auburn University and Masters of Literature degree from Boston University in 1993. She is a pastor's wife, mother to three boys and a homemaker in North Carolina. Ginny likes to sing and write poetry. She blogs at oneday-ginny.blogspot.com about life with her children.

Lynne Leite is a speaker, writer and storyteller. This is her eighth story to be included in the *Chicken Soup for the Soul* series and she hopes to contribute more! Her motto is, "Life is a series of stories meant to be told." Learn more at www.CurlyGirl4God.com.

Janeen Lewis writes and lives in Smyrna, GA. She has degrees in journalism and elementary education from Eastern Kentucky University, and enjoys writing about life with her husband Jesse and children, Andrew and Gracie. Several of her stories have been published in *Chicken Soup for the Soul* anthologies.

Amy Gray Light is pleased to have another story in the *Chicken Soup for the Soul* series. She and Excy run Wing Spur, a nonprofit sanctuary for wild mustangs. When she isn't messing around with the animals she likes to write stories and personal essays. E-mail her at orphicaeg@windstream.net or visit Iwonderwye.blogspot.com.

Lisa Littlewood is a freelance writer and full-time mom who lives near Buffalo, NY with her three energetic girls and a very outnumbered (and lucky!) husband. She enjoys writing inspirational and candid stories about her life as a mom and wife. Read more on her blog at www.littlewritermomma.com.

Cristina T. Lopez-O'Keeffe has been writing since age seven. Her poetry and essays have been published extensively online and in print, and she published her book *Finding Francis* in 2003. Cristina owns her own organizing business and lives in Stewart Manor, NY with her husband and their three daughters.

Patricia Lorenz is the author of thirteen books, has stories in over fifty *Chicken Soup for the Soul* books, and has been a contributing writer for the annual *Daily Guideposts* books for twenty-three years. Patricia is a professional speaker who loves to travel the country speaking to various groups. E-mail her at patricialorenz@juno.com.

Diana Lynn is a small business owner and freelance writer in Washington State. She loves writing and is so excited to be part of the Chicken Soup for the Soul family. E-mail her at Diana@recoveringdysfunctional.com.

Kate Lynn is an elementary school teacher in Colorado. She enjoys traveling, skiing, and spending time with family and friends!

Lisa Mackinder received her Bachelor of Arts degree at Western Michigan University. A freelance writer, she lives in Portage, MI with her husband and rescue animals. Besides writing, Lisa enjoys photography, traveling, reading, running, hiking, biking, climbing, camping, and fishing. E-mail her at mackinder.lisa@yahoo.com.

David Martin's humor and political satire have appeared in many publications including *The New York Times*, the *Chicago Tribune* and *Smithsonian* magazine. His latest humor collection, *Screams & Whispers*, is available on Amazon.com. David lives in Ottawa, ON with his wife Cheryl and their daughter Sarah.

Karen Martin loves traveling, sunshine and good stories. She'll interview anyone who will let her and writes for magazines and small business blogs. She adores her husband David and helps him run his chiropractic office. Learn more at www.karenthewriter.com.

Catherine Mattice is President of Civility Partners, a consulting firm helping organizations build positive workplaces (www.Civility Partners.com). She is co-author of *Back Off! Your Kick-Ass Guide to Ending Bullying at Work*, available on Amazon, and she published her story of resilience in *Chicken Soup for the Soul: The Power of Positive*.

Kate Meadows aims to help others communicate their life stories. Her essays have appeared in *Writer's Digest*, *Chicken Soup for the Soul: Thanks Mom*, and elsewhere. She is the author of *Tough Love: A Wyoming Childhood* (Pronghorn Press). She lives in Kansas City with her husband and two sons. Learn more at www.katemeadows.com.

Margaret Nava writes from her home in New Mexico where she lives with a rambunctious Chihuahua. In addition to her stories in the *Chicken Soup for the Soul* series, she has authored six books and written numerous articles for inspirational and Christian living publications.

Marc Tyler Nobleman is the author of more than seventy books, including *Boys of Steel: The Creators of Superman* and *Bill the Boy Wonder: The Secret Co-Creator of Batman*. His cartoons have appeared in more than 100 international publications. At noblemania.blogspot.com, he reveals the behind-the-scenes stories of his work.

Margaret Norway is a full-time college student in upstate New York. Her interests include music, foreign languages, and spending time in nature with her beloved Jack Russell, Ezra. Margaret plans to earn her BA degree in writing and to write fiction novels in various sub-genres. E-mail her at Margaret.norway@students.sunnycgcc.edu.

Elissa Nysetvold is currently studying chemistry at Brigham Young University. She is happily married and enjoys writing, reading, music, learning about science, and being outdoors with her family.

Linda O'Connell is an accomplished writer and seasoned teacher from St. Louis, MO. A positive thinker, she writes from the heart, bares her soul and finds humor in everyday situations. Linda enjoys a hearty laugh, dark chocolate and walking on the beach. Linda blogs at lindaoconnell.blogspot.com.

Molly O'Connor lives in rural eastern Ontario on a lazy country road where she can be seen out walking with her camera slung around her neck. When she is not writing, she is taking photographs of wild flowers or singing in a choir. She winters in Arizona. Read her blog at mollyswanderings.blogspot.com.

Caitlin Q. Bailey O'Neill, a six-time contributor to the *Chicken Soup for the Soul* series, married her prince charming in 2010; the college sweethearts now call Newington, CT home. E-mail her at PerfectlyPunctuated@yahoo.com.

Cynthia J. Patton is a special needs attorney, autism advocate, and single mom. Her award-winning nonfiction and poetry have appeared in twelve anthologies, including five *Chicken Soup for the*

Soul books, plus numerous other publications. She is completing a memoir on her unconventional journey to motherhood. Learn more at CynthiaJPatton.com.

Lisa Pawlak is a freelance writer and mother of two mischievous boys. Her work has been featured multiple times in the *Chicken Soup for the Soul* series. Additionally, you can see her life stories in the *Survivor's Review* and *Coping with Cancer* magazine. E-mail her at lisapawlak@hotmail.com.

Ava Pennington is an author, speaker, and Bible teacher. She has published numerous magazine articles and contributed to twenty-two anthologies, including eighteen *Chicken Soup for the Soul* books. She is also the author of *Daily Reflections on the Names of God: A Devotional* (Revell). Learn more at www.AvaWrites.com.

Tammy Pfaff studies journalism at Delaware County Community College. She is a wife and mother of four children. Tammy enjoys spending time with her family, writing short stories and devotions, scrapbooking and swimming. E-mail her at tammypfaff@gmail.com or visit her website at www.tammypfaff.com.

Mimi Pollack was raised in Belgium. There, she decided that she would one day marry "An American Boy." To this end, she studied English with great passion, and eventually met and married her (American) husband. They live in Florida, almost an old married couple after thirty years. E-mail her at mimi@pollackhome.com.

Shannon Scott Poteet loves being able to capture moments on a page and share those experiences with people she likely will never meet. As a wife and mother to three amazing children, she enjoys spending time with her family, reading, writing, and being outdoors.

Jennifer Purdie is a freelance writer. Her work appears in national fitness magazines and Southwest-based lifestyle magazines. She is working on her first two books: *Destination Race* and *Running with Penguins*. She holds a bachelor's degree from the University of Washington and a master's degree from the University of Phoenix.

Mark Rickerby is a writer, songwriter and singer. His stories have been published in four previous *Chicken Soup for the Soul* books. He co-wrote his father's memoir, *The Other Belfast*, and released a CD of songs for his daughter, Marli. For information on these and other projects, please visit www.markrickerby.com.

Ann Elizabeth Robertson retired from teaching art and English to work even harder at home. Whether she's teasing out weeds in her garden or those ever-growing ones in her writings, she's got dirt (or paint) under her fingernails and she's smiling. Learn more at www.annelizabethrobertson.com or e-mail her at aerobertson50@yahoo.com.

Sioux Roslawski, a third grade teacher, continues to dish out trouble... on a daily basis. These days, she cooks up stories with the help of her writing critique group, the WWWPs (Wild Women Wielding Pens), who also serve up generous dollops of "trouble." Learn more at siouxspage.blogspot.com.

John Scanlan is a 1983 graduate of the United States Naval Academy, and retired from the Marine Corps as a Lieutenant Colonel aviator. He currently resides on Hilton Head Island, SC, and is pursuing a second career as a writer. E-mail him at ping1@hargray.com.

Gretchen Schiller courageously continues to date while Mr. X-Lax continues his Book Tour elsewhere. Gretchen is an ex-wife, ex-pediatric nurse, ex-resident of Guatemala and ex-member of Weight Watchers. (Cake is simply too yummy!) Gretchen's humorous website, www.sassysinglemom.com, includes topics about motherhood, adoption, healthy co-parenting after divorce and of course, dating!

Thomas Schonardt dedicates this story to Laura Rose Miller, soon to be Mrs. Schonhardt. She is his backbone and has helped him through so much these past four years. Words cannot describe how much she means to him. Thomas loves her with all his heart. E-mail him at TSchonhardt@gmail.com.

Joel Schwartzberg is a nationally published essayist and author of the award-winning collection *The 40-Year-Old Version.* Joel's pieces have appeared in *The New York Times Magazine, Newsweek,* the *New York Post,* the *New York Daily News,* Parents.com, and other sources for people who read. Learn more at www.joelschwartzberg.net.

Marisa Shadrick is a freelance writer and speaker. Born in New York City and raised in Los Angeles, Marisa understands the challenges multitasking women face in a fast-paced world. Marisa encourages women to find their oasis in the desert and cultivate quiet strength through her weekly blog, "Lite Living."

A Realtor for thirty years, **Alvena Stanfield** used the housing industry's decline to explore her love for writing. She's published fifty articles, three short stories, belongs to several writers' groups and attends NKU's Creative Writing program. She's written two novels and a screenplay (not yet good enough, but getting there).

Diane Stark is a wife, mother of five, and freelance writer. She loves to write about the important things in life: her family and her faith. Visit her blog at www.DianeStark.blogspot.com.

Tiffany Stroud received her bachelor's degree in communications, specializing in journalism from Anderson University in 2011. She is a freelance writer, blogger and Army wife. Tiffany lives in Georgia, but is originally from Indiana. She enjoys eating ice cream, visiting beaches and playing board games. Visit her website at www.seeingsunshine. com.

Pamela Tambornino lives on a small farm in Kansas where her husband, two dogs and four cats rule. She teaches at a university in Lawrence and loves to write. E-mail her at bookwormbugg2002@ yahoo.com.

Tena Beth Thompson writes about life as she knows it. She has published her first book titled, *Separation Survival Guide: When Your Marriage Catapults into Limbo*. After twenty-four years of marriage to her high school sweetheart, she found herself divorced. She turned her misfortune into a positive opportunity to help others.

Elvira Van Horn received her Bachelor of Arts degree, with honors, in communications and a minor in business from Eastern Michigan University. She teaches eighth grade in Houston, TX. Elvira is also a recording artist and enjoys writing and composing music when she's not teaching. E-mail her at evanhorn45@gmail.com.

Carrie O'Maley Voliva is a public librarian in Indianapolis who enjoys writing, reading, music, biking, yoga, and spending time with her family. "Love, Loss, and Cake" is dedicated to her husband, Dustin, who swept her off her feet and out of "the dating game." E-mail her at carrieovoliva@gmail.com.

Samantha Ducloux Waltz offers readers inspiration, courage and a fresh perspective on life as the writer of more than sixty creative nonfiction stories published in *Chicken Soup for the Soul* and other anthologies. She has also published under the name Samellyn Wood.

S.M. Westerlie is an Army wife, mother, and writer from the Seattle area. She is currently earning a bachelor's in education from the University of Cincinnati. Westerlie is the author of *The (Tough Love) Military Wife Survival Guide* and *The Alliday Poem Book of Silly Celebrations*.

Janice Westerling is a San Francisco Bay Area writer who grew up in the Central Valley of California and attended Fresno State College. She is an avid hiker and traveler. Her work has appeared in *The Christian Science Monitor* and *The Coachella Review*. E-mail her at jwesterling@comcast.net.

Dallas Woodburn is a 2013-14 Steinbeck Fellow in Creative Writing at San José State University. This year she is doing a random act of kindness every week and chronicling her experiences on her blog, daybydaymasterpiece.com. Contact her and learn more about her nonprofit youth literacy organization Write On! at writeonbooks.org.

Sheri Zeck enjoys writing creative nonfiction stories that encourage, inspire and entertain others. She lives in Illinois with her husband and three daughters. She has contributed stories to Chicken Soup for the Soul, *Guideposts*, *Angels on Earth*, *Farm & Ranch Living* and other magazines. Visit her website at www.sherizeck.com.

Paulette Zubel is currently writing a novel on her blog. She is the author of *Canine Parables: Portraits of Life and God*, and her story "Treasure Stored in Secret Places" appeared in *Chicken Soup for the Soul: Answered Prayers*. She and her current therapy dog, Forester, enjoy working with third and fourth grade children.

Meet Our Authors

Jack Canfield and **Mark Victor Hansen** are the co-founders of Chicken Soup for the Soul. Jack is the author of many bestselling books and is CEO of the Canfield Training Group. Mark is a prolific writer and has had a profound influence in the field of human potential through his library of audios, videos, and articles. Jack and Mark have received many awards and honors, including a Guinness World Records Certificate for having seven books from the *Chicken Soup for the Soul* series on the New York Times bestseller list on May 24, 1998. You can reach them at www.jackcanfield.com and www. markvictorhansen.com.

Amy Newmark has been Chicken Soup for the Soul's publisher, coauthor, and editor-in-chief for the last six years, after a 30-year career as a writer, speaker, financial analyst, and business executive in the worlds of finance and telecommunications. Amy is a Chartered Financial Analyst and a *magna cum laude* graduate of Harvard College, where she majored in Portuguese, minored in French, and traveled extensively. She and her husband have four grown children.

After a long career writing books on telecommunications, voluminous financial reports, business plans, and corporate press releases, Chicken Soup for the Soul is a breath of fresh air for Amy. She loves creating these life-changing books for Chicken Soup for the Soul's wonderful readers. She has coauthored and/or edited more than 100 *Chicken Soup for the Soul* books.

You can reach Amy with any questions or comments through

webmaster@chickensoupforthesoul.com and you can follow her on Twitter @amynewmark or @chickensoupsoul.

Thank You

W e owe huge thanks to all of our contributors. We know that you poured your hearts and souls into the thousands of stories that you shared with us, and ultimately with each other. As we read and edited these stories, we were truly amazed by your wonderful love stories and your funny date experiences. We appreciate your willingness to share these amusing and encouraging stories with our readers.

We could only publish a small percentage of the stories that were submitted, but we read every single one and even the ones that do not appear in the book had an influence on us and on the final manuscript. We owe special thanks to our editor Madeline Clapps, who read the stories that were submitted for this book and narrowed the list down to a more manageable number of finalists and created the chapters and the intial manuscript. Our assistant publisher D'ette Corona did her normal masterful job of working with the contributors to approve our edits and answer any questions they had. Senior Editor Barbara LoMonaco proofread the stories along with our editor Kristiana Pastir, who also managed the process of turning a Word document into this beautiful book.

We also owe a special thanks to our creative director and book producer, Brian Taylor at Pneuma Books, for his brilliant vision for our covers and interiors.

~Amy Newmark

Sharing Happiness, Inspiration, and Wellness

R eal people sharing real stories, every day, all over the world. In 2007, *USA Today* named *Chicken Soup for the Soul* one of the five most memorable books in the last quarter-century. With over 100 million books sold to date in the U.S. and Canada alone, more than 200 titles in print, and translations into more than 40 languages, "chicken soup for the soul" is one of the world's best-known phrases.

Today, 20 years after we first began sharing happiness, inspiration and wellness through our books, we continue to delight our readers with new titles, but have also evolved beyond the bookstore, with wholesome and balanced pet food, delicious nutritious comfort food, and a major motion picture in development. Whatever you're doing, wherever you are, Chicken Soup for the Soul is "always there for you™." Thanks for reading!

Share with Us

We all have had Chicken Soup for the Soul moments in our lives. If you would like to share your story or poem with millions of people around the world, go to chickensoup.com and click on "Submit Your Story." You may be able to help another reader, and become a published author at the same time. Some of our past contributors have launched writing and speaking careers from the publication of their stories in our books!

Our submission volume has been increasing steadily—the quality and quantity of your submissions has been fabulous. We only accept story submissions via our website. They are no longer accepted via mail or fax.

To contact us regarding other matters, please send us an e-mail through webmaster@chickensoupforthesoul.com, or fax or write us at:

Chicken Soup for the Soul
P.O. Box 700
Cos Cob, CT 06807-0700
Fax: 203-861-7194

One more note from your friends at Chicken Soup for the Soul: Occasionally, we receive an unsolicited book manuscript from one of our readers, and we would like to respectfully inform you that we do not accept unsolicited manuscripts and we must discard the ones that appear.